Three Thousand Miles for a Wish

Safiya Hussain

New Age Publishers UK

THREE THOUSAND MILES FOR A WISH

Copyright © Safiya Hussain 2011

All Rights Reserved

Published by New Age Publishers UK, 4th Floor, Media Factory, Kirkham Street, Preston, England, PR1 2HE.

www.newagepublishers.co.uk

ISBN 978-0-9570960-0-4

Three Thousand Miles
for a Wish

FOREWORD

This book is a work of non-fiction. However, the names of characters have been changed to preserve anonymity.

I have made reference to Prophet Mohammad but have chosen to omit the words 'peace be upon him', which usually follow afterwards, for the readers ease and to preserve the flow of the story. Please include these words when reading if you wish to do so.

The facts in this book are stated to the best of my knowledge and recollection. If I have made any errors or caused any offence, I apologise in advance and hope to be pardoned.

For my mother, under whose feet lies my paradise

1

'PEOPLE HAVE GONE AND never returned alive'.

Those infamous words loomed over me as I stared at the murky smog. Fixated on searching for a speck of light. Something resembling a radiant genie. An Aladdin. That would tear through the clouds and say: 'you look desperate. Tell me your wish and I shall grant it immediately.'

Desperate.

'Be brave and may God be with you '.

Destroyed.

'Allahu akbar. Allahu akbar. Allahu akbar.'

I switched my gaze away from the window and shot a glance at the young man to my right. An African man. Rocking back and forth in his white robe. Cupping his bearded face with his hands. Fervently reciting *God is the greatest* in Arabic as though they were to be his last sacrificial words.

I dug my nails into the seat of the shaky plane. The one that my life now depended on. Recalling terror events that had occurred on planes in the past, I froze. Instantly regretting my earlier thought of wanting it to take a nose dive into the North Sea.

What the hell am I doing here?

The blood draining statements of those I had left behind played in my mind again as I questioned the sanity of the bearded man. Worse still – the sanity of myself.

'People have gone and never returned alive'. 'Be brave and may God be with you'. 'There will be three million people there, you're insane'.

'Allahu akbar. Allahu akbar. Allahu akbar...' He would not stop reciting. Would not stop ticking.

I licked my lips. Salt. Blood.

What would be a worse fate; to be blown up on this plane by the man on my right, to be killed like the others who had embarked on this voyage, or to continue living in the same hell I had been living in for the past year?

'*It is a journey of a lifetime*', they said. That century-old statement stopped me from running out of my seat. They said, '*it is truly the most amazing trip in the world*'. That stopped me from screaming for a reason I was unsure of. They said, '*it is a life changing experience*'. That reminded me why I had taken the drastic step to board the plane.

To save myself.

I was flying to Mecca, Saudi Arabia, to embark on the Hajj; the great pilgrimage. I had little idea of what it was and whether I was Muslim enough to go. But they said what they said. They said it was the land of wishes. And I needed a wish.

I needed a wish.

2

THE BABY IN THE aisle next to me began to wail. I longed to hold it. Not because it was crying. But because of the deceit it was about to live. The pain of life it would suffer.

It was at your age that my pursuit for happiness began. Is that not what we all do? Pursue happiness as soon as we are dragged out of our mothers' wombs? We come out kicking and screaming so I am unsure that the pursuit is one that we look forward to. Nevertheless, irrespective of desire or reluctance, the chase begins, as it began for me.

***

There are hardly any dolls, toys or hide-and-seek games of childhood. The pencils, the books and my father's three words, 'education, education, education', is all I seem to know. My childhood and youth is swallowed by the labour of learning. School, college and university – that is all.

Why do my parents push me to bury my head in books? I guess, as immigrants from a third-world country, it is because they did not have the freedoms of learning to read and write. Having lived a life of difficulties, they have this ideal that in a well-paid and respected profession lies the key to happiness. I suppose they know best.

I take the aspiration to become a lawyer; a well-paid and respected lawyer. I see in this ambition, my passport to success; passport to happiness.

I clamber through the thorns and over the pits of an unprivileged life. It is slow. It is painstaking. I hate it most of the time. I just want to play. Have fun. I wish I could be happy now. But my mother said I have to work for happiness.

So I do.

My young, yet mature eyes do not take themselves off the single vision that I have – the moment when I would graduate and be handed my passport to success; passport to happiness.

Twenty-two years old. The moment finally arrives. I throw my black graduation hat in the air. I throw it as high as my hopes. I laugh like the child I never was. With my passport in my hands, I lunge into the career I have always set my eyes on. I have crossed the finishing line and made it to my key destination. I brace myself for the promised fireworks.

Only a week into my life as a trainee lawyer and my parallel dream is awakened. A romantic dreamer, I often gaze at the sky not wanting to miss the moment when my Prince Charming would drop down from the heavens and land on one knee at my feet.

'Hello.'

That is all he has to say. My doors of paradise fly open. Clichéd as it is, he has me at 'hello'. He does not drop down from the sky but rather steps out of the office of a law firm near mine. Prince or no prince, like a burning meteorite shooting into the cool Atlantic Ocean, I fall in love for the first time.

Zameer.

A true artist of romance; he skilfully captures my heart in his hands and blows into it promises of everlasting love and laughs. He blows into it with such power that I am convinced it will soon burst like a star and release a thousand exotic butterflies.

It is wonderful.

A love that elevates me to another Universe. A love that makes me sing and dance under the roof of my house. A love that makes me shower every baffled stranger I pass with the cheesiest of smiles.

Intense. Passionate. Out-of-this-world. It is the epitome of love.

My passport to success is gripped in my hands. Love is gripped in my heart.

Life is amazing.

***

The ticking man stirred and I was thrown out of my thoughts. Shooting my bulging eyes at him I saw that he had quietened to an odd murmur. But his lips still moved. I did not quite know what to make of it. I did not quite know what to make of anyone on the plane; including my mother and father.

Unlike me, most of the women wore head scarves and most of the men wore beards. The look of unease on their faces whilst they clutched guide books on 'Hajj' made my stomach turn.

What has driven these people to embark on this voyage? Do they carry the remains of a broken heart, broken dreams like me? Are they travelling in desperation? Or am I the most sorrowful of them all?

'Assalaamualaikum, I'm sorry we couldn't meet in England!'

The appearance of a small man startled me. My persisting edginess on the plane was becoming exhausting. It was Layth, our guide. My father had arranged for us to be a part of his group and be guided by him through the mammoth journey of Hajj.

The fact that we needed a guide with us at all times said enough.

The seventh century rituals we were to carry out included; making our wishes at the famous Kaba – the black cube set at the centre of the Islamic world, the said wishing well – joining millions of crushing people from every nameable country, running up mountains, sleeping in hot deserts, begging on the grounds where the first man, Adam, is said to have stood, weeping on the land where the Last Day is supposed to take place, chanting, stoning pillars of Satan and partaking in a mass sacrifice of animals. I did not kid myself. I knew we needed much more than one guide.

He may have been short and old, but Layth's strong jaw, bulging arms and piercing grey eyes positioned him somewhat as a lion. *I wonder whether your arms will stop me from being crushed to death.*

'My wife!' he presented Daania – a shorter, plumper, female version of Layth – to us with misplaced melodrama. *Perhaps he's scared too.*

'We're landing in Turkey. Our next flight will be a few hours away, so I'll arrange a hotel for the five of us,' he said.

The rest of the thirty plus members of our group were to meet us in Saudi Arabia.

A weathered south-Asian woman shuffled down the aisle towards Layth. Taking slow, painstaking steps whilst grasping onto the edges of passing seats. Just like a woman in her seventies. In her white traditional south-Asian dress and loosely wrapped scarf she painted the perfect picture of a veteran Andrex puppy. Her struggling demeanour and grey wrinkled expression displayed a long life of fatigue. She hobbled past, her eyes downcast followed by her drooping lids. Each line on her face etched a trial and tribulation which had hardened into rods of steely determination. My gaze lingered on her. Slight sadness. Slight admiration. *Is this her final fight for a wish, just like mine?*

***

Monday morning, 7th January 2008 – the day 'amazing' turns to 'torturous'.

I swipe my card to enter the doors of my office for the third month and it suddenly hits me. 'This is shit.' Where on earth are the happy days that I have been waiting for all these years?

I feel nothing.

'I feel like a prisoner. A prisoner of the nine-to-five life. Nine to five, Monday to Friday; caged in by bars of paper and ink, suffocating in a grey office and slaving away meaninglessly. The days always end with no real satisfaction and I leave each evening with only the thought that the same laborious pattern will be repeated the next day.' My boss is out of the office and I make an early morning comfort phone call to my best friend, Sarah.

'That's really poetic ... but please! I don't want to think about it, we have the whole week to get through yet!'

I am confused.

Tightly clutching a coffee in my hand, elbows on desk, I stare out of the rain splattered window at the surrounding tall office blocks. As though a grim piece of art, I study the matted greyness and harshness of the shapes of the buildings whilst the caffeine awakens me. Awakens me to reality. The real world.

I sigh. The infamous despairing sigh is born.

'Is this it?' I ask Sarah. 'Is this it?'

She remains silent.

I hang up and it dawns on me. The same dawning feeling that hit me when my grandmother's life support machine was switched off and her death pronounced. She was never going to be saved. The fireworks are never going to be lit. My wait for them over these months was in vain. My anticipation over these many years, foolish.

This is it.

The strings of hope begin to slowly tear out of my veins as I look around helplessly at my damp existence. Is this what I had hugged those wretched books for, for twenty years of my life? Is this how it would be for the rest of my life – slaving away in a career that gives no sincere satisfaction? And for what – for the sake of making a living, to have roast chicken on the table, a mortgaged semi-detached house and a Ford car? Would I, like others, surrender to this type of hollow life and live only for the pricks of joy on weekends until death knocks on the door?

This is it.

What was I expecting? Am I being ungrateful? After all, it is much better than my last job as a checkout girl in ASDA. Am I seeking something that does not exist? Others find happiness in the smile on the boss's face, in helping clients win legal cases, in their wage packet as they take it home to their families. Should I be the same? Or maybe realise, like the majority of people, that life is just a big mortgage. Accept it with a shrug, a forced smile.

I try to accept it.

I try.

But I cannot shake the feeling of discontentment. I think of Oscar Wilde's words: 'to live is the rarest thing in the world. Most people exist, that is all.' I struggle to cope with that thought. The idea that I am here for the sake of making a living just to merely exist.

The sudden realisation of this hollowness smacks me in the face like a hard hitting truck. The parasitic disappointment sucks the life and vibrancy out of me instantly. Dispiritedness infects me and spreads its incurable disease.

This is it.

The dreaming of a young girl stops. The reality of an older woman sets in.

My pursuit of happiness was a lie.

This is it.

***

'An angel' I whispered.

Time almost stopped as the image in the mirror of the Turkish hotel stared back at me. The image of an angel. Her whiteness manifested the purity of a lone snowflake. Wings that could have flown her straight to the heavens. Her humility, the way she bowed her head, as humbling as an oyster in its shell. Her body, unadorned and in its simplest form was starkly beautiful. Her being displayed other-worldliness yet her feet stood as concrete as those of a human. Soul lay bare, visible to the whole world. She represented something. A truth.

I stared and stared at the girl in the full length mirror, unable to move. *Who is she?*

It had to be me, of course. Not an angel. I had changed into my ihram.

Ihram – the official state of purity of the mind, body and spirit. No person could visit the Kaba in Mecca and perform the welcoming ritual of Umrah without being in ihram. My mind had to be free of impure thoughts and my body clean and modestly covered.

Pure, I had not felt for months.

As the hot water of the hotel shower had touched my cracked face moments before and trickled down my body, I fantasised that it was washing away all the dirt, blood, tear stains. I imagined the anger, hatred and bitterness that discoloured my heart, being scrubbed away and sucked by the drain. I longed to be clean. Free of the marks of my grief, my loathing.

In my ihram I painted the façade of purity. Transformed as radically as the darkness of night turns to the lightness of day. Gone was the sexy leather jacket, five-inch heels, tight skinny jeans and 'rock chick' T-shirt. The messy black hair, red lipstick, mascara laden eyelashes, flamboyant fashion jewellery. It was all gone. All that remained on my olive skin was a white loose-fitting robe and white headscarf. My feet lay flat in brown sandals. That was it. Covered from head to toe. No flesh of mine was visible except that of my jewellery-less hands and my make-up-less face. I appeared as simple and pure as those drops of water.

I looked at the angel-like figurine as though the moon was placed metres away from me. At first, it unnerved me. Naked of my usual comforts, I questioned whether I would be able to walk out of the hotel dressed like this.

But I was not horrified. An eerie calmness fused itself within me. My humanness, my soul lay exposed yet I did not buckle. A strange sensation of warmth, security and liberation infiltrated my body. I was a nut cocooned in its shell away from the bad auras of the world. The insecurities. The vanities. The conformities.

I saw humility. Purity. Honesty. Freedom. I saw... me.

These white garments made me realise something. I was just another human being of the billions that had stepped on land. A being that had come into this life as a baby covered by a white blanket and would leave the world covered in a white shroud. This exposing white robe represented my birth and my death.

This is what I am... My mind, body and soul are all I have. A shattering realisation. An uplifting realisation. It seeped into me like a bitter-sweet injection of morphine. *I entered this world with nothing and I will leave with nothing.*

Instinctively, I bowed my head. Pure yet weak, liberated yet insignificant – I had been humbled.

I lifted my head up again.

What would Zameer have done had he seen me like this?

He would not have looked at me twice. Would not have desired this simple brown nut in its shell. Recalling the time I had sashayed past him in my black figure-hugging suit and clip-clop heels. I imagined walking past him for the first time in this baggy robe and these soundless sandals. Dressed like this, I would have been shielded from his leers. *Could this simple change of clothes have saved the crashing of my heart?*

'Women are like diamonds – their bodies are best covered, to protect them from the dirt of others, and only shown to special people. Our bodies are precious, fragile and delicate'. My mother was one of many to have made that acclamation.

'Pffft!' was always my response as I pulled up my skirt. But now, her words stared right back at me, puffing their chests, daring me to challenge them.

***

'That's my fiancé!!!' Only hours have passed, just hours, from that reckoning Monday morning when the piercing shriek of a hysterical young woman rips into my ears. She almost lashes at me in the middle of the busy city centre but in shock, I do not react. In fact, I do not move. Paralysed by the immediate pain created by the wrenching of my heart I let the icicle of betrayal slice through my bed of love as the scene becomes a suffocating blur.

Zameer has led a double life for months. He has been cheating on me. His declaration of love, a lie. All his promises of an eternal future, made in jest. From those wonderful heavenly skies of love, I am hurled onto the hard gritty ground of pain with a fierce and violent force. His blowing into my heart did now make it burst. Out came a thousand six-headed thorns.

It is an emotional, and even physical, pain that I have never felt before in my life, nor ever come close to. Its vicious teeth tear me mercilessly into shreds, like a blood thirsty tiger at a turkey.

If heart break could kill, I have been killed.

My year of hell has begun. Its birth stamped by this day. The day my passport to happiness is ripped out of my hands and love is ripped out of my heart.

***

'No, not you too,' shaking my head I coughed the lump out of my airways. Biting into my lip and blinking several times, I urged myself: *please don't cry. Please don't cry.* But the cumbersome emotion pushed the first tear over the brim and the rest followed in suit.

One look at my mother was all it took.

'Mum?' I whimpered mutely. With my stance poised at the bathroom door of the hotel, I quietly watched her as she stood with her back to me rummaging in her suitcase on her bed. The short, plump and sweet old woman had changed into the same white robe as mine. Her robe was too long for her and trailed a couple of inches on the floor. Small, round head covered tightly in a white headscarf, bobbing like a float on water, extenuating her large, puppy dog eyes. In her baby wrap, her death shroud, she appeared as vulnerable and weak as an old canary in a jungle.

Please. I begged silently, not wanting to see the vulnerabilities I had seen in myself, in her. *Not you. You're my mother.*

My mother, who bore me in her womb for nine months and soldiered through the discomfort, the sickness and the unmatchable pain of childbirth. The one who had brought me into this world and loved me more than herself, even when I vomited on her shoulders and urinated in her lap. My mother, who kissed my grazed knees when I fell, wiped my tears when I hurt. Who jumped from the comforts of her sleep and ran to my bedroom whenever I had a nightmare. This woman, who spent nights and nights on her prayer mat with her hands raised, begging God, to give me happiness above her own.

She was my Supermother.

Mum, please not you too.

My silent pleas were just that. Silent. It was too late. She was exposed before my very eyes. Stripped down to two meagre pieces of cloth, she no longer represented the strength of a backbone or the comfort of a pillow. She had been replaced by a mere human being. This great woman was just human. A worn out, weak, perishable woman.

I noticed for the first time, the puffy circles under her eyes, darkened from sleepless nights. I noticed the deep wrinkles around her mouth, etching each broken dream. I noticed her stature, no longer of a shooting stem but rather of an old drooping plant, hunched by the weight of her worries.

She had been suffering.

Despite the façade of bravado she had put on for the sake of us, I had always known, but had sharply turned a blind eye. Now, the curtain of my eyes was drawn apart and there was nowhere for me to hide from the harsh truths.

I saw that the woman who had given me her world, had been hurting, and I had done nothing to help her. I had not seen her laugh or smile much in the past and never questioned her. She had watched her dear ones die before her and I did nothing to comfort her, not even hug her. She had watched her friends and family betray her yet I did nothing to reassure her, not even smile at her. Her own son coldly walked away from her yet I did nothing to numb her ache, not even a kind word.

The sight of her in her ihram smacked that lost conscience in my face like a boomerang. The guilt, the deep realisation of her pain cut through my stomach. My eyes burned with the silent flames of my tears as I remembered I was possibly the biggest inflictor of her wounds.

They say that those who you love the most hurt you the most. She loved me the most.

***

'I want it!' I scream at her.

My sixteenth birthday is approaching and I want the latest Nokia mobile phone. The handset costs a hundred and seventy pounds.

'I don't have any money. It's all gone on the food, the gas bill and the engine for your dad's car. I'm really sorry. Please.' Her eyes water. She cannot bear the thought of not giving her favourite child what she wants. She wishes she could sew those cushion covers faster so she would make more money. But how much can she do? The whole day is spent on housework. The nights are spent sewing, at 60p per cover. She feels like a failure.

'I don't care. You're getting it for me.' I give her a threatening look before I walk out of the room.

She did not have any money. But she managed to buy it for me. Somehow.

***

Over the past year, I barely spoke to her without screaming at her. I was the drunken violent man. She, the innocent powerless child.

***

Two' o'clock in the morning and I have just come home after a night out with friends. My mother has been waiting up for me. She cannot sleep without knowing I am safe in my bed. I had ignored her seven phone calls. My mascara has run down my face. I spent my journey home in tears. I cannot forget Zameer.

'Why do you look sad?' My mother walks towards me.

'Get away from me!' I snarl at her and push her away. She holds onto the wall to stop herself from falling.

'I'm your friend. Will you be my friend?' She asks. My sister had been the last person to say those words to me. My mother follows me up the stairs with a pleading smile on her face. A love struck puppy.

I ignore her and slam my bedroom door in her face.

She sits outside.

I hear her sniffling.

Half an hour later, I climb into bed listening to those sounds until I fall asleep.

***

Her love for me was a vast ocean in comparison to the droplets of love I had received from anybody else. Had she known of my sorrows, she would have taken her heart out of her beating chest and put it in the space where mine had died, I am sure.

But I had stamped on her heart repeatedly as though it was an irritating bug. My behaviour, vile and nauseous. Its severity only became apparent to me now.

With my gut rinsing in guilt and pain, I wanted to run to her and hug her. I wanted to hold her tightly and squeeze her heartache away. Tell her that I loved her. Drop to her feet and beg her to forgive me for my callousness.

Her feet.

'Paradise lies at the feet of your mother'. That is what the last Prophet had said: keep your mother happy and paradise will be

yours. Mothers were given the highest status and to even 'tut' at them was seen as a grave sin. I had done more than just tut. I had driven over those feet with a truck repeatedly with such disregard that you might say I deserved to be shot and deserved hell. Despair just got more despairing. I longed for the ground to open up and take me away from my fate.

Go to her, my own feet cried out. *Say 'forgive me'.* I wanted to. I wanted to kiss those bruised heavenly feet as a frenzied act of love and remorse. But my cowardly paws would not move.

I do not know why.

Was it pride? The unbearable shame? The embarrassment of the sudden melodrama? The physical inability I have had for years to show my emotions to my family? Or was it the fear of being knocked back? Whatever it was, I was paralytic to this desire.

Instead I turned away and ran back to the bathroom floor. Gripping my stomach, I kneeled over as fresh tears stained my cheeks.

'Are you okay?' My mother tapped lightly on the bathroom door.

Just go to her. I jumped, rubbed my cheeks and splashed them with cold water.

'Just a slight stomach ache mum,' brushing past her, avoiding her gaze.

'Oh. Ok.'

As she turned her back to me once more, I sneaked a long gaze at her. Eyes throbbing. I lightly touched my chest with my fingers and made a silent vow. I vowed, from that day onwards, to never plunge my knife into her heart again and to stitch the rags of it back together.

I would start by holding out my hand and offering it to her as we undertook this hopeful quest together.

***

The lobby of the hotel was not as quiet as it was the night before. It was littered with, what seemed like, Turkish pilgrims. The Turkish flags on their backpacks above the words 'Hajj 2008' gave a clue. I watched them passively as my mother and I stood there with our travel luggage at our feet, waiting for my father. He had disappeared to receive help with his ihram.

My mother and I had made the requisite formalities of entering into ihram: performing two bows and prostrations to God and reciting short verses from the Quran. When stepping away from my prayer mat, my official journey to Mecca had begun.

A man walked towards us from a distance as though he had just stepped out of an ancient biblical scene. He wore two sheets of white cloth. One sheet was wrapped around his midriff covering him from his navel to above his ankles. The other sheet draped over his body diagonally. Apart from sandals, there was nothing more on him.

A tingle skittered along my arms.

It was my father in his ihram attire.

The simplicity and starkness of his clothing made him look astonishingly small. The two white shrouds turned him into a poor man. And a pure man. A man in need. A humble man.

He could have been a man from the cave man era or a man of the robot era; it would have made no difference. In fact, in these pastoral shrouds my father looked as though he was not part of any era. He was detached from life and on the brink of entering the realms of submission to God.

Gone was the strong figure that had brought me up. Gone were those powerful arms that lifted me to the sky when I was a little girl. Gone was the man who told my brothers off with his ferocious voice when they called me 'hairy Mary'. His once large, gorilla-like body now became that of a weak, defenceless old man. His greying hair contrasted harshly against the deep brown of his skin. He walked with his shoulders slumped, head hung low. I detected a slight limp as he approached us. This man was not the father I knew. This man was a mere mortal.

'What do you think?' Nervously, he adjusted his shroud on his shoulder.

Memories of my childhood as daddy's girl swirled around me as I continued to watch him.

Once upon a time I was the cutest and sweetest thing in his life and in return for my hard work of being cute and sweet he lavished me with gifts. The blue swivelling torch he had bought for me when I was nine years old, I still had. He had come home from work, found me in the kitchen drinking a glass of milk and surprised me with it. The yellow bumble bee on the front had caught my eye first. That bee had become my friend during the nights I would stay up late to read after the lights went out.

It had all changed over a year ago when I had become a

rebellious bitch with an 'and what?' attitude. Just like I had hurt my mother, I had hurt him. I dropped all the love he had invested in me down a hole and the special bond between us turned into a frazzled rope. Barely did I speak to him without looking at him with contempt.

When I saw him now, his old love looked at me the way an orphan child would look at his mother after years of abandonment. A face of scars and bitterness with underlying fleshes of hurt.

'You look like a cave man.' I fidgeted uneasily, biting my bottom lip.

Repeated shame and regret encircled me unrelentingly. *Can I seriously expect to go to God's land and believe my wish will be accepted when I have brazenly disobeyed his Quranic words?* 'Be kind to your parents... address them in tens of honour'. Tens of insults had been my only way.

Mum hates me, dad hates me and God hates me.

The journey had barely begun and already emotions that had never been unearthed began to weigh me down. Emotions that I did not want to discover.

I have no fight in me. I inhaled deeply and blinked thrice, urging the advancing teardrops to stop in their tracks. *Is this trip really going to heal my wounds or is it just going to create new ones?*

3

'LABBAIK ALLAH HUMMA LABBAIK.'

The poignantly harmonious voice stirred in my ears with a caressing golden sensation. The language was the most exquisite of them all. Carrying with it beautiful soul. And the words. The words were the most heart rendering words of the moment. Expressing what a thousand instruments never could.

I remained soundless. My eyes still shut with a slight sub-consciousness. They were just a few words. Yet they had the power to gently unveil my sorrows once more. They softly uncovered every memory I had ran away from. The evocative music kindled the grieving spirit that brimmed on the corners of my eyes.

'Labbaik Allah humma labbaik.'

Arabic for: *here I am at thy service, O Lord, here I am.*

The voice was emanating through the speakers of the plane to Saudi Arabia. It was the voice of an Imam. He uttered the words that we, as pilgrims, were to continue saying from the moment we officially entered ihram until the moment we set our eyes on the Kaba. It awakened the other sleeping passengers too.

We were flying over Saudi.

'Labbaik Allah humma labbaik,' he repeated again in his mournful, sentimental melody. The passengers, all pilgrims, now repeated after him. I was unable to follow with them. The powerful moment had captured me in its bars of poignancy.

'Labbaik Allah humma labbaik,' finally I whispered, my eyes still closed. 'My Lord.' I stopped. My throat tightened. The painful flashbacks of the year returned like haunting ghosts. The moment I threw my graduation hat up in the air. The moment I realised that my life was a purposeless cycle. The moment I discovered Zameer cheated me. The moments when I cried myself to sleep. The moments when I screeched that God had left me.

'He has called you'. My Aunt had looked into my eyes for a

long, hard moment before I had departed. As if reading the pages of my book. At my blink she continued. *'Allah has called you to his holy land to save you. He loves you'.*

To save me.

'My Lord...,' whispering again. I took in a quiet breath. 'Here I am.' With that, I opened my eyes and freed the tear that I had held captive for that long moment.

***

'I feel like God has betrayed me.' It is the first brazen statement I make to others in relation to God. It raises eyebrows. Causes shock.

Born into a Muslim family, I am taught from a very young age of the oneness of God; Allah, the book of guidance; the Quran, the teachings of the final messenger; Prophet Mohammad and the final destinations; heaven or hell.

'God can make all your dreams and wishes come true if you please him'. The words of my mother constantly ring in my head ever since a child.

Through the ups and downs of life these words play and replay. Always a vivid and ambitious dreamer, I will do anything to turn my aspirations into reality. My mother's words prompt me to 'please God' in order to gain fruits. The bud of this blind faith has been planted inside me and as I blossom with age, my faith blossoms in mirrored synch.

Every morning I wake up half an hour early before school to make extra prayers. I share my Dairy Milk chocolate with my little brother. Wash the dishes at night on occasions. Help my friends with their Maths assignments. Laugh politely at my father's poor jokes. I stay away from clubs and alcohol. Do not let my friends tempt me into smoking Cannabis. And I make sure boys never come too close to me.

I try my best to please God.

True to my mother's words, my wishes always take a noticeable shape. All that I ask God for, he seems to give me. A new dress when I am eight. Top marks in my A level exams when I am seventeen.

God accepts my wishes. I become accustomed to getting what I want, having things go well for me and feeling relatively comfortable. I have the firm belief and hope that, with God by my side, I can have anything. Am I simply lucky or does he actually hear my every wish?

Since that Monday, luck has disappeared and God does not seemingly hear.

It is the fourth week of my turmoil and like every day since, I sit on my prayer mat, raise my hands to God, with hot burning tears in my eyes, and beg him, literally beg him, to end the intense mental and emotional anguish I am going through. But the clouds of despair only thunder more and the sun of hope is nowhere in sight. The storms are here to stay.

In my time of most need it seems God has left. My life is falling apart around me but he is doing nothing to help me. He has turned against me. Failed to protect me. Abandoned me.

'Why?!' I scream out. 'Why make me suffer?! I am a good Muslim! Help me out of this!!' The echoes of my own lonely voice are the only response. A defeated deer, I crumble on my bedroom floor until sleep numbs me.

My hope in him comes crashing down along with my life. The comfort my mother's words once gave me, now make me feel sick.

The road to self-destruction and rebellion beckon me. My anger is menacing and with it, I snatch back the strong hold that I had on the rope of God.

In rebellion, in sheer desperation, I delve into an existence that defies the principles of Islam and morality. I enter the glistening and welcoming doors of a bitter-sweet sinful life.

I use men for their attention, their care, their money. Bunk off work to stay in bed all day or to go watch afternoon movies at the cinema. I take revenge out on Zameer by harming him however I can. Through threats. Abuse. Violence. I inflict my family and friends with bitterness and hatred. I am evil towards them. Deliberately. I dismiss my prayers. Hang out with drug-dealing violent criminals.

I scrounge for these little drops of joy amidst the incessant gloom.

Spending time with other men divert my thoughts away from the rat. Intoxications of any kind make me forget about my hopeless future. Acts of revenge on Zameer fuel the intense hatred I have for him – numbing those uncontrollable feelings of love that will not leave. My rising arrogance protects me from inevitable feelings of worthlessness. Abusing friends and family with my cruel words until they hurt gives me a sadistic feeling of power. Bunking off work relieves me from those feelings of imprisonment. Seedy clubs, bars, *shade me from the glaring realities of daylight. Refusal to make my obligatory prayers is my daring act of challenge to God.*

***

'Labbaik Allah humma labbaik.' The Imam led again.

'Labbaik Allah humma labbaik.' I repeated after him, like the others.

Raising my head, I looked around the plane. The sight of these white clothed pilgrims inside the modern, clinical aircraft was surreal. Every passenger was now in ihram attire. Women wore white robes and white headscarves. Men wore two white sheets and sandals, like my father. The chants turned the atmosphere to that of a mystical cult scene. But without the darkness. For the first time since leaving my house, I felt solidarity with those around me. We were all on this plane for the same purpose. We were pilgrims. Desperate pilgrims.

'Labbaik la shareeka laka labbaik.' *Here I am at Thy service and Thou hast no partners.* The Imam continued with the rest of the verses. His fervency grew in his voice and spread contagiously as we repeated after him.

'Innal hamdah wa nematah.' *Thine alone is all praise.* He powered over the noise of the aircraft with a serene strength and we followed with equal power. An unpredictable adrenaline gushed into my veins.

'Laka wal mulk.' *Thine alone is the sovereignty.* His voice wavered. Ours broke.

'La shareeka laka.' *Thou hast no partners.* Lowering his tone, he bowed his head, weighed down by the sudden emotion of the moment. We instinctively mirrored his sentiments.

The air was cogent. Strained. I exhaled a deep breath and turned towards the window.

'Labbaik,' he led again, determined not to allow his emotions to overcome him.

With each repetition the anticipation of the moment I would be stood before the Kaba grew. Each Labbaik drummed in my heart. An unhealthy anxiousness brimmed on its surface. Not quite believing that I was heading towards this sacred wishing well. *Me.*

***

I dance like a carousel to Justin Timberlake's 'Rock Your Body.'
The beats vibrate through the speakers of the club, into my veins.

In my little red dress I am having a blast and feel like I am on stage.

The DJ changes the track.

I stop. It is abrupt. A soft whimper escapes my lips. A heavy flood of sadness gushes into me. Weighing my entire body down. The music of the next track now shatters my ears. I cower to the floor with my hands over my face. The sparkling club lights pierce my eyes. The friends around me that I had hugged only moments ago now appear like rasping snakes and stinging wasps.

'What the hell's happened to you?' Several people ask me as I run out of the club. I must get away. I throw myself onto the doorstep of the exit and huddle in the corner. Ignoring them all. Staring out into emptiness, I fight off tears for the rest of the night. The bitter cold and icy rain drops touch my skin like both friends and foes.

What the hell has happened to me? I do not know. I do know. I have entered that all familiar deep and inescapable depression. That is what has happened. The sporadic attack that cripples me for hours. The one that takes respite in nothing but the lapse of time.

Hours.

I know that when the paralysing state passes and I am able to move my limbs again I will spend every moment like a drug addict on the hunt for heroin, frantically searching for a fix. Those fleeting pleasures that will provide me with that little bit of temporary relief. As every heroin addict would admit, that is all such pleasures are – fleeting. The short lived juices are always, without fail, followed by a powerfully crashing, longer lasting, taste of bitterness and sickness.

Men only make me feel more worthless. Pathetic. My vengeance only makes me feel like a helpless nutcase that will soon see the bars of prison. Lashings at my close ones later make me feel disgusted with myself. My avoidance of work ends with the worry that I will soon be fired and penniless. Seedy clubs make me feel dirty. My new ominous friends make me mourn for my old happy self. My defiance to God makes me feel guilty and alone.

Life should not have got worse than that day in January, but by the time months have passed, I am drowning in unspeakable despair.

I am in pain.

My heart and mind had taken a shattering of a mallet at the beginning of it all. But they have now taken an intense grinding in a nut mill. These instant pleasures are becoming my enemy. I am spiralling deeper into a filthy, helpless mess with each tick of the clock.

I am diseased.

The more I seek these dangerous joys, the more prominent the later desires are of slamming the book of my life shut. For good.

'Get out of here!' My inner voice warns me. But I cannot stop and go back. I am in a mess. Trapped by the lure of the short sweetness's of my nights, despite knowing that they will, moments later, transform into an intolerable bitterness of lows and regrets. I need those fixes that allow me to escape for a little while from the truths.

Nothing else will numb my pain.

Nothing else gives me hope.

It is a vicious circle that is dragging me deeper into a black hole.

I am trapped.

***

The sands of the Arabian Desert rippled artistically under the cloudless sky. The sun beamed on the smooth, yellow-golden dunes. Spotless, beautiful and picture perfect. There was a futile temptation to jump off the plane, land into the soft sand with a quiet bounce and run my fingers through the shimmering beads. Arabia already possessed the ambience of a holy country. Seemingly untouched and undisturbed by the impact of modern man, like our ihrams, it was simple and pure.

As the plane descended, the uninhabited desert land disappeared and we entered civilisation. The yellow glow remained as roads occupied by large, white trucks and dots of people now emerged. Buildings spotted the sides of these channels; some small, cottage-like structures and others, three-storeyed, white marbled mansions.

We continued to recite Labbaik, louder and more passionately as we descended further to land. The zeal of these strangers and the electric atmosphere they had created inspired me. The hairs on my arms saluted as the first trace of excitement trickled through my veins.

***

The cheery, kind and funny young woman I have once been loved for is being buried deeper into her grave as each day passes. She is simultaneously being resurrected as a teary-miserable-unpredictable-crazy-zombie-bitch.

I do not know myself anymore. No one else knows me anymore.

'Look at you. Perfect life. Good job. Excellent qualifications. A family that adores you. Friends want to be you. Men desire you. You're blessed and gifted. You have it all! I can't understand this depression you have?' Sarah, along with everyone else, does not understand.

What is wrong with them? Can they not see the place inside the chambers of my heart? I am fighting a war. A war that I have raised all my weapons to but it just hurls me back into the trenches. Leaving me to perish.

No, they cannot see. My words are not enough. My tears are not enough. Unless they step into my soul, they will never understand my sorrows.

'Sorrow is sorrow, Sarah. Sorrow is sorrow.' I give her a weary look and my infamous sigh.

Perhaps, another person facing the same episodes as me would not deal with these events as hideously as I am doing. Perhaps any other person would take heed from Aaliyah and her song 'Try Again' and simply dust themselves off and try again. But what does that matter? Is there not a reason why they say 'what one perceives as a mountain the other perceives as a mole, and what one perceives as a mole, the other perceives as a mountain'? A Somalian man, whose daily worry is for survival, would surely be disgraced watching the aspiring music star on X-Factor falling to pieces at the realisation that he will never make it to fame. Moles. Mountains.

'Surely you can at least relate to simple feelings of hurt, emotional agony, despair, depression? Whether you understand what triggered it or not, and whether there's a reason for it or not, it doesn't matter Sarah. Ultimately, it's all the same. Sorrow is sorrow.'

Sorrow is sorrow; and mine is consuming, destroying and boundless.

***

Every marbled square foot of Jeddah airport was crammed with pilgrims from all parts of the world. Tens of thousands of them, mirror images of the next; white robed, white sheeted, brown sandaled. All kinds of loud and noisy faces shoved past me; white, black, brown, serious, concerned or just plain exhausted. These being the first hints of the commotions to come, I furrowed my eyebrows with concern.

Jeddah airport only ever opened its terminals for Hajj. It was the only seasonal airport in the world. Its seasonal experience, or lack of it, was evident from the great hold up at the airport desks. The desks were being confidently manned by slim Arab men, who I was convinced were still in their teens. Dressed in long black robes and Arabian keffiyahs on their heads, they were the only ones who were not in ihram attire and thus carried with them an air of self-importance.

They took over an hour to open their checkout desks. From then onwards, we were passed from one desk to the next. The authorities seemed to need to stamp our passports several times, each stamping taking up to half an hour.

Layth took control of our passports and ordered us to stand by our luggage whilst he sorted the necessary paperwork out.

'Thank goodness we have Layth with us. I don't understand a word these people are saying and they're so rude!' I slumped on my suitcase besides my parents and Daania whilst watching Layth push through the crowds waving our passports in the air. There was no concept of queuing behind desks. The person with the strongest arms and sharpest elbows got his turn first, it seemed. Poor Layth, despite his bulk, his meagre height meant he stood little chance. *It looks like we're going to be here for a while.*

'You've got to be tough skinned, this is how it is.' Daania warned wearily.

The Saudi airport staff did not speak a word of English and their way of communicating with everyone was by waving their arms frantically and shouting 'yalla!' I figured that meant *this way*. There were no signs throughout the airport, nor any guidance as to where we needed to go. The electric and uplifting mood that I had experienced only moments ago on the plane had long fizzled out, and was now charged over with disorder and frenzy.

'Keep an eye on those.' Daania inconspicuously pointed to a group of Asian female pilgrims who were loitering around our suitcases.

I fired her a quizzical look.

'They look shifty, they might take our bags.' She said.

'What? Surely you don't get thieves here. The land of *holiness*?' Surprised that she would suggest such a thing.

'Of course you do! Watch your bags and belongings at all times.'

My naivety rapidly passed when one of the women rested her cloaked back on my mother's suitcase. Narrowing my eyes at the potential thieves, I hugged my bags.

Three young men had joined us and two of them were talking to my father. They were members of our group. The other apparent members of the group were nowhere to be seen. *God knows how Layth is going to find them in this mess.*

'How long to the Kaba?' I asked the tall, chiselled one. *Kaba*. It sounded unnatural on my tongue.

Mikaeel, his name I later found out, exhaled loudly.

A positive sign then.

'Several hours on the coach,' he said. In his two white sheets he looked rather Greek and Adonis-like.

'How many?'

'Six. Probably more.'

'Six hours??!' *Another six hours before I get to make this wish.* It was an agonising thought.

The various pilgrims around me were probably hit with the same news judging by their gloomy long faces; faces as long as the next six hours.

It had taken us a total of twenty four hours to get to Jeddah and in that period I had slept little, thought a lot and underwent an array of draining emotions. Now, I was uncomfortable, confused, tired, irritable, sweaty, emotionally exhausted and impatient to get to Mecca.

Mikaeel informed me that the Saudi Authorities limited the number of pilgrims able to cross the border each year to approximately three million and refused entry to millions of other aspiring pilgrims. It was a requirement that all applicants were Muslim too, which meant billions could never experience this journey. Weeks prior to the trip, each individual name had to be registered with them in order for them to organise the use of medical, camping and transport facilities for the pilgrims during the Hajj. The mechanics behind the pilgrimage were perplexing and so I contently sat on my suitcase, under the heat, and watched Layth fight in the queue for us.

Our miniature lion returned moments later. He looked haggard. 'We need to put our luggage on this truck.'

A rusty truck appeared. Open backed, carrying the number 34 on it. Two dark skinned, conspicuous looking men, dressed in blue uniforms hovered around the truck eyeing up our suitcases. 'They'll take our bags away to our coach,' said Layth.

I raised my eyebrows, not feeling comfortable entrusting these dodgy looking men with our possessions. Not now that Daania had instilled her cynicism into me. Anxiously, I watched the men load their truck with our suitcases and hoped that we would get it all back later – whenever that would be.

Thinking about it, it would not have been a great loss if my suitcase did disappear. I had packed very little and did not bring anything of value. A simple face cream, soap, toothpaste, a toothbrush, a comb, shampoo, my contact lenses and glasses. I successfully fought the urges to pack any make-up. I brought two Islamic robes and headscarves and a couple of trousers and t-shirts to wear underneath them. One pair of slippers and one pair of shoes I judged would suffice. Bar some books on Mecca and Hajj, that was it.

I left the luxuries of my life behind. There would be no need to impress anyone and no need to compete with anyone. Something I was secretly glad of. A life of simplicity and humility beckoned me, even if it was just for three weeks.

Our small group hung out in the vicinity of the vast airport waiting area as we anticipated the arrival of the coach. The sun shone through the open roof onto the dusty ground and lit up the surrounding small shops. Fruit, gifts, drinks, phone cards and other useful things that travellers would buy were being sold at these seasonal stalls. Benches were dotted sparingly and fully occupied by laying pilgrims. The carpeted areas were where most pilgrims sat – under the glaring sun, in simultaneous preparation for the mid-afternoon prayers. We joined them after having a quick half-body wash, as the five daily prayers were obligatory upon us, especially when in the state of ihram. Surprisingly, I still remembered how to make these prayers, albeit quite rusty.

When the coach eventually arrived at three' o' clock, three hours later than it was supposed to, we left the rest of the pilgrims on the carpeted mats whilst they waited for their assigned coaches. Our luggage had reappeared and was thrown on top of the vehicle and we were thrown inside.

A collective sigh of relief was let out as everyone – minus the rest of our group who were nowhere to be located – leant back and relaxed when the coach took off. I barely put my tired feet up when a burly man sitting adjacent to us chanted loudly: 'labbaik Allah humma labbaik!'

Anxiousness and excitement trickled through my weariness. *O Lord, here I am. Although I don't know how far I am.* I was looking forward to the moment that I would stand before the Kaba and say 'here I am, finally'.

The coach journey was, without doubt, one of the longest coach journeys I had ever been on. I burned from the forty degree heat and coughed in and out sandy dust that entered the – falsely advertised – air-conditioned vehicle. I failed to catch a nap with the coach rocking from side to side on the bumpy roads, as though for our amusement. We made several pit stops at road diners mainly to use the toilets, wash and perform our prayers. Cartons of small snacks and water were handed to us by Saudi authorities who parked up huge trucks storing these replenishments for the pilgrims who were on their way to Mecca. A nice gesture that briefly gave relief to my otherwise sapped and debilitated body.

As the coach drove up and down hills, my mood rose up and down with it. The sudden thought that I was approaching the Kaba would throw me upright and arouse me into raw and fervent recitations of 'Labbaik'. But there were other times when human fatigue overpowered me and I shut my eyes longing for nothing but to lie in my bed and listen to the pitter-patter of the English rain.

***

It has now been almost a year. I am still trapped in this deepening dark wilderness. I try to forget Zameer. I try to forget work. My days are spent scrounging desperately in seedy places for scraps of happiness. My nights are spent reeling from a deepened agony and hopelessness.

My heart struggles to beat with peace. My mind is a scrambled chaos. And my soul – destroyed.

What will my mourners say? 'It was not an earthquake which wiped away her livelihood that destroyed her. It was not a flood which washed her away from her home and family that destroyed her. It was not a brutal murder of her that destroyed her. No. It was the shattering of her dreams, the breaking of her heart and the demolishment of hope in God that destroyed her. Which is the more accursed event; the earthquake, the flood, the murder or this disease of the soul?'

***

'This is the long road, Ibrahim al-khalil, that leads to the Al-Haram mosque, within which the Kaba lies,' whispered Layth, ten hours later. He pointed ahead.

My eyes widened from either deliriousness due to lack of sleep or genuine excitement.

'Yep, we're in Mecca and we're nearly there!' he said.

The coach had slowed down. My heart skipped a beat. I lifted my body to peer out of the window.

The sky was black but the stars twinkled onto the land. It was one' o'clock in the morning yet the city was rip-roaringly alive.

The sandy grounds sung Arabia. Side-lining the road were tall well-built marbled buildings and small dubious hut-like stony structures. Knitted closely together, they resembled shanty houses amidst palaces. Some buildings were advertised in English; 'Al Humus hotel', 'Money exchange', 'Jubbah shop'. Others were signed in incomprehensible Arabic. The larger buildings were decorated exquisitely in patterned pale green and pink marble, edged in gold, with huge, fancy glass doors and glittering signs. I figured these were hotels. The smaller structures were not extravagant and more box-like, with open-faced, windowless entrances. Many huts were packed with garments filtering out on to the pavements. Smoke from cooking food escaped others. The architecture did not leave much to order or symmetry but was fascinating to my eyes, which had seen too many western brick buildings.

Above all, the occupants of this infamous road were bedazzling. The vicinity was crammed with tens of thousands of people, all of which I could not take my curious eyes off. Pilgrims walked alongside the coach and others leisurely away, dressed in Arabic robes and colourful North African gowns. The majority of pilgrims were in the ihram attire and walked rapidly forwards. I guessed many had just arrived and were heading towards the Kaba. I watched tribes of African men and women, peered at white blonde haired men, observed small Chinese women and gazed at south-Asian ladies. I had taken a dip into merged pools of Africa, Asia, Europe and America.

Old people tightly held onto walking sticks with one hand and the arms of their companion with the other. Disabled women dressed in white sat in wheelchairs whilst being pushed by sheeted men as they weaved through the crowds. I even spotted a few children – running down the road, being held by their parents or being carried on the shoulders of fathers.

This new world, this new existence was captivating. As the coach crawled forwards, I continued to gape out. There was so much to see. Owners of garment shops loitered at the entrances of their shops watching the life of Ibrahim al-khalil road unfold. Chefs of takeaways took orders from hungry customers. Small groups of women shopped, holding out scarves or dresses, deciding whether to buy or not to buy. Families paced in the opposite direction, with juices in their hands, looking rather unaffected by it all. *Hold up, how can they busy themselves with shopping when the Kaba is only metres away?* Bewildered. *How can they worry about eating when the great wishing well is just yards away?*

Those in their ihram attire were certainly touched. They scurried in the direction of the Kaba to catch it in time, as though it would disappear in a few moments like a UFO. Eyes fixed in the direction ahead. Their faces revealed excitement, nervousness. Their lips moved, informing God that they were 'here'.

In a few moments that will be me. Am I really here?

'Labbaik Allah humma labbaik!' chanted a bald man at the other side of the coach as if to answer my question.

'Labbaik Allah humma labbaik,' I repeated. *I am definitely here.*

'Where is it?' I asked Layth anxiously.

He laughed. 'You won't see it from here.'

I looked at him urging him to tell me more.

He smiled and turned away teasingly. Before I had the chance to pester him, the coach halted to a stop outside one of the tall buildings.

'We're here!' exclaimed Layth and jumped up.

I looked at my mum. She mirrored my ediness and lightly held my hand.

My first step onto Meccan land was with a heavy thud. A thud that reflected the weight of the emotions I had brought with me. A thud that jolted my entire body, confirming that all this was real.

The diverse sounds coming from all directions penetrated my ears. They were revived. Labbaiks of pilgrims. Cries of worshippers. Laughs of children. Clatters of pots. Horns of vehicles. Rustles of movement. Sizzles of frying meat.

Mecca.

Looking around me, I hoped to see something that would suggest where the Kaba was but there were no clues. We were still amidst shops and hotels.

I will soon know.

'This is our hotel.' Layth pointed to a building signed 'Al-Afas'.

Narrow in size, approximately seven yards in width. Its outer walls were covered in white marble stretching to fifteen storeys high. Directly adjacent to it was a fabric shop and on the other side was what appeared to be a laundry outlet.

Green uniformed hotel clerks whizzed through the automatic doors and without a word offloaded our suitcases and took them inside.

Inside, the large chandeliers hanging from the ceiling emitted a yellow glow which reflected onto the white marbled floor and walls giving the hotel a very Arabic ambience. A couple of golden sofas and an oak table filled the reception area. The small reception desk manned by a white robed, bearded Arab.

It was only a fleeting thought but if I was to confess I was disappointed at the adequacy of the hotel room that I was to share with my parents. The three beds, a large wardrobe, an air-conditioning unit and an en-suite bathroom were luxuries that I would have expected from a hotel in the west, not a hotel for pilgrims. The same disappointment would pass in an eager back-packer that came to know that he would be staying in the Hilton hotel and not in a tent. I desired an earthy and simple experience. These comforts made me feel, ironically, uncomfortable.

'Go put your bags down, have a quick wash and meet me here in five minutes and we'll make our way to the Kaba,' said Layth.

Five minutes. In five minutes I will be there. In five minutes I will raise my hands to God and will make my wish. Will it be a life changing moment?

After travelling for almost thirty six hours in anticipation of this moment, I was suddenly not ready.

***

'The tickets have been confirmed, we're going to Mecca for Hajj.' My mother walks into the kitchen whilst I am making myself a cup of tea.

It is four o'clock in the morning and I cannot sleep. She is up for the pre-dawn prayers. I have not seen her for any part of the day before, which is not unusual. My eyes are stinging from another teary moment having seen Zameer and his fiancée together in Starbucks that afternoon. I try to hide my face under the shadows of the dimly lit kitchen so my mother would not see the streaks of pain.

My parents are planning on going to Mecca for the annual pilgrimage. Like many people, they have harboured the wish to go for almost their entire life and finally, this year, their dream was becoming real.

I pause for a moment and stop stirring my tea.

Mecca. Hajj. Kaba.

These three words linger in the space of my mind. I do not know much about them, but I know that Mecca is in Saudi Arabia and is the holy land for Muslims. In Mecca lies the Kaba, the focal point of the Muslim world, which is a cubed monument that billions around the world pray in the direction of. It is in the direction of the Kaba that I have raised my hands and made my many prayers to God. I know Hajj is an intense five day pilgrimage that most Muslims are required to do at one point in their lives. Being sent to the local mosque from four-thirty to seven' o' clock every weekday afternoon between the ages of four and eleven taught me that.

'So kids', my Islam teacher, Mr Aryan, would always begin his classes with the same words. His little speech was as common as his daily greetings.

'In order to be a true Muslim, You must abide by the five principles of Islam. The first is to believe that there is no God but Allah, and to believe that Prophet Mohammad was his messenger. Yep?' Mr Aryan, throughout our seven years, never waited for our dopey little faces to nod in understanding but always ploughed on. 'The second rule is to perform Salah, the ritual prayers five times a day – at dawn, mid-day, late afternoon, sunset and after nightfall. Yep? The third is Charity, to give some of your money to the poor. Yep? The fourth is to fast in the month of Ramadan, from dawn to sunset. You lot are too young for that but when you're older this will teach you self-restraint and cleanse you. And finally... Hajj. Perform Hajj at least once in your lifetime if you have the physical and financial means. But not yet. When you're older. When you are *old enough to appreciate its magical beauty...'*

'Magical beauty...' The striking phrases used to describe the voyage of Hajj now beam at me. I heard a countless number of times that Hajj is a 'journey of a lifetime', 'a life changing experience', 'truly the most amazing trip in the world'. No mediocre words were ever used to describe it. They say that if a wish is made directly before the Kaba, then that wish will come true.

'Hajj makes a person as pure as a baby,' they say. As pure as a baby; imagine that. Would I be able to press the rewind button on my life? I think bitterly. Can I go back to my childhood and be taught how to enjoy Tennis? Will someone warn me, 'do not dream and hope in vain', before I close my eyes and make my dreams? Can I go back and save my heart from Zameer? Can I be like that sweet child that I was twenty-four years ago, the one that never knew heartache, never knew sorrow; the one that was protected from the demons of life?

My brewing tea is as dark and concealing as my future. The hot, obscure liquid is waiting to trickle down my throat and immerse itself into the shades of my inside. I gaze into it with the sore and forlorn eyes that have kept me up until such an early hour.

'I want to go,' it is barely a whisper.

The thought is as random and emerging as a rainbow amidst a storm. The idea of embarking on this 'journey of a lifetime' has never crossed my mind, but in this sudden moment I can think of nothing but to grasp this rainbow in my hands.

The land of wishes.

Am I running back to God? The one who I have rebelled against out of feelings of betrayal and hurt? I cannot answer the question in this moment, nor do I want to address it. But I am sure of one thing; the widening of my dark deeds has widened the small hole I was originally in into a gaping crater. I hate to admit it, but the picture of reality does not need a confession from me. I am in a more dismal place than before I turned my back on him.

A life-changing experience.

To retrace my steps and go back to my old self is inconceivable. I do not have the strength or the ability to pick up the pieces of my heart and put together the shards of my dreams one by one. Almost twelve months have passed and I have tried everything that I possibly could, to bring myself out of the despair that I am in. I have ripped my hair out searching for that peace, that meaning, that comfort. Nothing has worked. With my bare hands I try to climb out of this deep-hundred-feet hole but I only seem to dig further in the opposite direction, whilst friends and family look down, outstretching their unreachable hands. I need help from someone greater and bigger than a measly person. Could that be God?

I do not know.

'A journey of a lifetime', 'truly the most amazing trip in the world', 'the land of wishes'; the fairies beckon me with their whispers. Never have these claims been associated with any other trip. I need more than a holiday to the Bahamas. I need something that allures me with the promise of changing my life. Perhaps I need this.

The metal spoon in my hand bends as the hazy thought turns into determined need. I need to go to Mecca. I will make my wish at the Kaba. I will embark on this 'life changing journey' and maybe I will find a way out? Maybe it will work for me. Or maybe it will not. But I am a desperate woman. Crestfallen. Willing to try anything, even if it is as drastic as flying to Mecca.

The teaspoon flashes in my hands under the kitchen lamp. Is this my glimmer of hope? Hope, that perhaps such a journey would change my life, like it had seemingly done so for others? Hope that perhaps God will come onto my side again and grant my wishes if I make them at this holy land?

Possibly.

'I have to go.'

'You??'

'Yes.' It is a simple, soft plea. I turn to her, as a slow tear trickles down my face. For the first time in these few months my mother has been exposed to my pained face, the dark circles under my eyes, my grief-stricken expression.

She is stunned. This is not the face of someone expressing a whim. This is the face of a young woman who is experiencing severe mental anguish, for whatever reason, and is desperate to cure it before it kills her.

Three weeks later, I close the door to my house for the last time, ready to leave everything behind and embark on this journey to the 'magical' land. The mental torment is still as raw as my wounds. Thinking about the immediate past pains me. Thinking about the long term future distresses me. But for a fluttering moment, one feeling overtakes all those feelings that I have felt during this year. As brief as the chirp of a robin, it momentarily replaces the anguish. It makes me notice the subtle skitter of my heart, the slight alertness in my eyes, the faint spring in my step. It is a feeling that I thought had escaped me forever.

Hope.

4

'DO NOT LOOK UP.'

Fuelled by both deliriousness and sleep deprivation, my eyelids stretched wide apart as Layth repeated his warning. 'Do not look up. Not even to catch a glimpse of it, until we are stood directly before it.'

I wiped my forehead and nodded meekly.

Do not look up.

These four words shot my fear and anticipation up into the foreign skies above. *Fear? What am I afraid of?* I was not quite sure but part of me wanted to run in the opposite direction and not have to face it. The other part wanted to leap towards it faster than I could blink.

Stood outside the hotel, Layth had gathered my parents, Daania and I into a huddle to give us last minute advice before we made our way to the Kaba. The men who had arrived with us had already left and the missing members of our group were nowhere to be seen.

The black sky glittered with stars which shone on every inch of the city in sight. But, paranoia or not, they all seemed to pin-point their gaze onto me. They had watched my every move. From my life in England to my moments here in Mecca. Silent witnesses to the death of my dreams, broken promises of love and the rise of my rebellion. And they were now waiting for the rest of the story to unfold.

'Once we are there and we are stood before it, then look up slowly. And once it is in your full gaze, make your wish. For they say; the first wish that you utter when you see the Kaba for the first time will always....,' he paused, '...always be accepted by Allah.'

'Holy God.' I caught my breath. *Could this moment really be the most important moment of my life?*

'Let's go and stay with me as there will be quite a crowd.' Layth puffed his chest, turned around and stepped forward. 'Labbaik Allah humma labbaik,' he chanted.

My body tensed and I failed to move. *'Many have gone and never returned alive'. 'The crowds are fierce and over-zealous'.* The warnings crept out. The fear of not knowing what lay ahead paralysed me. *Will I be crushed in the crowds? Will something happen before I reach the Kaba which will spoil the moment? Will I be so overwhelmed by the sight of it that I pass out? Will I get what I came for or would I only face another crashing disappointment?*

'Come on, what's wrong?' My mother tugged at my robe.

Reluctantly, my feet lifted themselves off the sandy rubble. The fear was consuming but the desperation for a wish, which I had harboured for so long, prevailed. Too much hope rested on this moment for me to lose courage now.

'Labbaik Allah humma labbaik,' I stuttered. Breathing heavy. Head bowed. I walked along Ibrahim al-khalil road. Small tense steps. Heart pounding in my chest. A thousand emotions bubbled within me.

I was making my way towards it.

***

Thinking about the Kaba seemingly made even the most composed of people nervy. For Muslims it was *'the holiest object in the world'.* Golden framed pictures of it decorated mosques and the houses of Muslim friends and family I knew. Key rings, ornaments, books, mugs, pens were passionately embellished with the cube. It is in the direction of the Kaba that I had raised my hands and bowed my head over the years in prayer. Billions of Muslims all over the world had raised their hands and bowed their heads in its direction too. Prayers revolved around it and its symbolism, as seemingly did life.

But never had I known why the Kaba was so momentous until I had opened up a book on the plane and read about it. I was thrown aback by what I came to know. It said, when God created the world he had started it from the grounds of the Kaba. This cube was originally constructed by the first man and Prophet, Adam, and then rebuilt centuries later by Prophet Abraham. Its new purpose was to ensure that Muslims, no matter what creed, race or nationality, would use the Kaba as the single point of their prayers, remembering the oneness of God and come together at this one place on the planet both spiritually and physically. To unify humanity.

'Allah's blessings shine from the heavens directly onto the vicinity of the Kaba and then spread throughout the world from here', Layth had said.

No wonder people, with the belief it holds the key to their happiness, crossed oceans to be beside it. I envisaged the heavens opening and a ray of magical light beaming down from the skies on to the Kaba. With that concocted image, I guess, I too would have swum across seas to stand beside this promise.

***

The walk to the Kaba was a haze. Eyes lowered, I attempted to keep my vision intent only on the few paces ahead of me as we weaved our way forward. White hems of robed women and sheeted men fluttered past. Brown feet. Black feet. White feet. All rushing to make a wish. Chants of 'Labbaik' surrounded me. Fierce chants. Passionate chants. Almost wails.

I squeezed my mother's hand for comfort.

A few paces on, I could no longer resist. Curiosity begged me to push my eyes upward. My vision was immediately hit by a sea of white bodies. Loud, passionate, chanting pilgrims charged past us in their sheets, having lost any signs of composure. Others walked slower, seemingly foregoing consciousness whilst their lips moved rapidly. These foreign people were eccentric. I had entered another world. Frightened, I threw my eyes back down.

Seconds later the light enveloping me suddenly changed. The yellowness from the shops and street lamps that reflected on the sandy ground transformed to a dazzling luminous white. It shone into my eyes and I could not help but ignore, for a second time, Layth's warning not to look up.

I nearly lost my footing at the sight of what stood before me.

Metres away, lay the most striking building I have ever set my eyes upon.

'Here is the Al-Haram mosque. Sorry, you can look up at it, as the Kaba lies within it.' Layth faintly echoed in the background.

A colossal magical palace. My first thoughts.

An extremely grand, columned structure, three storeys high and seemingly thousands of metres wide, cemented in front of me. Its beauty took my breath away. Lavished in shiny white marble, its walls appeared to be lit from within the stone. Six large, exquisite minarets dazzled eloquently and soared into the glittering night sky. The tops of the storeys each rimmed elegantly with a white, glossy balcony that travelled all the way around the magnificent architecture. Several archways provided an entrance into the depths of the mosque. On the far sides were smaller archways but the most prominent were the three directly in front of us that emanated a green light from within.

The mosque stood apart from everything that surrounded it; like a peacock amongst mice. It stood with romantic grace, fantastic prestige and wild elegance. It blessed luminosity onto the faces of the people below it. So profound was its glow that for a long moment, I wondered whether I was still on planet Earth. Never had I seen a building with such a presence on the earth's surface. Its otherworldliness almost convinced me it was a palace of heaven.

Tentatively, I stepped up onto the immense marbled courtyard. Resting the soles of my feet, I imagined my spirit rising up a step closer to that heaven.

'We need to offer two nafil prayers before we enter the mosque,' said Layth. He looked at me and forced a smile.

Another delay. I coughed to get that ballooned heart out of my throat.

'The Kaba is inside, through the archways,' he pointed ahead.

Layth led us towards an outer wall of the Al-Haram. Having removed my sandals and shoved them into my backpack, I offered my two bows and prostrations with as much concentration as a child reading an encyclopaedia in a theme park. Nerves, fear, excitement – they were wearing me thin. I was desperate to move on.

Minutes later we proceeded towards the large archways. Layth gave his final piece of advice. 'Don't look up. Keep your eyes down until I say and keep reciting Labbaik.'

I sucked in a deep breath, pushed my shoulders back, lowered my head and grabbed hold of my mother's hand. 'Labbaik Allah humma...' I started again. Trembling involuntarily.

Here goes. This is it.

We walked.

'...Labbaik.'

Frantic thoughts rushed through my mind as the stars above exploded in synch. *Am I finally about to stand under the rays of God's blessings and make my wish? Are my problems about to end?* The thought sounded incredulous, yet hope flickered at its possibility. *What should my wish be?* I panicked, fearing that words would fail me when I needed them most. *Is God going to pull out all my sorrows and heal me?* A flashback of pain squeezed my heart. *What if he refuses to accept my wish because I've been so defiant?* The thought horrified me. I had come too far and hung too many emotions in the firing line to be able to deal with rejection now. *What if I am swept away by the crowds and crushed to death?* I tightened the hold on my mother's hand. It was too late to turn back. Death or no death, it had to be faced.

'Labbaik la shareeka laka labbaik.' I continued.

My movements controlled by the magnetic force of this gem as it pulled me through the archways, barefooted. The ground radiated a strong light and I felt as though I was floating on a soft bed of air.

'Inal hamda, wanih mata laka wul mulk, la shareeka la.' I repeated these words under my breath. I heard them in my ears. But from a faraway remote distance. The shoves, the pushes from the people next to me were barely acknowledged. I heard the roar of voices, feet and movement but I did not listen to them. Nor did I dare look up. Momentarily, I spared a thought for the blind as I underwent the torture of yearning to see.

Minutes passed.

The roar picked up in strength. I sensed more people. More activity. More rush. The noise was deafening. The sound of titanic waterfalls. The aromatic smell of street spices had long left and a raw, earthy smell had taken their place.

We were closer.

Exhausted beads of sweat rolled down my face. My hand throbbed. My fingers clasped tighter around my mother's. She returned the crushing gesture.

'Stop!' Layth shouted.

My heart plummeted.

'We're here, you may look up.'

My mother dropped my hand and I was left to stand on my own. It was time.

***

The gates of the inferno gape open. Hot flames lash and drag me inside unsparingly. Despair for life is as constant as the feeding of oxygen to my lungs. Each agonising hour is a crawling struggle through the endless stretch of thick and heavy anguish. My hope and motivation for even the simplest of things has been destroyed.

What is the point?

Once a firm believer of 'good things happen to good people', I now resent that statement.

My inner strength was once as tough as a rock. I was never one to feel sentimental often nor was I ever one to cry. I barely remembered the last time I had let go of a tear. But with my broken heart and broken dreams, even the unshatterable rock inside me shatters into a thousand pieces. I am in tears almost every day. With tears in my eyes I sleep in the long nights. With the same tears in my eyes I awake in the dreaded mornings.

My whole world has come caving in. It is burying me alive. And I do not know what to do to save myself.

***

'Labbaik,' I whispered.

My eyes fixed onto the ground. My body posed like a statue. Unaware of the beats of my heart. My hands would not move. My ears deaf to all that was around me. Movement totally failed me.

But my mind. My mind ruptured with once repressed thoughts. Flashes of past events jerked before my eyes. I saw myself curled up in bed with my duvet over me, sobbing throughout the night until my body forced me into sleep. My head on my desk; office door closed, staring at a bottle of paracetomols. The darkness of my eyes in the mirror night after day. Zameer's cold expression as he walked past me, as though he never knew me. My pained body crumbling to my bedroom floor in a fit of tears. Clutching my heavy chest. On my prayer mat, head bowed, hands raised, begging God to make things right. My desperate self, bowing in prostration, shaking my head with tears streaming down my face. Refusing to get up until God told me he had heard me.

'He has called you'. My Aunt's words played again. *'Allah has called you. To save you'.*

To save me.

'O Lord. Oh my Allah...' My face crumpled.

'My Lord, here I am...'

Slowly I lifted my head up. Eyes level. As the jewel of Arabia steadily unveiled itself.

Piece by piece.

There it was; the Kaba.

The most phenomenal and influential entity in the universe.

Instantly, it captured my whole being; heart, mind and soul. Past, present and future. It took my breath away with suave and undeniable charm. Possessed by the aura of mystery and sacredness, my earth stopped orbiting, my moon froze and all life paused.

Time stood still.

The fifteen metre black cube shrouded in its silky cloth shot a spectacular contrast against the surrounding snowy marble and graced my sight with a supreme elegance. Golden Arabic scripture 'laa ilaaha illAllah hu Muhammadur rasoullullah', *there is no God but Allah and Mohammad is his messenger*, ran across the ebony and flashed like a million miniature stars. Dazzling my eyes. The magnet towered over the hundreds of thousands of awestruck pilgrims. Proclaiming its prestige, magical majesty, as though it was its God-given right. It was a rich, jewelled king amongst poor unadorned slaves. A sensational ruby amongst dusty gravel.

Through the foreign people, the vast seas, the warm houses, the open roads, the shapely clouds, the flowing rivers, the bashful trees, the brazen fields, the inflicting rain, the dormant volcanoes, the scorching deserts – through it all – I had reached the core.

The centre of the world.

The Kaba.

My heart, I was sure, had burst. Overwhelming emotions splattered into my eyes. Immediately my vision blurred, flooded with tears. The rivers of blood in my body rushed to the sea of my mind. My throat constricted as I fought for painless air. My chest heaved. My legs trembled beneath me. I struggled to raise my shaking hands in front of me. The gesture of a poor beggar.

'Labbaik!' I exclaimed through my heavy sobs, 'O Allah here I am!'

In the intensity of that powerful moment my legs gave way. I fell to my knees. My white robe drowned my body. My hands raised. Head bowed.

It was the picture of a desperate woman. A scene that told of an impoverished girl who had travelled three thousand miles in desperation with nothing but handfuls of tears and a heart of pain, praying that God will save her.

My body shook wildly and through the medium of my uncontrollable cries I unleashed all the emotions that were within me.

Through my tears, I freed the hurt and betrayal I felt by Allah. Through my tears, I ripped out the heart that was broken by that horrible man. Through my tears, I shook out the frustration of my shattered career dreams. Through my tears, I screamed out the anger, bitterness and hatred that had consumed me for so long. Through my tears, I let out the fear of my perpetual misery. Through my tears, I let go of the sadness, the simple sadness that had been with me for a seeming eternity. Through my tears, I unveiled the rope of hope that I clung onto to get here.

Through my tears, through my wails, through my trembling body, through my pleading hands, I liberated my desires to dream again.

I wept.

I wept as the stars stood over me, the Kaba watched in silence and Allah waited patiently; 'Tell me. Tell me your wish…'

***

Words failed me.

Under the beam of God's showers, in a shroud, on my knees, hands raised, tears rolling down my cheeks with my eyes resting on the Kaba for the first time – words failed me.

Billions had come and made their wishes and now Allah was waiting for mine. Waiting for me to utter what I desired the most.

I longed for something that I was sure every person to have set foot on this planet longed for, and every person who will ever set foot on this planet will long for. I longed for something that no man and no woman could give me. Something I knew only God could ever give me.

'O Allah.' I took in a deep breath.

'I wish for…' I paused to regain some composure.

'O Allah, I wish for… eternal happiness… I wish for eternal happiness for me and those that I love.'

Not just happiness. Eternal happiness.

5

'SAVE ME.'

MY AUNT's words resonated in my head. '*He has called you. To save you.*'

'I've come at your calling. See my outstretched hands? See me on my knees? These tears? The hope in my eyes? I've travelled three thousand miles to call upon you. To pull me out of the darkness and carry me under your light. To save me. So save me!' I implored.

My knees did not shift from their place at the Kaba. I had much to say to Allah and much to ask for.

'Allah, please turn this frown into a smile. A smile that will last forever until the day I die. Give me peace in my heart. I could have every material thing in the world at my feet, but without this peace, I am lost. How do I get it? I feel empty. This despair is killing me. I don't know where else to turn but to turn to you... Heal me.'

I blabbered on.

'Will you love me and mend my broken heart? Don't let me shed another tear for Zameer. If you are by my side I can tackle the world, please don't leave me again.' My loneliness called out softly. 'If no one in the world loves me, I can still live on. But if you don't love me, how can I live?'

The prayers switched rapidly as did the seconds in my life. I feared I was losing time and opportunity.

'My soul is dark,' lowering my tone. My insecurities pressured me to believe that God probably hated me for my misdeeds. Bowing my head in shame, I remembered my infidelity, my vengeful attacks on Zameer, the abuse to my friends and family. All the other things that I was too ashamed to think of here. 'Pardon my human weaknesses.'

My mother and father caught the corner of my eye. My heart wrenched in pain at the sight of them. They were begging. My parents were begging. Standing with their hands raised in the air. Raised like slaves would to their master. Lips quivering, bodies shaking and pained faces streaming with tears. It was physically unbearable to watch. Never had I seen them like this. Never had I seen my father cry at all, not even at the death of his mother and father. And now here he was, here they both were, weeping as though they had just lost everything they ever had.

I thought of the heartache they might have repressed over the decades; the death of their young children, the death of their parents, the betrayal of their family and friends and other things I did not know about. Their expressions said what a thousand laments could not. Only now, in their late fifties, were they seemingly able to set the horridness free.

'Oh Allah,' turning my eyes to the Kaba again and shaking my head, 'look at them. They did not deserve that, surely?' The drops burned my cheeks as I recalled the hurt I had inflicted on them. 'I'm sorry for causing them such misery. They don't deserve such unhappiness. Please Allah,' pleading, 'make them happy. Take away all their pain and never let them see a dark day ever again.'

Moments later, my thoughts turned to the millions of people in the world who would give their limbs to be at the place I was. To be able to make a wish with hope that money could never buy. I said a silent prayer for those suffering from injustices, poverty, torture and oppression. I prayed for my loved ones and all the good people of the world, leaving out the evil and those that had wronged me.

Will he accept my wishes? 'Allah you are the greatest, you created this world, so surely you could in an instant, in the time it takes me to blink, grant me my wishes. Please do it.'

There were more things that I wanted to say but my mind was sapped of all its energy. 'Whenever I call upon you, will you hear me?' I stared at the Kaba with my glistening and faraway eyes. Waiting for an answer.

***

'Prayer is the most potent weapon of a believer; it can change fate while no actions of ours ever can.' Those were powerful words once acclaimed by Prophet Mohammad, and at that moment in time, when I made my wishes, I felt that my words alone did have the power to change my fate. Build new roads, open new doors. Knees on the hard marble, my being was sure that Allah was listening and I

blindly entrusted him to bring my wishes to a reality. Whether my mind was with me or not, I felt that with these prayers anything was possible and nothing was impossible.

God had never witnessed me utter a prayer with such sincerity. On an ordinary day, my lack of composure in such a public place would have mortified me. What must I have looked like? A woman cloaked in white, on her knees, with her palms outstretched like a scrounger, whilst she cried out uncontrollably. What must an outsider have thought seeing me like this? Did I look like a mad beggar that had escaped a mental asylum? In fact, I do not think mad beggars even behaved like this. Even they had their limits.

He is my master and I his servant. Feeling so small beside the Kaba, I began to think it for the first time. *Should I feel humiliated begging the one who created me and would end my life when he chooses? Am I not his servant; at his mercy? To plead with him is all I have left to help myself now, isn't it?*

I knew I would never beg a person like that. Not even if a psychopath held out a gun to me and threatened to shoot me if I did not beg.

But this was God.

And it felt rather liberating to forsake all pride and plead with the one that I believed had the power to help me.

***

'I really need this job. I might have to drop to my knees. Pull on their trousers. Beg them to give it to me.' I joke. I am on my way to Manchester for a job interview and have struck a conversation with a young man who sits opposite me on the train.

'Don't beg them.' *He tuts and pulls his blue hood down.* 'You're Muslim right?'

I nod.

'Never seek help from others in your affairs. Don't lean on others, even if it's a small lint of wood that you require – that's according to the Prophet. Ask only him.' He points upwards, to God I presume.

'Well, surely I need help from some people. Without these guys I won't get the job!'

'No, imagine this. You've bought a car. You'll tell me that you've worked for it, earned the money and paid for it. You'd say it was all down to you, yes?'

'That's obvious.'

'Ah, but no. Did you make these arms for you to work? Did you make these legs to take you to work? Make that brain that tells you how to carry out your work? Create the food that you eat which gave you energy, the seeds? Did you earn your birth in this country rather than in an impoverished part of India? Did you?'

Staring at the passing countryside I pause to think. Shaking my head, 'no,' I reply, knowing where this is going.

He smiles smugly. 'No? Then who has?'

'God?'

'Yup. God has ultimately, provided you with this car. Allah has created everything and therefore provided everything. He's shown you kindness. You've created nothing.' He leans back. 'Only ask God directly to give you this job. He may give it to you through the means of other people. But people are the tools for his gifts.'

'Well... ermm. You do know I was just joking about getting on my knees...?'

***

But he's right. No man and no woman in my life had managed to fix what was broken in me. *Sarah, Mo, Paul, Hannah, mum, dad – none of them.* People were useless when it came to the bigger problems in life. Could a person prevent the tsunami earthquake if the victims asked? Could Barack Obama prevent the economic crisis and give people their jobs back if they asked? Could you give me peace and happiness if I asked?

No.

Superman does not exist. Nor does Superwoman.

But God does.

Glancing at my hands, prayer slowly began to raise itself on my palms as a weapon, a shield.

If, to use these tools, it was a condition to kneel down with my hands outstretched to God, then I guessed I had to do it.

And so I did.

6

MY SENSES AWAKENED TO the unveiling of a surreal scene. A mass of foreigners swarmed around me like an almighty flock of white doves. Unlike doves, their collective roar was turbulent and intimidating. Chants, sobs, heavy footsteps, thundered through the air. Hundreds of thousands of pilgrims covered the vicinity of the Kaba, circulating it or stood making prayer.

It was two o'clock in the morning, yet sleep was the last thing on these people's minds.

'We need to perform Umrah,' Layth pulled us out of our daydreams. Every pilgrim who came here would have performed Umrah at their arrival – the necessary welcoming ritual, said to carry rewards and purification of the soul.

Nodding, I glanced at the torrent of pilgrims shuffling around the Kaba and took out the Umrah guide I carried in my pocket. It was drenched in sweat.

'First, we're to circulate the Kaba seven times, starting from this corner.' Layth pointed to one of the corners of the Kaba. It was packed with pilgrims reaching out to it as though it was distributing crystals. 'It's where the black stone lies.'

'The black stone,' I repeated, remembering that this is an apparent sacred piece. Briefly, I glanced into the crushed Umrah guide in my hands. '*Built into the wall of the Kaba, the stone was sent from heaven to Prophet Adam. It was originally pure white, but because it had been touched by so many, it turned black from absorbing their sins. We must touch it when beginning Umrah, as Prophet Mohammad had done by example.*'

The black stone was forty metres away from us. It was apparently the size of a football and I tiptoed to take a look. Instead I saw hundreds of wild pilgrims piled on top of each other outstretching their hands, scrambling to touch the stone or, if they were extra daring, to kiss it. An attempt to have their sins absorbed.

'We can't touch the stone.' I looked over at my father with terror. 'Those people will crush us to death!'

'No we're not going in there! It's ok to just kiss your hands and point to it from a distance.' He shouted over at me. 'Don't forget to say, bismillahi Allahu akbar wa lilla hil hamd, each time we pass!' Meaning *in the name of Allah, Allah is the greatest and all praise is for Allah.*

'Come on, and make sure you hold onto each other!' Layth bellowed.

Daania held Layth's waist. My mother clung onto Daania's robe. I clutched my mother's arm. And my father gripped my shoulder.

We followed Layth through the entranced crowds that positioned themselves on the outer edges, and into the perilous core of the swirling masses. Thousands of these indistinguishable zombie-like pilgrims formed a thick rim around the Kaba and squashed themselves into one another uncomfortably. They shuffled slowly and forcefully, moving their lips and staring at the black cube. Layth led the five of us into an area of the human wheel that was dangerously unfit for even a small child. With hesitancy and an inevitable squeeze, we wedged ourselves into the cog.

'Labbaik!!'

Immediately, I was thrown side to side by waves of bodies as we inched forwards in an attempt to orbit the Kaba. Where there was once air to breathe, there was now a hairy arm, a big torso or a sweat-drenched leg. My suffocation was unnerving. There seemed to be nothing beyond the swarm of people. I felt bodies in front of me, to the side of me, behind me. The thought of these random strangers pressing themselves against me sent a queasy shudder down my back.

'Labbaik!' The random shouts were ear shattering.

Big cave-men-type pilgrims in their two bare sheets chanted 'Allahu akbar', *Allah is the greatest*, so intimidatingly that for a second I worried they were warriors on their last ritual. The small Chinese women were frightening. In their pale robes with the flag of their origin printed on their backs, they travelled in chains. Seven to ten of them, digging their nails into each other's shoulders, not allowing anyone to break through. Chihuahua-like in appearance, their strength was as mighty as bears. Large, black women, dressed in black robes, loomed over me. Now these were bears. Big bears that made me cringe in dread at the thought of their big feet crushing my flea-sized toes.   Small, white bearded Turkish men, who paced measuredly along the far edges, read from their books with a calm eeriness, as they crept forward amidst the rush. Young, excited, European men skipped like kangaroos and skilfully broke through the crowds leaving turmoil behind them. Asian pilgrims shuffled along in a zombie-like fashion; lips moving, eyes fixated on the Kaba. Younger, white ladies tightly held on to their dear ones, like children. Blue eyes wide open. Anxiety, awe. Tears running down their faces.

'Labbaik!'

My deep fears of being crushed did not take long to multiply. The flow of our movement was disrupted by a train of passionate men that suddenly cut across the wheel to touch the Kaba. This turbulence caused those ahead to stop in their tracks. The hundreds behind them, including us, stopped too and we all collided into each other like dominoes. My body squeezed with the weight of others.

'Aargh!' I shouted as my feet got trampled on and I resisted being pulled to the ground.

Panic and frenzy flooded in. Pilgrims pushed each other apart using their elbows. Others chased after their disunited members. I watched in horror when, in that instant, my group members were washed away from me into the sea of pilgrims.

'DAD!' I cried out, thrusting bodies away.

I was on my own.

It hit me how alien this country was. How alien the people were. I feared being lost for hours. Even days. As I had forgotten where our hotel was or what it was called. Unprepared for distasteful events, I had no mobile and no money. Panic levels high, I searched frantically for a familiar face. But each dot of a person looked exactly the same. Tens of thousands of men fretting in their white shrouds. Tens of thousands of women bobbing their scarfed heads indistinguishably.

'MUM!' Not a head turned my way.

The perilous upheaval took several minutes to return to a forceful shuffle. My body was drenched in sweat that would have been worth ten intense hours at my local gym. A heavy humidity hung in the air. Breathing was difficult. Unwillingly, I was carried forward with the current as I continued to look for a recognisable face, forgetting my reasons for being there. Performing Umrah was the least of my worries.

A few gasps later I caught a brief glimpse of a bald head swivelling from side to side.

'DAD! OVER HERE!!!' I jumped up and down and waved my hands in the air.

Metres away, but he somehow caught sight of me and tore through the crowds like a tiger through a bush field.

'I can't do this dad!' letting out my frustration when he finally got to me.

'Shush! Come on you'll be ok, not got long to go.' He reassured in vain. I knew that we had hardly circulated a fifth of one lap.

I submitted to being pulled forwards as he led us to the others.

'Why do we it?? Walk around this?' I asked him, dodging toes and robes. The act of circulation was bizarre to watch but stranger to perform.

'It's just a ritual!' He shouted over the commotion despite being only an inch away from me. 'It started with Prophet Adam, after he was thrown out of the Garden of Eden. When he was in heaven he had constantly heard the sounds of Angels circulating the throne of Allah in worship. He wanted to hear these sounds again, so Allah told him to build the Kaba and circulate it whilst saying 'glory be to Allah', 'All praise be to Allah', and 'Allah is the greatest'. Since then it's become a sacred ritual.'

'I bet it wasn't life-threatening at that time!' I retorted.

Following the initial scare, there were many other upheavals and hysterical moments. The turbulences sent my heart leaping in dread and body juddering with the fear of being crushed. At all times I remained as drenched as a wet sock and as tense as a steel rod.

After our second lap, anxiety began to mingle with growing adrenaline.

The Kaba.

I am walking around the Kaba.

Gazing at it, I was mesmerised once more by this black silk-clothed cube. It was not of a significant size. Merely fifteen metres in width and twenty metres in height. Yet its presence was unmatchable. In that moment it appeared to be the most beautiful yet simple structure I had ever set my eyes on. The black silk cloth drew my mind like a magnet to a piece of iron. The Arabic scripture; *laa illaa ha illallahu mohammadur rasoolullah*, was woven on the top of the cloth in wholesome gold thread, reflecting the worth associated with the phrase; *there is no God but Allah, and Mohammad is his messenger.* As we edged around, a sparkling golden door gleamed at me; the entrance to the Kaba. Its intense luminosity bedazzled my eyes. I wanted to enter it and see what was inside.

I watched the hundreds of people gathered along the walls of the Kaba. Kissing it with their lips. Touching it with the palms of their hands. They behaved as though they were worshipping the Kaba itself, despite it only existing as a pinpoint for the worship of God. But I longed to do the same. Not to worship it but to touch it. To feel the silky cloth between my fingers. Run them along the golden calligraphy. Cling onto it. Hold my face against it. My body. They were ruthlessly clambering over each other to get a feel. It was a need for them. But a danger to me. An impossibility.

The Kaba was situated in the middle of the mosque, in the open-roofed courtyard. I glanced upwards and briefly watched the night sky and sparkling stars. It was as though the heavens had opened up at this spot and shone its light onto its black gem. I gaped through the opening searchingly. 'Oh Allah... are you there?' I presumed he was. And so I spoke to him. I spoke to him about my year, about now, about the future. I continued to speak, until a realisation hit me.

The first man of this world, the progenitor of human race, stood here.

Adam; Arabic for *man*.

My mind wandered into the realms of the deepest philosophies ever known to man. And I asked myself the billion dollar questions again. *Why did God create Adam? Why did he create me?*

***

'Why am I here?' I ask, Zain, a friend of mine.

'Erm, to have a laugh?' We are in a bar having a drink. Year 2008.

'Tut. Noooo. I mean why do I exist, why am I here? Why are we all here?' asking him again.

'That's deep shit. I don't know. Does it matter?' He picks his glass up and slouches back into the leather couch.

I look at his disregard with melodramatic disbelief. 'Does it matter? Hell yes! Our first words as babies should not be 'mama' or 'dada', they should be 'why? Why the hell am I freakin' here?' Isn't that the most fundamental question of all time?'

He shrugs his broad shoulders and sips.

I sigh and shrug mine too. 'Whatever, get me another drink.'

***

It seemed crazy now, that I never did bother trying to find out. The biggest question I have ever asked, yet I did not search for an answer. I am not sure why. I guess other things took over; what am I going to wear tonight, chicken pasta or tuna pasta, who killed Den in Eastenders, will Rachel and Ross in Friends ever get back together?

***

Channel surfing; I stumble across a guy on TV, coincidentally a week prior to my flight. He is stood on a pedestal giving a speech to hundreds in an audience. The spark in his eyes catches my attention. My finger hovers over the channel button on my remote, curious to know what he is talking about.

It is probably the most important channel surfing moment of my life.

This man enlightens me like no other. 'Allah says, 'I have not created man and jinn except to worship me'. There. There! There, in chapter 51 verse 56 of the Quran, is the sole purpose of our existence. We are here to worship Allah.'

In that instant, the scholar on TV opens the curtains of mystery.

He continues. 'Our main purpose is not to enjoy ourselves or merely exist but it's to worship Allah. He'd created angels to worship him and praise him. Then he'd created jinn to do the same. And finally he created man to worship him too. We worship Allah because it's for that reason we are created. As our creator he is worthy of unconditional worship. Allah is our king.'

This man does for me what my teachers, parents, friends never did. He answers the biggest question I have ever asked, and will ever ask, in six simple words.

Why are we here? 'We are here to worship Allah'.

It begins to make sense. The prayers, rituals, which I had followed blindly for twenty-four years, now have some logic to them. Twenty four years later I see the purpose of my existence.

Twenty four years later.

He sheds further light and explains how my world, my life, came to be. 'Before man was created, Allah assembled the angels, made of light, and thousands of jinns, made from fire. He told them that he was about to create man from clay.

'*The angel Iblis, disapproved stating that man is inferior and would stray from his purpose. Nevertheless, Allah created Adam and gave him more knowledge and ability than the angels. Due to this superiority Allah ordered the angels to bow down to his new creation. Iblis was the only one to disobey Allah and refused to bow down to Adam. He thought he was better than man. Allah then expelled Iblis from heaven and deprived him of his blessings.*'

Who's Iblis? I wonder.

'*Iblis, now Satan, asked that he be given respite until the Day of Judgement, and in the meantime vowed to lead Adam's descendants astray and show Allah how inferior and disobedient mankind will be. Allah accepted saying that if any do disobey then they'd be sent to hell with Satan.*'

I press the volume button on my remote.

'*Adam was given a female mate, Eve, to expel the loneliness and granted them heaven, allowing them to do anything but eat from a certain tree. Satan soon tempted Adam and Eve into eating from the forbidden tree.*'

'*Ah, the tree,*' *I say.*

'*They begged Allah to forgive them. He accepted but sent them out of heaven and onto earth instead to be tested as ordinary people for an amount of time and then be recreated again and judged on the Day of Judgement for their good and bad deeds, which will lead to either heaven or hell.*

'*On earth, Adam was sent guidance by Allah and thus became a Prophet. He passed God's messages onto the rest of his descendants, teaching them to worship Allah, do good deeds and stay away from the whisperings of Satan.*'

It is quite a story that happens to tell me more, in a few minutes, than what I had ever been told at the mosque.

***

And here I am; where all the action took place. I'm walking around the Kaba just like the first man had done.

Wow.

A far cry from walking down the small, cobbled streets of wet England.

My thoughts were interrupted by two hands that tightly clasped my steamy shoulder. I tensed and swivelled around. The fearful green eyes of a small, light skinned, old, frail lady looked up at me.

Of Russian appearance, her face broke into a wrinkled smile. She said something in a language that I did not understand.

I guessed she was looking for cover from the aggressive pushes of the other pilgrims. 'Sure you can hold onto me, but beware, if I go down, you'll be coming with me!' I cracked a smile back. *There are hundreds of languages in the world but a smile speaks them all.* It was the first smile I had given anyone since my journey began and despite the frenzy, it felt nice.

'What's that?' My mother pointed to a golden stool and glass box besides one of the corners of the Kaba.

'Prophet Abraham's footprints imprinted in stone are in that box.' Layth shouted over at her. Sweat streaming off his face. He looked like he had just stepped out of a shower.

'Why are they in the box?' I shouted at him over the roar. The footprints were huge, probably twice the size of twelve's.

'They were created when he stood on the ground and invited people to perform Hajj after he built the Kaba. His footprints were set into the ground and have remained since.'

Gazing at the footprints, I transported back in time and pictured myself in that group which Prophet Abraham called out to.

I understood Abraham was one of the main Prophets in 1900 BC during the days when idol worshipping was rife. I came to know that Prophets, messengers, had been sent by God throughout history to guide people to worship. But they were all human, just like me. I was surprised to hear a couple of years ago that the Prophets in Islam were actually some of those people mentioned in the Bible. Jesus as Prophet Isa. Abraham as Prophet Abraham. Moses as Prophet Musa. Noah as Prophet Nooh. David as Prophet Dawood. Virgin Mary as Maryam. There seemed to be a great overlap between Christianity, Islam and possibly Judaism.

An acquaintance of mine, Pete-turned-Aryan, had converted from Christianity to Islam three years ago. When I asked him what made him convert he replied; *'I've done my research. Read the Bible, Torah, Quran and looked into Hinduism. I spent over a couple of years reading into these religions, and the evidence, for me, weighs stronger towards Islam'.* He went into the details of history but he soon lost me with the complexities and my mind consequentially switched off.

Admittedly, I had never troubled myself with trying to work out which religion was the 'true' religion. It was not out of arrogance or ignorance but merely because time was not spare. It would require years and years of intense research, which I did not have the time for and ultimately I believed would not help me make a crystal clear and absolutely perfect decision.

I confess, I could not rationally explain my reasons to stick around with Islam rather than divert to another religion or none at all. I presume most people of any faith would admit the same. How many have researched into all the religions and sciences, studied the encyclopaedic books comprehensively, and then come to an informed decision? I guessed not many apart from the likes of Aryan.

There are two matters that I felt were best left to the heart. Those of love and those of religion. And I had left the matter of religion to my heart. My heart told me that Allah is God and in my heart of hearts it felt right. That was simply it. It may not be enough for some but that was enough for me.

***

Time had escaped me during the moments I spent circulating the Kaba and thinking. I could not be sure whether I had spent minutes walking around it or whether it had, in fact, been hours. With a slight relief, we began to squeeze out of the masses. Drops of sweat and tears left as souvenirs.

Legs on their last threads. Holes burnt into my vision. Cheeks itching from scalding tears. Head spinning like a disco ball. But I was raring to take the next step.

'Next ritual is to drink water from the well of Zamzam.' Layth informed. 'You're all ok so far yeah? You've done well.'

We piled our weight on to each other as we waded out of the wheel

'Why are we drinking this water?' It was a little easier to talk to Layth now that we were away from the grinding crowds.

'Simply to commemorate the events that occurred leading to the discovery of the well. It's a ritual. Do you know the story behind it?'

'Ermm, not really. Meaning no, actually.'

'Want to hear it?'

'Yeah. Go on.'

'Well, before the Kaba was rebuilt by Prophet Abraham, and during the time when Mecca was just an uninhabited desert, Prophet Abraham, who lived in Palestine, one day brought his wife, Hajar, and baby son, Ishmael, to Mecca. He made them sit under a tree on a high hill called Al-Marwa. He left a bag of dates and some water and then left them there. He told Hajar that he was doing this because Allah had ordered him to do so.'

'What? He just left them there!?' I interrupted.

'Yeah, because Prophet Abraham had another wife. She'd given Hajar, her slave, to Prophet Abraham as she wanted him have a son, which she herself hadn't given him. Hajar gave him a son, Ishmael. His first wife then gave birth to a son too, Isaac. She then became very jealous of Hajar and Ishmael, fearing that Ishmael would become a leader of the nation rather than Isaac. So he sent Hajar and Ishmael to Mecca to protect them from his first wife, as Allah advised.'

'Ok.'

'Prophet Abraham put his faith in Allah, raised his hands to the sky and asked Allah to sustain them and travelled back to Palestine.

'He relied on a prayer to Allah to keep them safe in a parched, abandoned desert??'

'Yeah... but listen to me. Let me finish.'

'Carry on then.'

'The water and dates ran out and Ishmael became distressed from the heat and thirst. Hajar became worried and ran from the As-Safa mountain hill to Al-Marwa, looking for water or help. She ran back and forth seven times until she fell to the ground and began to pray to Allah for help. Then, either Ishmael had been kicking the ground or angel Gabriel had come and scraped the ground, either way, the earth began to spurt out water. It was a well and was given the name Zamzam, which means 'stop' in Arabic, which were the words Hajar cried out fearing that the stream of water would run out. The well meant that Hajar and Ishmael were sustained and the area around it became a vibrant town, Mecca.'

'Wow. That was lucky,' appreciating Layth's explanation as it made the ritual less confusing and more meaningful.

'Not lucky. It's Allah's sign. The water from the well still flows today. After all these years of consumption by millions of people every day, the well in this desert land has still not dried up. It's near the Kaba, but it's now been covered. For ease of the pilgrims and to avoid fatal accidents, the water is pumped to there.'

Layth pointed to an area a few yards away which consisted of a wall with numerous taps attached to it. I was expecting to see a gaping well with people scrambling around it for a drink. Initially disappointed but that swiftly turned to relief. I would rather not have been a witness to the horrors of people falling into a well for a glass of water.

Layth handed me a plastic cup of Zamzam water. 'A cure for illness, thirst and hunger.'

I turned to face the Kaba and raised my glass to my lips.

'Make a wish before you drink,' said my mother.

I wished for the detoxification of my body, both in the literal and spiritual sense. I refrained from gulping it down in one go. Instead, wanting to be on my best behaviour, I took three sips at a time, remembering that Prophet Mohammad had said that this was the dignified way of drinking and quenches the thirst better. The cooling sensation on my lips, tongue and throat gave a deep refreshing pleasure. For natural water, it was strangely sweet and I soon tapped my cup for more. The sweat I had lost earlier needed replenishing.

Feeling mildly re-energised, we offered two bows as was customary and prepared for our next step which was to walk from the mountains of As-Safa and Al-Marwa seven times, as Hajar had done. Layth explained that it was to commemorate the trust she put in Allah.

'This is Mount As-Safa.' He led us to a slight sloping area within the mosque. The ground was tiled with marble and the area was walled off into a long, narrow gallery which led to the other mount.

'Ermm, this doesn't look like a mountain to me,' giving Layth a dry look. Disappointed by the manufactured and polished marble, and the general unearthliness of the 'mountains'.

'Yeah I know. It's changed now, to preserve it and make it safe. The slopes represent the hills.'

When we reached the peak of As-Safa, which was, of course, a remarkably easy mountain to climb, I opened my guide book and followed the instructions to the ritual. 'O Allah,' I murmured, 'I perform this ritual between Safa and Marwa to please You. Make it easy for me and accept it from me.' I then recited a short verse from the Quran; 'Indeed Safa and Marwa are among the Signs of Allah.' I raised my hands, said 'Allahu akbar,' *Allah is the greatest,* three times, before 'climbing' to Mount Al-Marwa.

The distance between As-Safa and Al-Marwa was half a kilometre. An unquestionably exhausting walk. My bare-footed thuds on the hard marble floor sent a jolting pain through my feet, my calves and into my thighs. The vibrations of a concrete digger. The pressure to walk without stopping was driven by the floods of pilgrims behind us. My pain was muffled somewhat as I envisioned Hajar running up and down these mountains all those centuries ago.

Surreal it was, to see thousands of pilgrims pass this gallery only to commemorate Hajar's actions. But stranger it was, to see men, some of which I would have betted were chauvinists, do this to remember the actions of a woman.

I turned to glance at my mother. Being an unfit woman who suffered from weak bones, diabetes and other illnesses it appeared that she was not finding it easy. Her face was streaming with perspiration and her headscarf had been dragged to the side, covering half her eye. She left her mouth half open as she struggled to take in breath.

'Are you ok mum?' Worried, I held her hand.

'Yes, come on don't stop!' she shoved me forwards. This steely determination came as a surprise. On a normal day at home she rarely wandered around the city centre without making several stops for rest and a McDonald's. But here, she charged down the track with her chest puffed out, shoulders pushed apart, like a true athlete.

My father too was not a healthy man and his efforts painted an exhausted picture. His small, greying beard was soaked wet, as was the rest of his body. The two white sheets he wore had loosened out of position and were on the brink of unwrapping. I hoped, for the sake of humanity, that they did not unravel before our eyes.

On our stops to Al-Marwa I uttered the same supplications as those made on As-Safa, before heading back to As-Safa.

On our seventh trip the pain in my legs and feet became agonising. I bit my lip, squeezed my eyes shut and compelled myself to continue despite the excruciating pain each hard step gave. I could not remember the last time I had pushed my body to such an extreme. My personal trainer at the gym would never have dared test my stamina this way. I longed to drop to the ground and surrender to the trampling of those feet behind me if it meant my legs would have respite from the torment.

Think of Hajar. Think of Hajar. Think of Hajar. She did the same on an empty stomach, on steeper, rocky mountains and under the scorching heat.

When we reached Al-Marwa for the final time I released a puppy whimper and collapsed to the ground. Had I had the might, I would have demanded a trophy and applause for running this marathon.

'Hey, it's not over yet. We need to snip our hair.' Layth smirked as he watched the rest of us sprawled on the floor like dried up slugs.

'Don't worry,' he noticed the look of alarm I faintly mustered. 'You women only need to cut a fingertip of your hair. Men usually shave full heads.' He paused. 'Oh and before you ask, because I know you will, I don't know the reason behind this one. Prophet Mohammad did it and so we follow his example as there is probably some wisdom behind it,' shrugging his shoulders.

Daania went over to a tall Sudanese woman who had a pair of scissors in her hands, and pointed to my mother and I.

The woman strode over to us, with a conspicuous glint in her eye. 'Cut? Cut?' she hissed pointing to her scissors and snipping them in the air. Reminding me of Freddy Kruger.

'Erm yes please, but be careful.' I lifted my headscarf a little from the back to reveal the ends of my hair.

She jerked my head back and grabbed all my hair with a stern force.

'Whoa. Whoa! Easy! Not all of it!' I snatched my hair back and gave the twisted Sudanese a horrified look.

'Hah cut cut.' She flashed her oversized wonky teeth at me, teasing me to come back to her.

With no comfort from the others, I reluctantly handed a small clump of hair to her whilst guarding the rest of it with my hands. She snipped a little off with a face of masked innocence.

'Jazakallah', *may Allah repay you*, I said and quickly pulled away from her before she got carried away in the moment.

'It took three long hours but our Umrah is complete. Congratulations!' Daania slapped my back.

'Ow.'

'I can't believe it.' My mother was in a daze.

'What an ordeal.' Breathing a loud sigh of relief I sprawled onto the floor again.

'This is just a small taste of what lies ahead with Hajj. This *ordeal*, was it worth it?' Daania asked.

A surreal and elating experience. Travelling to this monumental land and making my wish to God made me feel greatly accomplished. Witnessing things of historical significance, I had become a part of history myself. Stepping on the same grounds as the first man of the planet was something I did not expect. I had performed the arduous ritual of Umrah, an act that was said to contain great virtues and dispel sins as fire removes impurities. I made the most passionate prayer I had ever made to God. I drank the famous Zamzam water. All this I had just done, at the centre of the world.

'Was it worth it? Ha. Need you ask?'

A thirst itched in my mouth. A thirst for more of this action.

It was five a.m. but the desire to sleep had escaped me. I was fuelled by pure adrenalin. I wanted more. Dead legs I might have had, but I did not want to leave. With my blistered feet I wanted to run back to the Kaba, touch it, sit beside it, engulf myself in its nightly beauty. I wanted to drink more honey Zamzam water, close my eyes and splash it on my face. I wanted to skip around the vast Al-Haram mosque and breathe in its magnificence. I wanted to walk the plains of Mecca that the Prophets had walked on, see what they saw and feel what they felt. I wanted to stand in the highest minaret, look down on the city and like a delirious woman who had drunk too many bottles of exhilaration, shout on the top of my voice, 'ALLAH, HERE I AM!!!'

7

'I HOPE YOU AREN'T walking out like that.' My mother looked me up and down disapprovingly and watched me hover towards the hotel room door.

Khaki trousers. White T-shirt. Hair dripping from shower water.

'Yes, yes mum, I know.' I replied drily. 'I must remain modest because I'm a woman and I wouldn't want to be the cause of men going crazy with lust.' It was the morning after and we were no longer required to stay in ihram. 'I'm looking for a towel.'

'You do enough of that at home, please don't cause havoc here.' she said tiredly.

I cringed. And shot her a did-you-have-to-say-that-in-front-of-dad look. 'Ahem... no. I don't want to be pulled up by the Saudi authorities for wearing a skimpy T-shirt, anyway.' I was not joking, the rules were strict here.

Adequately covered in a robe and headscarf, my parents and I made our way up to the thirteenth floor to the dining area of the hotel – which was just a large canteen-like room with thirty or so wooden tables and plastic garden chairs surrounding them. Garden chairs. Some of the hotel residents had already filled a few of the seats. A buffet breakfast was neatly set out along the side of the room near the entrance. Food contained in shiny metal tins.

I opened one of the containers to be met with the sight of the runniest rice pudding ever. Another metal dish was filled with crooked, toasted bread. Adjacent to these was a steel barrel of tea.

'Is this what we're having for breakfast?' I already felt distaste.

'Tut. Be happy with what we've got. I hope you aren't going to show ingratitude to Allah in Mecca as well.' My mother pursed her lips.

With a loud groan, I picked a plate up and slopped some of the goo onto it along with a piece of disintegrating plywood. Hoping my mother did not play the worn out record again; the one about how people would give their fingers in exchange for the food that we had.

'Dear. Allah hates the ungrateful.' I was just about to sigh when I realised that was not the voice of my mother. Her voice was gruff, but this was a lot gruffer.

I turned around and saw an old man behind me, later known as Mr Raul.

He smiled, triggering numerous wrinkles to mimic the action.

I smiled back at him sheepishly.

He took that as an invitation to speak some more. 'You know dear, in the Quran Allah says the ancient Pharaoh and his people were enjoying great wealth, but they still showed ingratitude to Allah, so he replaced it with drought and hunger. He got angry and they became regretful.'

'Oh did they.' I feigned interest. Looking for a polite exit.

'Wouldn't you be angry if you baked a nice cake for your lovely mother here and she said eeeeeee I don't like it.'

I laughed immaturely at his squeaky 'eeeee'.

'Would you not be hurt and angry?' His tone became deeper, but his smile did not fade. He reminded me of Mrs Clark, my school head teacher. She always had a smile on her face when telling the kids off. Her face would turn bright red in anger but her smile would never disappear. She was an odd ball.

'I've cooked for this *lovely* mother in the past and she's told me my food is crap many times.' Laughing, hoping he would have a smiley harsh word with her too.

He stopped smiling and so did his wrinkles.

'Erm, but yes you have a point. It's hurtful. You're right.' Feeling like a spoilt brat, I stepped back, watching my mother scuttle off.

'Don't be ungrateful to Allah and his gifts, my dear, it is rude,' he said and slowly shuffled away.

I bit into my toast using my strongest back teeth and scurried to the table my mother was sat on.

I knew my moaning was going to be the most difficult thing to eliminate on this trip. My ingratitude was perhaps my biggest vice, paired with my impatience. Every morning I open my overfilling wardrobe and cry out '*I have no clothes!*' I go to lavish dinners and acclaim '*there's nothing to eat!*' Only hours after I had bought my brand new MINI Cooper I had watched a BMW Convertible 6

Series speed past me and whined *'I want that car!'* I couldn't help but complain. No matter how much I reminded myself that my mother was right, I should be thankful, it did not stop my dissatisfaction. I am sure it was a medical condition I had.

Fearing God's anger and Mr Raul's ability to read my mind, I looked down at my plate of cardboard and gruel, and forced myself to think appreciatively. Trying my best not to give away any signs of thanklessness I shoved the food down with a fake smile.

Truth is; breakfast was puke-worthy.

'Our group!' Layth joined us for breakfast with Daania. He waved his arms, as was his thing, at the rest of the robed diners.

Mr Raul, the old grateful man, was part of our group. He sat on a table with an old lady who was dressed in a black robe and headscarf. She appeared to be his wife. Accompanying them were two young women and one young man, all in their twenties or thirties – the old couple's children? They were Indian and from the snippets of conversation I could hear coming from the table, I figured they were from London.

On another table sat three couples and a man. Two of the couples and the man in their forties, the other in their twenties. They were of Pakistani origin and spoke English but with a Scottish accent. They laughed and joked amongst themselves whilst eating small cakes.

'Where did they get those cakes from?' I asked Layth. Feeling rather jealous.

'I don't know. They must have bought them.'

A middle aged couple, heads joined together, sat on another table talking quietly. Next to them spread the muscular frame of Mikaeel and the other two men we had met at Jeddah airport.

On the larger table sat a group of ten young Asian men all dressed in white robes, white turbans. Each had their heads lowered into their plates, seemingly in a world of their own. For a bunch of young lads they were eerily quiet. An older man, with a long white beard down to his navel, ate with them. He seemed like the boss.

'Ignore them. They're a little extreme,' Layth whispered conspicuously when he caught me staring.

'What do you mean?'

'Just ignore them.'

I kept looking. They were not doing much except staring into their gruel-filled plates. Bored, I turned my gaze away.

'So how did everyone get here without your help?' Dubious of Layth's leadership abilities.

'Long story, don't ask. They've all come on different flights from different parts of the UK. But anyway people will tend to do their own thing at their own times. We'll probably see these guys more during the actual Hajj. We five will stick together. I'll show you around.'

'Aw that's nice of you,' smiling at him warmly. I liked this guy.

Sipping on my tea I continued to watch my acquaintances-to-be. The cackling cake-eating Scots were already annoying me.

***

Today I was sober. Not drunk with the extreme and severe emotions of yesterday. I was itching to see the Kaba again but this time with my sedated eyes.

After breakfast Daania, my mother and I stepped out of the hotel onto the vast Ibrahim al-khalil road – my father and Layth had gone off to exchange some money.

With deliberation and calmness, I took in my surroundings. The infamous road was not the same as it was last night. Mecca did not carry the heavy, sombre intensity of that night. Today it was vibrant, bright, animated.

The picture perfect sky, a soft clear blue with not a hint of cloud. Revealing the wholesomeness of the sun, which beamed down on the sandy, once desert, ground. Its scorching forty degree heat penetrated my robe and burned my skin immediately.

Down below, the road was packed with pilgrims. Most heading in the same direction as we were. Forgetting what we were shuffling towards, for minutes I just stared at this setting and these fascinating people as Meccan life tantalisingly unravelled itself.

Large African women in their long, traditional, colourful dresses strode leisurely in big groups and despite the ferocity of the crowds some even balanced huge baskets on their heads. Just as they would in Africa. A group of Nigerian men sat on the side of the road adjacent to the rows of buildings. They huddled around a white paper laid on the floor containing broken pieces of meat and cooked bread. Early lunch. A couple of pale-skinned men bent over on the edge of the road with a small water bottle. They poured some of the water into their palms and rubbed it on their arms and feet. Washing for prayer.

Some people dotted themselves in corners and quiet, darker patches. They laid out pieces of rugs besides baskets that contained their belongings, and sprawled on the ground attempting to rest or sleep amidst the hustle and bustle. Others hovered around the small garment shops alongside the road whilst shop attendants invited them inside. A stark contrast to those entranced pilgrims who were hurriedly walking towards the Al-Haram.

Hotels and food huts laced this stretch. The smell of meat and spices wafted up my nostrils alluringly. Egyptian, Indian, Pakistani, Turkish, Arabic, Brazilian, Swiss and African takeaways, accommodating all the cultures. There was even a KFC.

Attempting to mentally block out the high and modern buildings, especially the Hilton hotel, I imagined this road being just as vibrant thousands of years ago, after Hajar discovered the Zamzam well, with similar huts and food stalls.

I continued to watch on until the Al-Haram mosque entered my vision.

Sucking in a much needed breath I paused to adjust to its grandeur and might. Even in broad daylight, amongst the riveting people and the tall buildings, its presence was all-captivating. A befitting attention-seeker. It instantly tore me away from the hubbub of the surrounding goings-on. Even the smell of spices disappeared underneath the wing of its aura.

The vast courtyard resembled a sea of moving white and black seeds. Sixty-four golden entrances stood around the mosque, yet even so, thousands of people were straining to get through the two entrances in sight. The same was probably taking place at the other entrances. Thousands of others opted to sit down along the outer walls of the mosque or on the courtyard under the sun whilst making supplications to God.

I stepped onto the courtyard. My heart skipped a beat. I had the urge to leave those two snail-paced old ladies by my side and jump over the crowds to see the Kaba right away. A look at my hobbling mother and hump-backed Daania sent a desisting wave of compassion into me. *I can't leave them to fend for themselves.* Remembering that the Last Prophet had placed great emphasis on showing respect and kindness to the elderly, simply because of their age and neediness. *God's watching me too.* Shaking off my impatience, I matched the pace of the two silent women.

Together, we weaved through the crowds, frequently stumbling over the arms and feet of those who had resorted to planting themselves in the middle of the courtyard. In fact, there was barely any space that was not hoarded by a pilgrim. If this was the state of the courtyard, I dreaded to think what it would be like inside. My face was already streaming with perspiration and my muscles resumed the tenseness of last night.

Half an hour later, we reached the nearest entrance. Its door gleaming in patterns of golden swirls and circles. On the top of the doorway hung a golden plate with the engravings of the infamous statement *'there is no God but Allah and Mohammad is his messenger'*. I inhaled, savouring the moment we stepped through the grand opening and into the home of the Kaba.

An echoing roar blasted my ears. Louder than the sound I would hear if I stuck my head in a tumble dryer. I was met with the sight of pilgrims overfilling the mosque. Not a marble tile could be seen. I had not looked up when I had entered the mosque last night but I was certain that it was not as crammed as this. Pilgrims stuck to each other and to the walls like jam. The mosque could hold two or so million people and I figured that that enormous number of people were all present.

Deflated, I turned to ask Daania how on earth we would tear through these people and get to the Kaba. But I stopped, knowing she would not have heard me above the deafening howls. We were at a complete standstill. I looked on in dismay as others surrendered and stopped in their tracks to sit down on top of those already seated. I dreaded having to sit on the round, big-lipped woman by my feet.

I have to see it again.

I have to see it again.

Stepping on my toes, I peered over the bobbing heads in an attempt to catch a glimpse of it. We were too far. There were too many pillars obscuring my view.

'We'll shuffle forwards inch by inch! Eventually we'll get there, even if it takes us hours!' I shared the idea with my mother but she did not hear. It was hardly a master plan but what else could we do.

The further down we moved, the greater the force of the bodies became. I was now pathetically clinging on to both my mother and Daania. These two ladies might have been old but they were sure built like oak trees.

We soon became part of a moving raft of people. Paddling ourselves inwards. Some jumped off and sat down wherever they could, not having the will to go on. The echoes from the crowds, the heat from the hundreds of thousands of bodies, the nervous anticipation of seeing the Kaba again – it all amplified feelings of exhaustion.

Through our labour the mosque's interior was left to be admired. Enormous chandeliers and golden droplets of bulbs draped down from the high ceilings. Glossy white marbled walls polished like mirrors. Marble floor as buffed as an ice rink, despite the millions that had trodden on it. Along the far ends of the mosque lay golden bookshelves with rows of Qurans resting on them. I could not begin to count the number of arches and white-gold pillars that were within my vision alone. They lined in a hundred or so straight rows but circled to make arched exits into the open top courtyard, where the Kaba lay.

As precious as a large diamond, every surface of the mosque was polished and glossed by hundreds of green uniformed janitors – care that reflected its beauty, history and spirit. Without doubt, it was the most grand but delicate building I had ever set foot in.

'Let's just find a spot here! We'll never get to the inner courtyard, there are too many people!' Daania, who had visited Mecca numerous times, had surrendered like the others. She was about to ruin the moment for my mother and I.

'No!' I shook my wet head adamantly. 'We have to go in, I want to see it!' giving her a warning look.

'We're not sitting here, we're going in!' My mother spoke up and attempted to charge forwards into the back of a broad man.

Ignoring Daania's mumbles, I too pushed forwards a little harder and faster into my mother. All in vain.

After two hundred metres of peering from side to side like an excited and impatient child I finally caught a glimpse of its black silky cloth. My heart leapt. A smile broke on my face. 'Mum, did you see it?' Not waiting for an answer, I jumped into a momentary gap in the crowds.

It took an hour to get from the entrance of the Al-Haram to the point past the final archway and onto the inner courtyard. Up until this point I was seeing the Kaba grow slightly bigger but had not seen it in its completeness. Now, as I got past the final archway, I saw it in its entirety.

'Subhanallah,' *Glory be to Allah.* I whispered subconsciously, my senses bewitched by this one jewel. The sun's rays lashed down onto its mysterious black cloth. Golden scripture sparkling. The blue sky floated above the Kaba like an angelic halo. Nothing could match the atmosphere surrounding this monument at that moment in time. Hundreds of thousands encompassed it, raising their hands towards it, bowing before it, signifying its majesty. Tens of thousands of others orbited it as though their lives revolved around it; which in a way, it did.

It does feel like the centre of the world.

Our raft had lodged at this point. Complete deadlock. There was no way to pass the human iceberg. The majority of our passengers had stopped in their tracks and either found a way to crouch down or made themselves comfortable in a standing position. Those behind me continued to irritate by pushing us forward.

There were ten steps that led down to the base of the inner courtyard. We were at the top. I spotted three women at the bottom of those steps begin to get up to leave from where they were sitting.

God let that space be ours! I pulled the two old ladies with me. 'Come quick!'

We managed to dive into our newly acclaimed seats before anyone else got the chance.

'Phew! Good work!' My mother wiped her forehead with her sleeve.

The hard marbled floor pressing against my bottom, the heat of the sun, the pressure of those around me and the deafening roar made it all rather uncomfortable. But the Kaba's presence soon made me oblivious. Mesmerised, I simply stared and talked to Allah.

'Subhanallah,' I whispered again.

***

'Say subhanallah' Sully, an old friend, says to me.

'What? why?' I ask him, confused.

'Just say it, go on,' he presses.

'Erm, ok, subhanallah.' It is usually an Arabic word uttered when overwhelmed by beauty.

He laughs. 'Allah has just planted a tree for you in heaven. If a person says subhanallah, his reward is a tree in heaven.'

***

'Subhanallah, Subhanallah, Subhanallah.' I could have sat on the solid marble floor staring at the Kaba all day and every day, tirelessly creating myself forests.

'Daania, why is it that I cannot tear my eyes away from the Kaba? I feel like I could sit and stare at it forever. I mean, aesthetically, isn't it just a cube with a black cloth around it?' The three of us had hardly said a word to each other since entering the mosque.

'Oh no. It isn't just a cube with a black cloth around it, it is the *Kaba*.'

'Yeah, but why does it have this... hold over me?'

'I don't know. So many members of our groups over the years have asked me the same question. It's got this hypnotic effect which only Allah knows the reason of. A lot of things in life can't be explained using our five senses. I guess, just accept that it is what it is.'

'Hmmm.' I looked on, enchanted. As odd as it may sound, immersed in a reality-stroke-fantasy moment, there is no other place on the planet that I would rather have been. Not even on a Caribbean Island. At this place, peace and tranquillity besieged me like no other.

***

'Oh...' Still sitting on the step, I gasped. The hairs on my arms stood on end as a new realisation sieved into my mind – a thought which I was surprised had not hit me the night before.

Maybe it was the humidity in the air or the emotions of the place but my eyes instinctively watered.

The greatest man, according to many, to have ever walked on this earth, placed his feet where I placed mine. The man who, according to worldwide reports, was said to be '*the most influential man in history*', walked where I had walked. The man, who is said to be the most beloved of God, made prayer in the same place that I had made prayer.

Prophet Mohammad, the last prophet of Allah.

I might not have known much about the other Prophets, but I knew about this Prophet more than I knew about some of my own family. As I grew up, Prophet Mohammad, his message and his example were all I ever seemed to hear about. '*God loves him the most*', they said. '*Muslims love him the most*'. In fact, they seemingly love him more than they love their own parents and children.

When powerful statements like that were made and when the world went into a shocked uproar at the parody cartoon drawings of him by a Danish artist, I could not resist the urge to find out more about him and know why this man was rated so highly. Rated higher than any other being.

As I sat on the step, I recalled his famous story.

Up until the age of forty he appeared to be an ordinary person, albeit the fortieth or so descendant of Prophet Abraham. Born in Mecca, in the 6th century he became an orphan child at the age of six. Before his prophethood the goodness of his character was recognised by the citizens of Mecca as rare. Special. In solitude, he led most of his pre-prophethood life, disturbed by the destructive events taking place in his country. Wars. Murders. Adultery. Idol worshipping.

For years he would travel to the nearby cave Hira to contemplate and worship God. One day, at forty, the angel Gabriel appeared and passed a short message from Allah to him. He then continued to visit him and in segments revealed the words of the Quran in a bid to guide people and answer the conundrums of life.

Mohammad had become a prophet of Allah.

Prophet Mohammad was to be the last prophet to be sent by Allah in a final attempt to save mankind from the pains of hell. It then became his arduous and life-threatening mission to reveal the message of the Oneness of God and pull people out of their darkness, into the light.

His devotion to his quest was remarkable and seemingly worthy of awe. The Quraish tribe, his enemies, had once offered him all the wealth and status that he wanted if he gave up on this mission but instead he said *'I swear by the name of God, that if they place the sun in my right hand and the moon in my left hand in return for giving up this matter, I will never desist until either God makes it triumph or I perish defending it'.*

A scene that was re-told time and time again when I was a little girl was about the time he walked home for miles and continually pelted with rocks by his enemies, until he was covered in blood. Yet he said not a word to them. Moments later Angel Gabriel came to him and said *'Allah has sent me to you so that you may give me your orders. If you wish I will bring together the two mountains that stand opposite to each other... to crush them in between'.* But

Prophet Mohammad rejected this offer and said, *'I rather hope that Allah will raise from among their descendants people as will worship Allah…'*

'He's my idol. I want to be like him'. People uttered these words because he was said to be a man with the most perfect character. *'The most gentle, noble, modest, brave, kind and giving'.*

But what brings tears to millions of eyes when his name is mentioned and what brought my eyes to water at that moment, was his profound love for mankind. His love for us. For you. For me. Yes, he loved me. Why did I believe that? Because he is said to have spent nights and nights prostrating to Allah, not rising for hours, his face drowning in puddles of his own tears as he wept and wept, crying out *'My Ummah (people) Oh Lord, My Ummah! Save them'.*

As I watched those treading slowly around the Kaba, I imagined him in front of me; on the sandy ground outside this cube all those centuries ago. I imagined him, dressed in two plain white sheets. Feet left bare. On his knees. Prostrating. His slender body bent forwards. Palms laid flat on the ground beside his head. Face pressed into the sand. His dark beard immersed in a pool of his tears as he sobbed uncontrollably. For hours. Begging Allah to save us.

I imagined the burden he felt, as the chosen one, to spread the word. The mental agony; having seen a glimpse of hell and heaven with his own eyes, having had Allah speak to him, knowing the truth of this life and what lay in the hereafter. I imagined his severe despair for those who rejected his pleas, for those that laughed and for those generations to come that would not hear him as he would not be there to speak. Thinking what he always said: *'by him in whose hands lies my soul; if you knew what I knew, you would laugh little and cry much'.*

I imagined how his heart was breaking as he realised that people will stray away from God, away from the heaven he had witnessed, blindly walk on a path that led to the torturous doors of hell. The hell that he had seen. I imagined how he might have longed to live forever, to run around the world, shaking each and every person, until they saw what he saw.

I imagined his cries thunder through the layers of the earth and shake the skies above, as he pleaded with Allah, *'My Ummah! Oh Lord, forgive them! My Ummah! Save them!'* He begged for everyone. He begged for me.

His persistence, his prayers and his love for humanity pushed the message of Islam through the generations until it reached me and a quarter of the world's population today; over a billion people. Because of this man and his legend I was a Muslim. Because of this man, I may be saved from the bad of this world and hell.

How could I not love this man?

***

The sound of loud heavy wails tossed me out of my thoughts. They came from someone nearby. I turned to see.

To my side, a couple of metres away, sat a black man. A grown man crying like I had never seen before. I broke away from the spell of the Kaba and watched him.

Dressed in a brown Kanga, he sat on his knees with his hands raised. Trembling. Weeping out loud. His cries reminded me of the shriek of a crow whose baby had been snatched away. The toughness of his dark skin showed resilience yet the wearing of his elbows, feet and hands revealed that the fight had not been without wounds. The crevices on his face unveiled decades of pain and sorrow. He cried out in a language that was foreign to me. Each tear that fell from his eye lashes opened a page of a sorrowful story before it dropped onto his lap. A few people looked at him but most continued with their own prayers. This man was having a breakdown right before these thousands of people yet no one did a thing.

'Stop, please stop.' My eyes, helpless.

He let out a startling shriek. The shriek of a man taking his final breaths.

This man is going to kill himself with his cries. What has he done? I longed to reach out to him and hug this big stranger. *Has he committed an enormous crime and is begging for forgiveness? Lost his wife in a tragic accident?* Catch his tears. *Is he all alone? Is he in physical pain?* Understand his story. *What? What is it?* But I merely looked on, like the others, knowing I could not go up to him and comfort him. Because he was a stranger.

Memories of my own miseries rose, to compare themselves. *Would I want this man's problems instead of my own? Maybe I should look at those below me who are less fortunate, like the Prophet had said. It'd give me some perspective. Control my sadness. Why am I so upset, anyway? Because Zameer cheated on me and because I don't like my job? This man has probably suffered years of poverty, torture, oppression and here I am whining about my deflated ego.* 'Oh my God, I'm pathetic.'

I knew full well that I would soon forget about what I was witnessing and resume with my self-pity, as was always my natural human pattern. But for the moment I welcomed my pain with contentment. I accepted that I was lame.

'Mum, why is he crying?' She was also quietly watching him.

'Sigh... Allah knows,' throwing her eyes onto her lap, not wanting to watch.

Nor did I. It was easier to ignore him. 'How many people do you think have come here?' I ask.

'Ermm... Millions?'

'I wonder whether at least one person from each nationality has... oh!'

A woman jumped in front of me, knocked my knee, and surged forwards into the mass of standing pilgrims.

A small child, wrapped up in a piece of cloth, clung onto her back as she clambered over others with her arms outstretched.

She's going for the Kaba. A thick, heavy, crushing cog of pilgrims circulated the Kaba. *There's not even an inch spare! Surely she must know that.*

'Oh my...'

I feared for the Persian woman and her child, as I watched her break through chains that the strongest man in the mosque would not have dared tackle. *These two are going to be crushed.*

She disappeared into the masses.

'No...' *The baby.*

I jolted up in horror, foregoing my seat. Fearing that her or her baby had been engulfed, pulverised. The crowd circulating the Kaba was sent into turbulence as people stopped in panic. They shoved and pushed. I strained my ears for the sound of dying screams.

I waited. No sign.

A few seconds passed.

A white outstretched hand emerged from the swarm. Her child still clinging onto her neck. She ripped through the remaining human fences and threw her palms onto the silk walls.

She had made it.

I caught a glimpse of her face before she became one with the crowd again. She was laughing. Or was she crying? I was not sure. But the look she had was distinct. A look of pure exhilaration.

'That woman is insane!' Her incredibility sent trembles through my feet. In this random burst of madness, she had risked the lives of herself and her child. To touch the Kaba. It was absurd.

Yet, that final image of her ecstatic face hung in my mind. Envious. In comparison, my faith was subdued, composed, plain average. I could not help but desire to feel what that woman felt.

***

A short while later I did feel something.

During the midday prayers, with the Kaba dawning over me, I prostrated.

I bent down on my knees, placed my palms flat downwards, put my forehead on the hard ground and closed my eyes.

It was the most humbling act of them all.

Malcolm X had admitted that this act was the most difficult thing to do when he first embraced Islam. An act that destroyed all arrogance and pride.

I felt what he felt. Stripped of the cloths of my pride and arrogance and left with a naked humbleness. Acted out by billions of people, it was the physical symbol of pure devotion. According to the Bible, Jesus too had apparently fallen on his face in prostration to pray to his God.

The thought of prostrating to a man or woman made me shudder unpleasantly. *Would I prostrate to my mother as a symbol of my love? To a lover as a dramatic act of devotion?*

No.

But I prostrated to God. Because I felt like his servant. He, my master. I did it for him, without instinctive feelings of humiliation. He gave me life, and I felt he had the power to give me the happiness that I came for.

The coolness of the marble ground radiated through my forehead and sent a refreshing flow of humility through my mind. The mask of my ego fell away. In this greatest act of submission, the position of my body told of my vulnerability. Yet in my psyche, I was strangely invincible.

For that passing moment, nothing affected me.

Feeling as though God was with me. Had formed an unbreakable shield around me. Not a thing could touch me. My heartache fell to the ground. The memories of pain engulfed by the layers of the earth. I did not care for the pangs of hunger, the miseries of poverty, the fallings of sadness. The future I worried not for. And the past, I had no resentment for. I was fearless, untouchable and so incredible that I was sure, I was sure I could walk through a blazing fire and emerge unscathed. I could step onto the stormy seas and run on their ominous waters. I could jump off a cliff, spread my arms and fly on the wings of a thousand angels.

For that moment, just for that moment, I would have been content with taking my last breath there. Because that breath would have been of the purest of air. And in that act of complete submission, I was so sure that Allah would have smiled at me and welcomed me through the dazzling gates of his heaven.

For that brief moment of my life, just for that brief moment, I did not fear death.

8

IT TOOK ME A while to come to terms with the idea that life actually continued as normal outside the vicinity of the Kaba. It went on.

It was four o'clock in the afternoon and we had spent hours beside the Kaba. All ordinary human needs had escaped my mind. Hunger, thirst, tiredness – vanished.

However, Daania's grumbling stomach had had enough. 'Let's go out get some air, stretch our legs and find food.'

Straight off the sandy tracks of Ibrahim al-khalil road, very near to the Al-Haram mosque, we were immersed into a modern, lavish and westernised shopping centre. Just as large and developed as those shopping centres in the UK but with an elegant Arabic twist. High ceilings decorated in gold. Chandeliers filtered from the tops. Walls, flooring, layered with white and cream coloured marble. Escalators hummed courteously. Glass shops glistened with Arab prestige.

The shopping mall hosted all types of retail and food outlets. Next, Claire's, McDonalds, Burger King, as well as the Arabian places. There were souvenir shops, doughnut shops, coffee shops, gadget shops, book shops, even a large supermarket which sold all the foods ASDA would sell.

Not a poor person crossed my path here. All the shoppers, who walked with their noses slightly in the air, had money in their pockets. There was none of the chaos that I had become accustomed to in the parts around the Al-Haram. The shopping centre was extremely calm and civilised. Pretentious.

A dazzling array of small Arabic perfume bottles set up in one shop window caught my eyes. The bottles; exquisite, delicate and extravagant. They contained men's perfume, *ittar*, which the shop owner had mixed himself. I picked up a tiny bottle, the size of a little finger. Made of glass and a golden metal, in the shape of a drop, red crystals embedded in its lid. 'The Musk of Arabia.'

'How much?' I asked the perfume man.

'One hundred and fifty riyals,' he replied stiffly. *Thirty pounds.*

I threw him an incredulous look. I had come to the country with the preconception that items would be a lot cheaper here than in Britain. It was a travel from west to east, after all. I guessed not.

I turned to Daania. 'Haggle with him?'

Most traders in Saudi Arabia could be bartered with, I was told. I did not know the first thing about the skill. My past attempts have either embarrassingly made salesmen laugh at me or resulted in me giving up in exasperation and being ripped off.

'Brother, one hundred and fifty riyal for a tiny bottle. Oh ho.' She stepped up to the mark. 'That's ridiculous. Take one hundred, brother.'

I sniggered at her calling this man, who was at least forty years her junior, a grandson, 'brother'. But it was the apparent Muslim thing to say and was done a lot in Saudi. Every Muslim was a 'brother' or a 'sister' to the other no matter how different they might look to one's siblings or whether the 'brothers' or 'sisters' had ever met before.

Brother shook his head arrogantly, taking his traditional Arabic headdress, the keffiyeh, with him. I saw how his baggy white robe did nothing to hide the shape of his large belly. He continued his task of mixing bottles of perfume together as though he was not bothered whether he took our custom or not.

I had formed an attachment to the bottle and wanted to buy it as a gift for my younger brother. I was in a righteous mood.

We continued to look at him, waiting for a verbal response.

He sighed. Unsettled by our stares. 'One hundred and thirty, no less.'

It was hardly a discount and by this time Daania had already wandered off to the jewellery stall. I took it.

We moved onwards to a shop that displayed the most exquisite women's Arabian robes, jubbahs, I had ever come across. The one in the glass window caught my eye. Flowing black silk, encrusted lavishly with diamonds around the waist, neck and arms.

'Mum, that's so beautiful,' I gushed. 'Who says modesty and glamour can't come together as one?'

'Seventy five hundred riyals!' The shop attendant shouted out from inside.

Fifteen hundred pounds. I raised my eyebrows. 'Who would buy that!?'

'The wives of the Arabs, like those.' With a sprinkle of jealousy, my mother pointed to a bunch of haughty looking women in the shop. 'Arabs are filthy rich and their wives spend all day shopping, buying extravagant items. Probably to numb the feelings of being controlled by their husbands.'

'Footballer's wives do the same, I bet. Shop all day to numb the pain of their cheating husbands. Victoria Beckham.' I remarked, my mother's jealousy spreading.

It was clear that women did not have much freedom in Saudi. I saw no female drivers or shop attendants. As a bit of a freedom fighter, I carried a slight resentment for Arab men. But, the women seemed to be happy enough enjoying a life of shopping and dining out. So who would I be to get the banners and protest boards out?

Prayer beads were sold in almost every shop. They were shopping necessities. Plastic beads. Steel beads. Rare stone beads. Even diamond beads. Traditionally used to keep count of the number of glorifications of Allah a person would utter. The extravagance and expense of some the beads reflected the worth and sincerity the Saudis and tourists attached to their worship. Some went for tens of thousands of pounds.

Browsing, my eyes caught a small shimmering box sat on the counter of a souvenir shop. Made of a dusty metal, it was engraved with intricate patterns and encrusted with blue and silver gems. It rested on four steel curved legs. An art of nobility. It possessed the imagery and aura of ancient and enchanting sacredness. It gazed at me with supremacy. And mystery.

I opened the box with intrigue, bracing myself for a bedazzling light from the jewels of a treasure chest. There were no jewels, no diamonds, no rubies. Inside the enigmatic box, was, what some would say, the answer to the mysteries of life. The Quran. The book's cover was engraved with the same metal and encrusted with the same gems. I opened the pages and on its silky white papers were the words of the Quran in beautiful Arabic calligraphy. Remembering that I was in the required state of cleanliness to touch this book, I graced the cover with my fingers. I had discovered an antique and blessed treasure. The delicacy and primeval beauty of this item was the perfect metaphor to reflect the Muslim sentiments towards the Quran and its words.

'That's beautiful,' whispered my mother. She reached out and lightly touched it.

'How much?' I asked the shop attendant. *No doubt expensive.*

Before he could reply the voice of an Imam rang from the speakers of the Al-Haram minarets. It was the pre-call for the afternoon prayer. Frenzy seeped into the shopping mall. The shop attendant snatched the Quran from my hands.

'Wait...'

'Come back later.' He pushed us out and pulled his front door shut within seconds.

I watched in confusion as the other shop keepers threw their customers out of their shops and locked their doors. The escalators had come to a halt. The nearby juice stall stopped serving. People hurried in all directions with their prayer mats tucked under their arms.

'It's time to pray Asar. Quick, let's run and see if we can get a place at the mosque!' Daania ran like I had never seen her run before. Like an oversized ostrich. With the little choice that we had, my mother and I ran after her, passing shoppers who had laid their prayer mats on the shopping mall floor.

We slid down the stopped escalators and reached the exit. The sight threw me back. Masses of dots scurried, like ants to sugar, towards the mosque.

I shook my head. 'We'll never get into the mosque, mum.'

'Quick! Quick, move!' She said, hobbling forwards.

Bravely, we joined the herds. Holding each other's hands, we pushed forward, squeezing through whatever gaps and spaces we could find.

I was still yet to make one of the five daily prayers at the mosque behind the Imam. The desire in these people made me now want to experience it.

All five obligatory prayers were led by an Imam, the leader of the mosque, at specific times. Praying behind an Imam at this mosque in unity with many others was said to carry much greater reward than praying in isolation. It was important for men to pray at the mosque and less so for women, as traditionally their domestic commitments were taken into account.

Somehow, we reached the courtyard of the mosque. As far as the eye could see, the crowds had come to a standstill at the entrances of the mosque. No one could make it inside now, and if they did, I imagined them standing on each other's shoulders. Or climbing up the pillars.

Hundreds of police officers had emerged and were doing their best to restrict the number of people that went inside.

'Allahu akbar! Allahu akbar!' A melodious sound materialised from the top of the shooting minarets of the mosque. The power, the harmony of the Imam's voice left me momentarily dumbstruck. It must have stirred every part of Mecca.

It was the Azaan; the call to prayer.

Prophet Mohammad had called people to prayer in this manner and ever since it has been repeated in mosques all over the world. Five times a day, minutes before the due time of prayer.

As though someone had pressed the 'pause' button on an old video player, every moving person stopped in their tracks.

The Imam continued to sing out, in Arabic.

> 'Allah is the greatest. Allah is the greatest.
> I bear witness that there is no deity of worship except Allah. I bear witness that there is no deity of worship except Allah.
> I bear witness that Mohammad is the messenger of Allah. I bear witness that Mohammad is the messenger of Allah.
> Hasten to prayer. Hasten to prayer.
> Hasten to success. Hasten to success.
> Allah is the greatest. Allah is the greatest.
> I bear witness that there is no deity of worship except Allah.'

Daania whipped out a small prayer mat out of her backpack and laid it down horizontally over a small space for the three of us to share.

Like rowdy children in a playground turned obedient children in a school assembly, each and every person of the millions in the mosque, on the courtyard and on the surrounding roads stood still on their prayer mats. They waited for the Imam to lead the prayers.

The boisterous bustle quietened to a hushed murmur. Astounding, how the city of millions had come to an instant standstill.

Every activity, every movement and every sound had stopped.

***

The look of disdain on Mr Aryan's face when I ask him 'why do we pray and why do we pray like this?' is one to remember. I am eleven years old. In quiet bafflement, I have been watching the other kids standing, bowing and prostrating whilst whispering Arabic verses. It is not the first time I have found these silent, robotic movements rather strange.

Mr Aryan, my Islam teacher is a stern and orthodox man. I wait for him to say 'oh just do it and don't ask me why.' But his bearded face slowly transforms to a rare softness.

'The purpose of it is to worship Allah. If these prayers were not made compulsory then would we use our own initiative and worship him? No.' He answers for me. He always does. 'Allah at first told Prophet Mohammad, peace be upon him, to tell people to pray fifty times a day. Fifty!! But knowing that this would be too difficult for the average person, he managed to have it reduced to five.'

'But why do we pray in this way?' I ask him again, this time mimicking the aerobic actions, almost falling over.

'It's just the manner in which was told to us by Allah through Prophet Mohammad. Each action shows complete submission to God. Sometimes the reasoning behind certain rituals can't be understood by us. A ritual is a ritual, just as a rule is a rule and a law is a law. Now come on, get up and offer your Salat.'

***

Disciplined. They all looked so disciplined. Perhaps the purpose of the obligatory prayers was to, as I think Mr Aryan was trying to say, instil a discipline of worship?

Waiting for the Imam to begin, I likened God's command to me to worship him five times a day to my parents' command that I went to school when I was a little girl. Often, I did not want to go and would rather have watched Tom & Jerry on TV or played out on my brother's bicycle. But of course, my parents knew what I did not realise. They knew that school would give me a better future and so, out of love for me, compelled me to go. Even if I kicked and screamed.

Is it the same with prayers? Quite honestly, I would much rather stay in bed at five in the morning or enjoy my time out with friends in the evenings uninterrupted, than pray. But perhaps Allah knows what I do not. Maybe he knows that the more I worship him, the better my life would be. Maybe he does not want to see me go to hell, so out of love for me, compels me to remember him five times a day? I know I would not have the discipline to worship on my own accord.

Admittedly, this sort of faith abidance can be seen as a chore, just as I had found school to be a chore. But, grown up, I became thankful for the times that my parents dragged me to school, forced me to do my homework, eat healthily. *Would there be a point in time when I'd be thankful for the rules God compelled me to obey?*

'Allahu akbar,' the Imam began. I, with my near and far neighbours, followed his lead.

Standing upright with my head bowed, I placed my hands on my chest, one over the other. The prayer was conducted in Arabic, as they all were, and involved the recitation of excerpts from the Quran. I did not speak or understand Arabic well, but there are certain sections of the Quran that I understood.

Just as it was custom to recite before carrying out any task – driving, eating, working – the Imam began with the well-known phrase 'bismillah hira maan niraheem,' *in the name of Allah, the most beneficent and the most merciful* – Always uttered to gain God's blessings in the task ahead. He then began reciting Al-Fatiha, the opening chapter of the Quran. I listened to his sweet tone.

> 'All praises are for Allah, the Lord of the universe,
> The most beneficent, the most merciful,
> Master of the Day of Recompense,
> You alone we worship, and You alone we ask for help,
> Guide us to the straight path,
> The path of those on whom You have bestowed Your grace, not the path of those who earned Your anger, nor of those that went astray.'

After another Quranic recitation under our breaths and the Imam's 'Allahu akbar', *God is the greatest*, we went into a bow.

He was the conductor. We the orchestra.

We recited 'Glory to my Lord, the Great,' three times. At the Imam's 'Allahu akbar' we stood up and said 'Allah accepts any who are thankful to him; our Lord, praise be to you.' At his next 'Allahu akbar', on cue, we went down into prostration reciting thrice; 'glory to my Lord, the most high.' 'Allahu akbar' again, led us to sit up. 'Allahu akbar' once more, we fell into a second prostration, reciting thrice; 'glory to my Lord, the most high.' His following 'Allahu akbar' sent us standing again. We repeated the same pattern as before, three times, with extra supplications when sitting down after the fourth and eighth prostration.

Back at home, I had made reasonable effort to make some of my five prayers. But my hectic lifestyle often took over. Towards the latter part of the year, the wayward part, I had given them up totally in brazen defiance.

Now, as I stood on Daania's prayer mat, I wistfully recalled the feeling I had had standing on my own blue prayer mat in my bedroom, before I had ripped it up. Stepping onto it was like stepping into a faraway, serene and tranquil bubble. It had room only for me and my Lord. An escape from the clatters and dramas of my life. The bubble always popped as soon as I stepped off the mat. Momentary it might have been – it was what I needed to break away from the rush of the world. And reality.

Standing in Mecca, on this green velvet mat, I realised how much I had missed that escapism. How much I might have needed it through my unruly months.

It was much better here. The devotion of these people was inspiring. Petrol to an almost burnt out match, it sent a vibe into the core of my own commitment and inflamed it into a thousand flames. I was not stood alone within the four brick walls of my bedroom. I was stood in the great outdoors with millions of people from all walks of life. It was still me and my Lord in the bubble but, I was not lonely.   There were millions of bubbles around me. I felt wonderfully united with these strangers in globules. We were a bubble team. I bowed when they bowed. Prostrated when they prostrated. We were perfectly choreographed as though we had rehearsed together for years. The synchronisation was spectacular. But we had never met each other before.

I itched to be a bird. To take a bird's eye view.

Hotel staff, shopkeepers, cleaners and even the policemen had dropped everything to worship their Lord. These devotees had brought this vibrant city to a complete standstill. Just like my life in England orbited around day and night, their lives orbited around Fajr, Zohr, Asar, Magrib and Isha; the five prayers.

As soon as the prayer ended, people stepped off their prayer mats. The city came out of its peaceful coma and 'pop' went millions of bubbles. Herds rushed out of the mosque. Shopkeepers scrambled to serve customers who had already got there. Hotel staff went back to scrubbing the floors. Chefs hurriedly flicked their

stoves. Policemen put their hats back on and shouted 'yalla!'
Life resumed until the next prayer.

***

We took cover from the flock of pilgrims exiting the mosque in the
street bazaars.

'Now this is the culture of Mecca. Where the *raw* trade takes
place. It's very similar to what it was hundreds of years ago.'
Daania led us into the narrow side streets off Ibrahim al-khalil road
where the rougher, less tidy stalls and shops stood, and illegal
traders sat.

'Yalla! Yalla!' were the constant shouts that filled my ears as we
meandered through the bustling and dusty streets. The call of shop
keepers persuading passers-by to take a look in their shops. The
unlawful traders who sat suspiciously cloaked on the floor with their
bric-a-brac sprawled around them did not make any verbal
advertisements. They attempted to lure shoppers with their eyes
whilst keeping a shifty look out for policemen.

A captivating atmosphere. It was without music or dance yet –
with the clatter of pots, passing of colourful cloths, sizzling of meat,
laughs of shoppers, jumping of traders – it exuded the vibrancy and
life of such entertainment. A stark contrast from the shopping mall.

The stalls and shops were crammed, noisy and chaotic. With the
lively buzz in the atmosphere, it was a far cry from the calmness of
the expensive shopping centre. A wider range of people hovered
around the small stalls and the rugs on the floor – where temporary
traders lay their goods. The poor shopped here for the cheap items.
The rich, for the culture and customs. Colourful jubbahs, crockery,
sandals, prayer beads, picture frames, clocks were being sold like
auction material; swift and impulsive. Every structure, every
moving figure, every activity intrigued me and so I stared like a
tourist, not buying anything but merely wandering through this
enchanting trade festival.

The aroma emanating from grilled chicken and peppers in the
takeaways soon stirred a sensation in my stomach. 'I'm hungry, let's
eat,' I said to the other two. 'I thought you were too, Daania?'

The two women were bent over a stall sifting through
headscarves, picking them up and dropping them to the dismay of
the stall man who had, only moments ago, folded them into a neat
pile.

'Women! Food!' That finally got their attention. My mother knew not to toy with me when I was hungry. She flicked the headscarves away dismissively as the stall man jumped to catch them and re-pile.

Queuing up at KFC, I was struck at how, outside the realms of the mosque and the equality of the ihram, the poor and the rich quickly became separated. Water and wine.

Within the mosque, it was impossible to know who was rich, who was poor. Each person, indistinguishably, prostrated to the same Lord, in the same direction, sat on the same floor, drank the same Zamzam water. Each wore the same types of robes and behaved in the same humble manner. King or servant? My guess was as good as the ones next to me.

But only metres away from the cocoon of the mosque the sad truth was exposed.

Never had I seen such extreme poverty and wealth in such close proximity. High above where I stood, flourished the king of Saudi Arabia's royal palace. Directly below it lay hungry beggars from third world countries.

Those who could, flashed the crisp green of the riyal and bought the finest of food, clothes and accommodation. Those that could not, took the place that they had been accustomed to all their lives. Dark, dirty corners. Watching rich passers-by in silence.

Most of those who sat on the edges of the road appeared to have made these dingy spots their homes. They could not afford the comforts of a roofed hotel or a soft bed. They must have come in extreme hardship. Spent years scrimping and saving little amounts of money for it to one day become enough for a plane ticket to Mecca; the land of wishes. Their passion, drive was admirable yet their evident struggle was disheartening.

Why did that woman, who composed herself so snootily, whilst she exchanged her dollars for riyals at the money exchange bureau before heading to Turkey Delights, deserve more than that woman who was hunched on a tattered rug near the gutters with a cup of free Zamzam water and a thin piece of bread in her hands?

And what about me? How is it that I'm able to queue up for a hot chicken meal? Do I deserve better than these at my feet; these that are clearly more driven Muslims than I am? Is this glaringly obvious inequality, justice?

It disturbed me.

This road was a perfect example of the wider world itself. I longed to go back to the safe haven of the mosque. That extraordinary place that momentarily shielded my eyes and ears from the harsh truths of life.

'Sigh... Mum... Why do bad things happen to good people? You always tell me Allah is good, then why does he allow such injustice in the world?'

That image came back; the one I had seen on BBC news when I was ten years old. A young Muslim boy in Ethiopia. The distinct way his body lay on the arid ground, unclothed, bar a dirty rag to preserve his modesty. It was heart-breaking. The extent of starvation was evident. Sharp jagged ribs, sunken cheeks. His eyes were lifeless and I was sure it meant that his soul had died. He was dying of AIDS. A young innocent child. A young innocent *Muslim* child.

Forcing the upsetting image out of my mind, the same anger welled up inside me as that I had felt during the times of my own mental agony. I was angry that Allah had allowed me to feel pain when I was sure that I had been a decent Muslim. Angry that there were devoted worshippers of Allah who sat on the dirty ground beside me, whilst wrongdoers in other places of the world laughed in speeding red Ferraris. Good people. Bad People. Angry that Allah allowed that famished Ethiopian child to suffer when he was as blameless as a child.

'It is a test. Allah is testing us all,' my mother said in a quiet confident tone.

'A test??'

'He allows good people to suffer through torture, poverty, loss, job redundancies, exam failures to test whether those people will react by losing hope in him and rejecting him or whether they'll stay faithful and patient with the belief that his help will come.'

***

'You know Sarah, I've been waiting for God to bring 'the one' to me for ages.' I push my lasagne away from me. Too love-sick to eat. *'I knew he'd bring him to me one day.'*

'Wow...' Even Sarah cannot eat her dinner. *'I've never seen you like this. You look so in love.'*

'I am...' My eyes mist over. *'Zameer's perfect. Everything I want. I mean, he's short and no Brad Pitt... but other than that, just perfect.'*

A couple of months pass and I find myself screaming 'Allah, you've betrayed me!!' as I pull at my prayer mat attempting to shred it to pieces with my hands.

'Grrrr!!' I try again, feeling my fingers burn.

And then search for a pair of scissors.

'You tricked me!!!' My tiny eyebrow scissors are the only ones I can find in my bedroom and I begin to cut up the blue mat inch by inch.

'You let me believe he was the one and all along he was a dirty lying rat! How could you let me hurt like this!' Aware that, with my frazzled hair and bloodshot eyes, I look like a psychopath, I continue to cut tiny pieces out of the mat.

Finally I give up and throw the whole thing into the bin.

***

Test. My mother's words buzzed in my head. *Have my sorrows been a test? Was it not betrayal but a test to see whether I would be a dutiful Muslim when things went wrong for me? Was Allah there all along watching my reaction to his test?*

'When good things happen to bad people, it is again, a test. A test to see whether those people thank Allah and worship him when life is jolly. You know, even the most loved of Allah, the Prophet, was tested. When he was tortured by his enemies, even he cried *'when will come the help of Allah?* "

'It was a test?' *Has my shredding of my prayers meant that I have failed?* 'All of this is a test?' I asked.

His eyes. 'That Ethiopian boy was being tested?'

'What Ethiopian boy?'

'No.' Daania shook her cream scarfed head. 'When a person goes through hardships it's sometimes a punishment from Allah, rather than a test. A punishment for sins that person has committed.'

'Oh...' disheartened.

'No, no, but that's good! Punishment in this life is better than punishment in hell. Prophet Mohammad said if Allah wants good for a person then he hurries with his punishment in this life, giving them a chance to repent, rather than holding back until the severer punishments of hell. Hell, where repentance will be too late.'

I knew that I had never been a perfect Muslim, just a decent one. *Have I sinned and been punished? Should I feel guilty and apologetic? Have these poor people come with skeletons in their closets? But surely the Ethiopian boy had done nothing wrong?*

'But I don't understand. Are these poor people being tested or punished for sins?' I asked.

'Allah knows best. Everything happens for a reason. Punishment or test? We can only speculate. He knows which it is.' Daania sighed. She was approached by a young girl, with half her left arm missing, begging for money.

I took some riyals out of my pocket and handed them to her. *Poor thing.*

'There's no need to be sad about these things.' My mother patted my back ushering me to move forwards into the queue. 'With hardship comes ease, as Allah says. Always remember that eventually things will balance out.'

'What do you mean?'

'Well, this life is not it. When you put this life and the afterlife together, then the good people will always come out on top. Always. Those who've been through the toughest tests but remained faithful to Allah will be rewarded the most. Justice will rise on the Day of Judgment. Good things will happen to good people in heaven. I promise you. Allah promises you.'

'Promise?'

'Promise.'

I guess this world is no place for justice. Innocent children will continue to be killed by diseases, landmines. Evil men will carry on oppressing with a smile on their faces and swords in their hands. The good will continue to suffer, being too weak to cry. And even my misery, God forbid, may continue.

But I wanted to believe that there will be justice one day, even if it is in the afterlife. I wanted to believe that Allah is just. That good people will be rewarded with good and bad people will be punished with bad.

My mother's and Daania's words were comforting.

I stepped forwards in the queue before anybody cut in.

I was surprised by the sudden idea that the infliction of my pain may not have been as a result of God's betrayal or desertion.

Looking at those around me, it did not feel like the right moment to be selfish and think about my own problems. They were bigger victims of pain. I put thoughts of myself to the side.

Their time will come. They aren't suffering in vain. That Ethiopian boy is on his way to heaven.

Pity reined in, I watched an old black woman eating a stale piece of bread on the ground. *Yeah, this life is so unfair. But I hope the afterlife is where everything will be set right. Where fairness will prevail. Their time will come, but until then, the game continues.* Snug answers to my bitter questions. I desperately wanted to wrap my questions in the warm duvet of the justice-will-be-done answers and hide away from the despairing scenes around me. And so I did.

I moved forwards in the queue and studied the menu. 'Didn't someone once say, *'one will not be a true believer unless he loves for his brother what he loves for himself?'* I asked my two companions.

'Prophet Mohammad,' they both nodded, clearly impressed.

I ordered four chicken burger meals.

I walked over to the old, bread eating woman and sat on the dirty ground beside her. *What is good enough for her is good enough for me.* I handed her one of the red boxed meals and smiled. She hesitated, cracked a big-lipped smile back, and took it from me. We chomped in pleasant silence, ignoring my mother's and Daania's incredulous looks.

I cannot end the sorrows of the entire world for I am a mere human being. But, what I can do, is put an end to one person's misery for at least a few moments, just a few moments, whilst we await the day of justice.

9

'THIS IS IT. THIS is where it happened.'

High above, despite the blinding sun, a small, dark, oblong shape emerged, contrasting ever so slightly against the grey rocks of the large mountain. The cave. It was hardly distinguishable. Merely a black dot amongst a mass of grey. Like lips, large, thick, slate-like slabs encircled the mouth of the cave, setting out an entrance. None of us dared climb up the treacherous mountain and enter the cave, like he had done. Hundreds of us simply gazed up at it in awe, from a safe distance.

'Cave Hira!' Since the beginning of our tour of Mecca, which Layth had arranged for our group, this little man, the tour guide, had done well in keeping us on our toes despite the fact that we had been dragged out of our beds at six in the morning. To capture our attention he had come equipped. He carried with him at all times his microphone, his booming Arabian accented voice and his outrageously pointy beard.

'It looks a little small?' I had expected its size to match its historic significance.

'It is small cave,' his English broken. 'About four yards and two yards wide. Prophet Mohammad spent lots nights in Cave Hira. All alone, worshipping Allah and thinking about troubles of world. This is that cave, dear brothers and sisters...' The guide paused theatrically. Waved his arms upwards. Took a deep breath. Raised his voice. '...Where Quran was first revealed to man Mohammad and this is where he became Prophet!'

His melodrama had the desired effect. Most of us knew about Cave Hira, but we still gasped as though hearing it for the first time.

'This is where he saw Angel Gabriel, right?' I asked Hooria, the youngest woman of the Scottish group.

'Yeah, where the message of the Quran was passed to him.' She took a Kodak camera out and snapped several pictures. 'Can't believe we're stood here to be honest!'

Like the fairytale of Cinderella, the story of Cave Hira was one of the most frequently told stories I grew up hearing. I had not known that the cave still existed. I had always thought the cave to be a component of a historical story that had no remnants left in the present. Seeing it felt strange. I would never see the actual ballroom where Cinderella fell in love with her prince because that story was just a fairytale that stopped on the last page of its book. The story of Cave Hira now differed, because I was standing directly below the cave and seeing it with my own eyes. Where the Cinderella tale stays in the fantasy world, the story of Cave Hira leapt out of the books and came alive.

The cave and mountain An-Noor, in which it was embedded, appeared untouched by man. It could not have changed much in the last fourteen hundred years from when it was first discovered by the Prophet. I wanted it not to be a tourist site, so that I could climb up the mountain at a steady pace and in silence, sit in the cave like Prophet Mohammad did. Contemplate in isolation whilst watching the moon. To feel what he felt.

Unable to stare into the blinding light from the sky for a second longer, I dropped my neck and adjusted my eyes. There were perhaps hundreds of other little tourists at the foot of the large mountain staring up at the cave. They looked rather bewildered. Binoculars were peered into and cameras flashed – paparazzi-style.

Apart from a quiet murmur coming from these tourists, there was not much noise. Magnifying the vastness of the mountainous desert we were in. I inhaled, deep, and savoured its earthy smell, as the morning sun, which could have set a forest on fire, frazzled my red nose.

Only two miles out of Mecca, yet there were no signs of civilisation. Just tourists, coaches and portable stalls.

Small, cheap items were being sold by the local tradesmen and women at the stalls. Dates, prayer beads, fruit and souvenirs – the kind that end up cluttering your shelves at home.

My eyes caught those of a mother and daughter who were sat on the ground, having laid out a mat with prayer beads on it. They peered at the customers of other stalls whilst their own goods remained untouched. I guessed people, like me, were now fed up of filling their shopping bags with prayer beads wherever they went. It was difficult to avoid these blobs on strings. I shrugged my shoulders and walked over to the stall. They were just poor people trying their best to make a living somehow, not having the luxury of state benefits and going on the dole.

'Assalaamualaikum.' I smiled, uttering the Islamic greeting which every Muslim is sure to understand. It replaced the general 'hello' with *may peace be with you*. 'How much are your beads?' pointing to a bunch of limp beads knotted in tatty brown string.

'Ten riyal,' the lady said. She had a soft voice. Her brown eyes hoping for a sale.

I did not need them – an image of me struggling to zip my suitcase over spilling with beads popped up – but I bought them anyway.

***

Our tour guide seemed to have lost his enthusiasm by the time we got to the next stop. He did not bother to tell us one of his animated stories. Or even just tell us where we were. The stifling heat and foggy dust in his coach must have hindered him.

The rocky and sandy piece of land that we stood at was almost derelict, bar a few huts and tourists. Some gathered around a large rectangular area that was enclosed by a rusty metal fence. Within the enclosure were fifty or so jagged gravestones. A make-shift graveyard.

'...battle of Uhud.' I overheard a tour officer of another group explain the significance of this place as they gathered around him and looked out at the gravestones with interest. Our own tour guide had wandered off to a portable juice bar. 'The Qureshites, who were non-Muslims, marched here with three thousand of their men to annihilate the Muslims, their religion and their Prophet. Seventy of Prophet Mohammad's men died here. This was jihad for them and they died as martyrs.'

Jihad. Martyrs.

As though a landmine had been placed in my path, those words instinctively made me stop in my tracks. Since the terrorist attacks in New York on 11th September 2001, whenever these controversial words were uttered in my presence a distasteful queasiness crept into me. Remembering the attacks, the later consequences. And that I was Muslim.

***

I am typing up a report for my psychology A-level coursework on a computer in the college library. The TV screens above suddenly turn on. SKY news. All the students and staff stop what they are doing and gawk up at the screens as a clip of two planes crashing into the New York twin towers is shown. Repeated again and again like a recurring nightmare. It is when the news reporter utters the words 'Islamic terrorists' that I bite my lip and furrow my eyebrows.

Through the rain, I walk home feeling confused. Ashamed. Is what the reporters say true? Does Islam allow such attacks to be made in its name? The Islam that I had been taught only ever stressed the importance of good morals – give to the poor, smile at others, be gentle, say kind words, do not show anger, be generous, be helpful. I have never heard of jihad and certainly do not know its meaning.

'Islam does not condone the attacks!' Muslim representatives are interviewed by TV channels and newspapers. For years, the blame, the defences do not end. Relieved that the Muslims were rejecting the accusations, I take it to be the truth and brush my doubts into a cobwebbed corner of my mind.

***

But there was something wrong. The way the tour officer said 'jihad' stirred that unvisited corner of my mind, disconcertingly. There was something not right about the way he said the word. He said it with unreserved passion.

He continued to speak. 'It says in the Quran that should one perform jihad then that person will be rewarded with the forgiveness of his sins and admittance into heaven.'

The group started to disperse and I noticed the tall figure of Mikaeel left behind. Stood beside the fence, he looked at the gravestones absentmindedly.

'They're jihaadi's?' I asked, cringing at the sound of the word. I had grown to hate it.

'Ah yes, of course.' I liked his voice. Deep, rich, educated.

'Hmmm… Controversial.'

'Ermmmm, why do u say that?'

'I don't know. *Jihad,*' wincing at him.

'This jihad isn't controversial,' pointing to the gravestones. 'I bet you're going off what you've heard from the media, eh?'

'I don't know.'

'No, go on. Tell me'

'Well, news reporters tell us Islam condones jihad and terrorism. Imams tell us it doesn't. Who do we believe?' I felt deflated by my rising doubts. The entire meaning of my journey was about to be destroyed.

'Listen, jihad simply means, *striving in the way of Allah*. That's it. It doesn't mean *killing* like many people think it does.'

'I thought it meant *to be at war* or *to be a warrior*?'

'Not at all! Jihad means, making an effort to please Allah by following the guidance of the Quran.'

He raised three of his fingers. 'This effort may be with the inner self of a person, through making a personal effort to cleanse ones soul by doing good, worshipping Allah, abiding by his rules.' He pulled a finger down.

'Or, this effort may be verbal, through saying kind words to others or perhaps, teaching others about Islam.' He pulled the second finger down.

'Or, this effort may be physical, through helping the poor, building mosques or defending Islam from the physical attacks of people, who attack Muslims because they are Muslims.' With that he pulled his third finger down. I noticed there was no wedding ring.

'So how were these people here jihaadis?'

'These men, who'd fought in the battle of Uhud, had performed jihad through physical effort. The third one. They had strived for Allah by fighting those who had come to attack them and their people simply because they were Muslims.'

'That's fair enough.'

'They didn't give up their faith like they could easily have done so to save their own lives. Instead, they fought against their attackers, keeping their faith in Allah. In other words, they strived for Allah – jihaadis.'

I nodded.

'Jihad isn't evil.' He continued. 'Prophet Mohammad allowed a battle against those who physically attacked the Muslims because of their religion. But he warned his soldiers not to ever bring harm to a child, woman or old person during their battles. Even trees. Fruits.'

'Hmmmm, I don't like any form of violence.'

'No, you're not understanding.' His thick brows furrowed, taking his hazel eyes with them. 'It's the same permission given to British soldiers by the Queen or Government to fight those countries and kill those that have wronged Britain and its people.'

'Yeah, like the World Wars.'

'Yeah! During World War II, German armies physically attacked Britain, British people. The British responded by attacking the Germans with the same guns and bombs. All to protect their country and people. Men were urged to join the army and fight for their country. Some of those people that were killed by the British army happened to be innocent women and children. But that's war. Those that died fighting in the war became war heroes.'

'Yeah, they did. They were heroes. Saved the country.'

'And this is exactly what happened in the battle of Uhud. An army of non-Muslims came to physically attack Muslims and Islam with their swords. The Muslims responded in defence of their religion, lives and people by attacking the direct perpetrators with swords. These here that died fighting in this war are war heroes. *And Allah will give them heaven.*'

'That type of war is a necessity. It's a classic case of kill or be killed.'

'Exactly.' He dusted sand off his bulging arms, getting ready to leave.

'Hey hang on.' Not wanting him to go. 'Ermm... what about the 9/11 terrorist attacks??'

'Oh, don't get me started on them...'

'Why?'

'They were just twisted bastards! The New York terrorists weren't jihaadis.'

'No?'

'These Muslim terrorists were not physically attacked by the Americans they had killed, were they?

'Well, obviously not.'

The muscles in his jaw throbbed. 'The New York terrorists killed people without good reason. They murdered innocent people and tried to justify it with our religion. You know, they've committed an enormous sin and I can imagine no end for those people except hell.'

'Well, they think they're getting virgins in heaven!'

'Ha. God says in the Quran that the sanctity of life is so precious. If a person kills another without a very good reason then it is seen as though he'd killed the *whole* of mankind. That's how bad the attacker's actions were.'

My father began to approach us from a distance, whistling with a guised casualness. It was comically obvious what he was doing.

Typical dad. He thought I was flirting with Mikaeel and was coming to put a stop to it. Lest he become a grandfather of an unwanted child.

Mikaeel whipped his sunglasses back on and prepared to walk off. 'I don't know about you but when I was younger I was constantly told that Islam teaches us to be kind to everyone, Muslim or non-Muslim. Jews, Christians, Buddhists, Hindus, whatever. Be their friends and don't be unkind, for it is a sin.'

'Yeah me too.'

'So it's ridiculous to think Allah condones the killing of innocent non-Muslims.'

'Now that you tell me that, it does... I feel a lot better now, thanks. For a minute, I was contemplating taking the next flight back to Manchester!' I laughed, relieved that the God that I had begun to put so much hope and expectation in did not side with the bombers. Having travelled three thousand miles in search of peace, I was in no mood to be friends with Osama Bin Laden.

'Just remember one thing,' Mikaeel stopped, swivelled on his heels and raised two fingers forming a 'V'. 'Islam means peace.'

***

Perturbed by the haunting and secluded windy road that we were now driving on, I demanded an answer from Layth. 'Where are we going?' Huge mountains loomed over us, darkening the land in a flash. It was still the morning, but we seemed to have immersed ourselves into a cold, wintry evening.

'Just wait.' Layth croaked with a psychotic-murderer smile on his face.

'Layth, stop looking at me like that... Will you tell me?'

He gave me a sideward glance and said nothing.

The coach juddered downhill for a few mysterious kilometres, reminding me of a horror movie. It creaked to a stop when it reached a point where the surface of the land was flat. The driver slithered the coach around so it was facing the upward hill. The mountains gnarled at us.

The tour guide rose in the dark. His energy had returned. It must have been in the juice. 'This is valley of the... jinns,' he whispered ominously.

Jinns. I gulped.

'All you will know that jinns are another creation of Allah. Jinn means 'hidden'. They made of smokeless fire. They came before Prophet Adam and like me and you, made to worship Allah. Now this is scary bit… jinns live *side by side* with us…'

A cold shiver ran up the back of my neck. I found my father's sleeve. *Did he really have to bring us here to tell us this story?*

'We can't see jinns, unless jinns make themselves seen. But they see us…' In the murky coach he stared at us. His eyes beadier than before.

'They have powers where they can travel big distances in super speed. They make themselves look like anything, a tree or… a person.' He squinted at each of us as if to determine who was a masked jinn and who was not.

This guy is creeping me out.

'They are also able to possess our minds and bodies.'

'Poltergeist,' someone whispered.

'These jinns been given powers to test them, so that Allah can see if they use these powers for good or evil. Most jinns are evil and Prophet Mohammad, peace be upon him, warned people not to hang around in areas like graveyards, ruins and… deserts.'

'What the hell are we doing here then?!' I whispered out loud. I rocked in my seat, itching to leave. I wondered how we ended up like this. Stopped in the middle of nowhere with this eerie and totally weird tour guide, who I feared might have been a jinn himself.

'Why you laugh??' The tour guide pointed his microphone at someone at the front of the coach. I could not hear his response.

'Jinns are explained in Quran! So you should believe they exist!'

'There are a lot of things that we people cannot see, hear and understand.' Mikaeel spoke up like the geek that sat at the front of the class. 'Just because we cannot see, hear or understand something doesn't mean it doesn't exist. Some things require us to have blind faith. Like we do in dreams, thoughts and feelings.' As always, he spoke sense.

'This place has lots jinns,' revealed the guide. 'They do not like people come here. My driver has switched coach off. He has foot on brake and will not touch accelerator. Now watch how coach is pushed *uphill* by itself. So hard, that my driver will have to control speed with brake.'

We all gasped as the unignited coach began to pick up speed up the hill on its own.

'This is by force of jinns!' The tour guide shouted over the racket of the speeding vehicle. I feared we were about to shoot off a cliff. 'The jinns are pushing coach away from their valley! Come have look, if you do not believe!'

Would jinns, the hidden mysteries of the supernatural, flash their powers so openly? Despite my blood running cold, curiosity pushed me to my feet and I tiptoed to have a look.

Just as he had said, the driver had the gear stick in neutral, the keys out of the ignition, his foot lightly on the brake. My eyes caught the speed dial. It was showing 70mph. We were going uphill at 70mph in a coach that was switched off and being controlled by the driver using the steering wheel and the *brake*. 'Oh my God...!'

'Please can we get out of here now, already??' Iraj, the older lady from Scotland, stammered what our clattering teeth were struggling to say.

Bizarre as it may seem, I believed in jinns.

The existence of jinns explained a lot of the notorious mysteries to me. It gave reasoning to real life accounts of exorcism, fortune telling, voodoo, black magic, witchcraft, poltergeists and ghosts.

This belief in jinns arose fifteen years ago.

My eyeballs began to crack as I attempted to fight off a familiar consuming sadness.

***

It is a summer's day. School holidays. 1994. I am cheerfully playing outside my house in the street with my sister. We are both eating the fruity ice pops we had bought from the corner shop for 5p. Playing a bit of Hopscotch. I am ten years old, she is fourteen. And although she is older than me, she is my bestest friend in the whole wide world.

All of a sudden, she lets out a piercing shriek. Her red ice pop drops to the ground. Splatters onto the pavement. Like cold blood. Startled, I freeze and watch her. Unable to move. She is looking upwards, towards the sky in profound terror. Her face turns white. Her eyes bulge out. She raises her hands and arms as though shielding herself from something that is towering over her. Without further warning, she drops to the ground. And passes out.

I did not see what she saw.

A few frantic moments later, she regains consciousness.

'What happened? What did you see?' I ask her.

'I don't know... it was something that looked like a... scary

angel... Smoke? A ghost? I don't know how to describe it... I can't remember anything else... I am so scared.'

I am scared too.

***

To the rest of us it was unheard, unseen, unknown.

'I think it was a jinn she saw', my mother said to me a couple of years later. What else could it have been? An irrational hallucination of a perfectly healthy young girl? Given everything, I think it was a jinn too. A work of black magic. Witchcraft. Or something similar.

Whatever it was, it struck again a few months later. The same way.

This time it was less merciful.

This time it killed her.

My sister, my bestest friend in the whole wide world, had been killed.

10

THE COMMOTION WAS STARTLING.

We were barricaded outside our own hotel. Ahead of me, to the left of me, to the right of me, everywhere, were a shocking magnitude of people. Hundreds of thousands had laid their prayer mats on the road whilst a swarm of people struggled towards the Al-Haram mosque. Like starlings returning to their roosts.

A couple began to lay their prayer mats on the bottom steps of our hotel whilst my parents and I stood on the top step. Our jaws dropped as we looked on in dismay at the pandemonium.

It was Friday; midday.

Friday – the holy day for Muslims. The midday prayers on a Friday, Jummah, are the most important of the week. All over the world, Jummah seemed to do the unthinkable. It coaxed the most defiant of Muslims out of their shells and into the mosques. During these weekly congregations people would meet others in their communities they would never ordinarily cross on a normal day. The reasons why these prayers were given such extraordinary importance, I did not know.

Here in Mecca, this was certainly no ordinary day and this was certainly no ordinary scene. Every occupant of the city had stepped into the limelight to pray Jummah in the Al-Haram mosque or anywhere which was remotely close to it. Including the steps of our hotel.

'This is impossible!' My father huffed. 'I'm going back up. I'll pray in the room.' He swung around back into the hotel, his blue prayer mat dragging behind him.

'Mum?' I shouted over the rumble.

'Today's our only chance to pray Jummah here. Oh Allah...' Her disappointment was undisguised and mirrored my sentiments, doing nothing to reassure me.

'But where are we going to pray?' As far as my eyes could see, there was not a spare square inch for us. We probably stood more of a chance swimming to Australia than getting into the mosque.

'Oh God.'

'Mum, you're going to have to say more than 'oh God'.' I contemplated laying my prayer mat on the shore of the narrow steps of the hotel, like others had. That option was soon swept away as I was abruptly shoved sideward by two women who decided to do just that. I was left standing on the foot of someone else's prayer mat with the tide at my feet.

The crowds drummed. The sun sweltered. I frantically scanned the vicinity searching for an opening. A scrap of land amidst this ocean of pilgrims.

I gasped, catching sight of a small gap towards the far edge of the road directly opposite to where I stood.

'Mum, there's a small gap over there!' To get to it, meant we would be wading through bodies of already seated people. 'Let's go for it!'

Not waiting for a response, I sucked in and stepped into the ocean, on my toes, holding onto the tightly wedged pilgrims.

It was worse than an assault course of nets, ditches and tunnels. With each step I cringingly fell into laps, crushed feet with my knees and dug my heels into hands.

'Sorry. Sorry. Oops. I'm so sorry,' praying that this clumsy moment would end.

But no one slapped me off or told me to get lost. They just watched me with amusement. The space I was heading for was only yards away, yet it seemed as though it was a torturous mile away. It was more exhausting than wading through water, mud, sand. I was literally wading through people.

Ten minutes, I had only reached a quarter of the distance. I was steaming under the ferocious sun. Overly tensed legs aching. Will weakened to the strength of a hair.

'Really sorry. So sorry.' I wanted to throw in the towel and give up. Turning around, I saw my mother blunderingly following me, stuttering apologies on her way. I contemplated turning around and going back to the hotel room to pray, like my father.

No. The thought of not praying my first and only Jummah prayer within the hemispheres of the Kaba and with its Imam niggled at me. Shaking the discouragement off, I winced and clawed forward. *All these people can pray here, so why can't I?* 'Sorry!'

My heart did a somersault when I noticed two big-hipped

African women heading for my space. I was so near it. They were not as delicate in their scramble as I was, and ruthlessly shoved people aside with their ploughing hands and rural elbows. Gritting my teeth, I quickened my pace.

Out of breath and panicky, I got there just a couple of seconds before them. One of the women glared at me with her big black eyes. She flared her nostrils. A livid baboon. I heard her shouting something at me in an unfamiliar language.

'I was here first!' I shouted back indignantly.

Effortlessly, as though swatting a fish, she flicked me aside and sat down, pulling her companion down with her. I looked down at her in disbelief.

She had bullied my space from me. My temper shot to my fins. 'Oi!!' Furious, I clenched my fist with a fired urge to thump her on her big back.

The eyes around gawked at me to see what my next move would be. *You should've brought popcorn with you!* I felt like screaming at them. *Maybe nachos!!*

Embarrassed, my temper dropped. It would have been more awkward if I got angry in front of my spectators. The hypocrisy of punching her just before I was about to pray, I imagine, would have been unforgivable. I sulkily turned away. Truth was, these women were three times my size and monstrous. I knew I did not stand a chance in hell.

I was the better yet wimpier person that stood uncomfortably between the laps and backs of four strangers. Although thankful that I was not wearing a short skirt, the situation was hopeless. Behind me were endless rows of seated strangers that I could not look beyond. I was stranded.

'Why did you let them take our space??' My mother finally caught up to me and looked peeved.

'I didn't *let* them take anything!'

'Allahu akbar. Allahu akbar.' I panicked as the Imam made the call for the Jummah prayer. Waves of people rose in preparation with an almighty surge that almost knocked me off my feet.

'We're in the way of people. We need to move away from here whether we get a space to pray or not!' My mother shouted above the gushing stirrings.

'Oh!' A glimpse of sandy earth sparkled before me. A Treasure Island. Through the movements of rising people, I saw a space a couple of metres away along the edge of the gutter. It was about two feet wide and six feet long. I worked out that my mother and I could squeeze into that spot if one of us sat in front of the other.

What other choice is there? With a muttered growl, I ushered my mother to follow me as I slashed through the congregation with a new found zeal.

We were welcomed at this golden spot by a stifling and repugnant stench coming from the adjacent gutter. 'Ohagh...,' almost reeling backwards with nausea. My hand shot to my nose, closing the inlets to this stink and saving me from passing out. Through my watering eyes I saw that the edge of the road curved downwards where it met the gutter. The ground I was supposed to be praying on was littered with remnants of mouldy food and other dubious specimens. Cream bits. Brown bits.

'I can't pray here mum? Someone will end up nudging me into the gutter.' My frustration was wavering towards a full blown hissy fit.

'Come on! At least we've found a space. Thank Allah.' My grateful mother laid down her green mat in front of me.

'Allahu akbar!' The Imam began to lead the prayer.

I wished for an instant Radox bubble bath as I laid my prayer mat over the dirty ground. Thankful that to pray on a clean mat was obligatory and I had brought my pink one with me.

I bowed in sync with the millions of others that pooled around the vicinity of the mosque, willing myself to dismiss what was to the left of me.

A few moments later, I immersed my mind into the shielding bubble of prayer. As I went into prostration on the ground, amidst the toxicity of the gutter and rotting scraps of food, I tried to work out whether I was feeling ridiculously humbled or ridiculously humiliated. Pride, embarrassment – they slowly left me.

Ridiculously humbled.

In the hush, I almost laughed out loud at the irony. At home, I often skipped Jummah prayers for trivial reasons. To lunch with friends, run errands or to buy that pair of shoes I had drooled on in Debenhams a few days earlier.

Less than a week had passed from those days and here I was willingly risking a sideward nudge into a repulsive sewer for the sake of praying Jummah. I had been brought down to earth and dumped right next to a foul gutter. Yet I still went down on my knees and prostrated to God. It felt like madness.

***

That night, time stood still.

It was our final night before our Hajj journey was to begin. Three o'clock in the morning. My parents and I sat under the dark sky in the inner courtyard of the Al-Haram mosque beside the Kaba.

'It is at night that Allah is closest to the earth and more accepting of prayers. When people sacrifice their sweet sleep in order to talk to him.' My father had attempted to numb my gripe as I grumbled out of bed at two o'clock in the morning.

The mosque was unusually quiet. There was a beautiful cool aura of tranquillity hanging over us.

Would sitting on a beach in the Maldives whilst watching the sunset give me the same serenity? I had had so little peace at home. My heart had been constantly restless. An unexplainable restlessness. But here I felt peace. An unexplainable peace.

In that moment, I hoped time would never end. Longing to stay cocooned from the outside world. I flicked my prayer beads as I indulged in contemplation. And self-pity.

Thinking of the past. I wondered why God had ignored me when I was most in need. Why he allowed me to suffer so mercilessly. I gazed up at the silent stars in the sky. A slow tear of memory rolled down my cheek. 'Why?' I whispered.

'It's a test or a punishment'. As if on cue, my mother and Daania's words played in my mind. Then replayed. I had not thought about what they had said since they first spoke those words.

Is that what it is? Have you inflicted me with a crap job and a crap Zameer to test or punish me? I moved my prayer beads, absentmindedly. Remembering the many nights I would look in the bathroom mirror and study the patterns the running of my mascara made under my eyes.

If it is a test then surely I've failed. I've done all that I shouldn't have done; I lost my faith in you and walked the path of sin. I saw the lies to my boss – *'What's wrong with you?' 'Erm... I've really hurt my back. Can't move',* hoping he could not hear the fairground rides from the toilets I was hiding in – the abusive text messages to Zameer – *'I hope you get run over by a big Carlsberg lorry. Why don't you just die?'* – the missed prayers, the cheating, the men. *I've failed. You must hate me.* I sighed.

Or were you already unhappy with me and were punishing me? What had I done? Thinking about time before January 2008, I guessed I was not always perfect. There were prayers I missed to watch Hollyoaks Omnibuses, pre-marital relations – Zameer, low tops, bullying my brother for his BMX bike, stealing Jelly Babies from Woolworths… The unrealised deeds crept up like mud men in a swamp.

'Heck,' biting my lip, suddenly feeling rare emotions of remorse and guilt. 'Test or punishment, either way I have sinned. You must hate me?'

What a shit life. I ran my sleeve against my cheeks. *I can't win either way. If I sin I get punished. If I don't sin I get tested. And for what? What am I pedalling on this vicious cycle for? For a painful existence until I die? How crap.*

'Are you ok?' My father asked.

'Yes…' Unlike before, I was no longer embarrassed to shed a tear in his presence. 'Dad?'

'Yeah?'

'Tell me what you used to tell me when I was little.'

'What's that?' scratching his beard.

'Tell me about heaven.' I yearned to hear his cuddly and comforting words again. The ones that always put a smile on my face no matter what was going on. I wanted a life better than this.

Mildly surprised at my request, he paused for a moment looking at me reminiscently and then laughed lightly. 'Come here,' he ushered me closer to him and put his arm around my shoulders.

'Heaven…' He stared up at the sky and smiled.

A child again, I mimicked him by grinning and looking up too.

'See these tears you just cried? You will never cry those in heaven. In heaven there is only happiness. And that happiness is forever and ever. There will be no war, no hatred, no worries and no injustice. There will only be peace.'

I tried to imagine a world without fights, without sadness, without evil. It was impossible to depict such a clean vision.

'In this life people die. In heaven no one dies. In heaven you will see your sister again.' He rarely mentioned her.

My eyes misted at her memory. Hurt would not have been hurt, had she not been taken away from me.

***

'Weeeee!!' My head spins, the living room swirls and my laughter ripples off its walls. 'Weeeeeee!'

'Again! Please do it again!' Jumping up and down I pull on my sister's sleeve, wanting her to twirl me around again.

'No it's my turn now!' My younger brother takes Nafeesas' arms and wraps them around his waist.

With a huge smile on her face, a smile that I have never ever seen fade, she picks him up and spins him around the room.

'Whoooo!! Whoooooo!'

'Me, me, me next.' I yank my brother out of her grip and stand poised with my back facing her front.

'Okay, you ready?' Nafeesa says. She is just as excited as I am.

'I want ten spins, because I'm ten years old.'

'Just ten, because I'm feeling dizzy now.' She wraps her arms around my waist, 'hupp,' and lifts me up.

And twirls.

'Weeeeeeeeeee!' giggling, my legs fly out with the force of the wind underneath them.

'One....!' she pants.

This is better than the merry-go-round at the park.

'Two...!'

'Weeeeeeee!!!' hoping that she starts counting in halves, like she always does, to give me more.

'Three...!'

'Weeeee!' It is so much fun.

'Four...!' She counts.

Little do I know that tomorrow there will be no spins.

No her. No spins.

'Four and a half...!'

*** * ***

'You will see me and your mum again, after we die.' My father continued.

Please... don't say that. I glared at him.

He swiftly moved on. 'Allah says that in heaven there will be rivers of water, milk, honey and wine. We will wear silk clothes. You will wear beautiful silk dresses. We will all be like kings and queens. You will be a beautiful princess, more beautiful than any girl on this planet!'

I giggled.

'In heaven you will get whatever you ask for. You will only need to think of it and Allah will give it to you. Go on. Tell me what is it that you would want?'

Laughing, I opened the gates and let my imagination roam the vastness of my fantasies. As far as they could go. 'Ermmm I want my own island, with a beautiful beach and palm trees. I want an endless supply of chocolates! I want to swim with dolphins. Be a beautiful princess, more beautiful than Kate Moss and Naomi Campbell. I want a bed made of just white roses!' My excitement was contagious. 'And I want to fly like a bird! I want to sing better than Leona Lewis and Mariah Carey! With giggles in my tummy, I want to laugh ecstatically all day and every day. Forever!'

'Is that it??' He mocked. 'Honey, your imagination is far too limited. And I mean *literally*. Allah says that heaven is beyond *anything* that humans can imagine.'

'What does it look like? Is it white? Like a soft bed of clouds? Are there waterfalls? Birds I can fly with? Unicorns? Juicy fruits? Beautiful people?' The thought of it made me giddy. 'Dad, I think a small bar of Galaxy chocolate is *heavenly*.'

'Ha. Anything that we can have on this planet means that it is not *heavenly*. Heaven is something a zillion times greater.'

Darkness passed over his face. His voice lowered in sombreness. 'But then there is the alternative. The fire of hell. People in hell will be made to drink boiling water and blood...'

'Dad!' I yelled, feeling sick. I pulled myself away from him. He had grown fangs. 'This isn't part of what you used to tell me!'

'No, you were too young then. But now, you should know that there is no middle ground in the afterlife. The *only* alternative is hell. You should know about it. The bad will wear clothes made of fire...'

'Dad!'

'...be bitten by snakes, be whipped continuously, be dragged...'

'Please stop! I don't want to hear it!' I raised my hands to my ears.

'Well, you need to know that just as there is heaven, there is hell too.'

'Well I don't want to know,' desiring to live in blissful ignorance of hell.

'Hell is *forever*, where there will be torture totally unimaginable and unknown to this world.'

'Ok. Ok. I think you've made that clear, thanks for ruining my mood,' I muttered.

'You want heaven, yes?'

'Yes.'

'Then it's simple. For zillions of years in heaven you only need to spend seventy or so years of your life, or however long you might live, making sure you keep Allah happy. That a flaming good deal, or what?'

Thinking. 'Yeah. It is.'

'Keep him happy and he will give you an eternity in heaven. Make him unhappy and you will regret it for more than… well, more than forever.' Despite his words dampening the fuzzy feeling I had only moments earlier, there was genuine care in the tone of his voice.

'How? How do I make him happy?' pouting and looking down in my lap.

'Worship him and stay away from bad things. Simple.'

Shaking my head despairingly, I recalled the time I threw my prayer mat into the bin and dived into a life of the night. Regret washed over me. I dripped in an awkward guilt.

'Otherwise it's hell?' An alarming fear turned me cold. A fear that I would never be that floating princess in heaven, but would spend an eternity burning at a stake like a witch.

'If you have sinned… then repent.' He saw through my concern.

'He has called you to save you'. My aunt's words again. *Has he called me here to give me the opportunity to repent? Is this how he wanted to save me?*

For the first time since I had arrived in Mecca and for the first time in months I looked up at the dark sky and uttered the words 'astagfirullah.' *Allah, forgive me.*

With the despair of my life in my chest I had staggered to Mecca for a cure, but now I feared that I would leave this city not with a cure but something worse.

A greater despair.

The despair of my afterlife.

11

TONIGHT MY JOURNEY OF a lifetime begins.

The Kaba stood before me. I stood before it. In my white ihram attire once more. The essence of my trip, the crux of the saga had finally arrived. I had clung onto the hope that this journey would change my life. Rip the despair out of my heart and hurl it out into space. *Make or break.* I feared that should I return the same as or worse than when I had arrived then I would not be able to keep my pedal on life.

My heavy reliance on Hajj made me nervous and jittery. I was excited at the possible discovery of a miraculous cure but I dreaded more, the possibility of a head-on crashing disappointment.

The night sky was as dark as coal. The mosque, eerily quiet and bare. There were very few pilgrims present as the majority of them had set off to begin their preparations for Hajj. The atmosphere was no longer vibrant. Instead, a strange sombreness hovered.

'Yes, it will probably be the most difficult journey you will ever make, but I'm with you all the way, Allah is with you all the way'. Layth had prepped the group with last minute advice before sending us off to pack and get into the requisite ihram. The tension had been choking. Each of us wondered what trials and tribulations the next five days would bring and whether we would come out as one of the lucky ones. Alive.

Am I really ready for this? Do I even know what I'm getting myself into? Like a man about to marry, doubt flickered in my mind and I found myself getting cold feet. *What am I doing?* I suddenly felt the urge to run out of the mosque and take cover under my duvet.

'Make your intention.' My mother poked my arm.

Biting my lip, I laid my prayer mat on the floor. The state of ihram had to be entered into once more, but this time with the intention of performing Hajj. As I bowed and prostrated, the steel balls of my chained apprehensions weighed me to the ground. 'Allah please make this easy for me and my family. Let us take from it what we came to take from it.' My whisperings faint-hearted.

'Labbaik Allah humma labbaik…' I had entered the state of ihram. With steps filled with burdens, I walked away from the Kaba. Fear, doubt, nervousness, excitement. Whatever I felt, it did not matter. It was too late to turn back.

My Hajj had officially begun.

***

We walked like an army of pilgrims on a mission to spirituality. That is what we were.

'Hajj is a prolonged act of worship of Allah with various rituals throughout the journey, which Prophet Mohammad had begun.' Layth explained as we, the group, hurriedly followed his sandals down the sandy track of Ibrahim al-khalil road. Our rucksacks dragging behind us. 'It's the most significant act of worship that brings Muslims from all over the world of all cultures, race, colour, background and wealth together and makes them unite and worship Allah, through this testing journey, as one. King or slave, we will all be the same'

Our first stop was to be Mina. Mina was apparently a barren desert outside of Mecca a few miles away. We were to camp out and spend the night and following day doing nothing but busying ourselves in the worship of God. I did not know the significance of spending time in Mina, but I presumed it was merely a place to aid our complete submission to Allah.

Like the change from summer to winter, the commerciality of the city disappeared. No one wandered around the shops anymore. Nor did the shop keepers beckon passersby. The muffled noises of our footsteps and those of the hundreds of thousands of pilgrims who were marching towards Mina at the same time as us created a solemn mood. The sight of the pilgrims in their ihram attire, their sincere recitation of Labbaik and the intent look on their faces as they advanced into the night created a feeling of tenseness and spirituality in my own walk. Whilst I walked, I tried to imagine Prophet Mohammad walking just like us. Like me.

'Ouch!' I stumbled forwards, almost falling flat on my face. A jagged rock had caught in between the soles of my slippers and feet. I yelped and hobbled in pain.

'Ah, should have worn shoes.' Hooria tutted then winced.

'I know. Tells you a lot about my preparation,' Looking down at my beach slippers with disdain, I allowed the pain to ease for a moment.

'So... Hajj eh? What's your story?' I asked her.

'What do you mean?'

'Well. Why? Why are you here?'

'Erm. Well, I got married a couple of months ago to that lucky chap,' she pointed to a skinny brown guy who walked slightly ahead of us with Layth, 'and this is a sort of honeymoon...'

'Didn't fancy Mauritius then?' *I thought honeymoons were to relax with your honey.*

'We've both had a bit of a... dodgy past... and we're hoping that Hajj will allow us to start on a clean slate and start our marriage with God's blessing.'

'Ah... interesting.' *Dodgy past. I wonder what she means by that.* I thought about asking her, but stopped myself. It was probably best not to be nosey and interrogative. 'We all have our reasons.' I thought of my own.

'What are...' *yours.*

'So are you nervous?' I stopped her mid-sentence. Not giving her the opportunity to peel the skin of my past.

***

'What if you get trampled and die!' Sarah says.

I shrug my shoulders. Slumped on the pavement outside her office. I did not go to work today and instead have been waiting for Sarah to come out for her lunch.

'It's drastic! Things can't be that bad?' Her thin, brown eyebrows rise in worry.

'They are Sarah, they are.' I hand her a Greggs pasty. 'I can't live like this anymore. I feel I'm a mess. I can't bear sitting at my desk staring at my computer screen for hours and The Grime haunts me day in day out. I just feel so sad.'

'Who's The Grime?' She looks baffled.

'You know who it is! I can't bear to say his name.'

'Za...'

'Yes! Don't you dare *say his name in my presence!' I glare at her.*

A driver horns at us as he drives past in a van. 'Piss off!' I stick my middle finger up at him.

She pulls me close to her. Smelling of Hugo Boss and cheese pasty. 'Are you sure?'

'I have no choice. It's this or the end...'

***

'Yes, I'm nervous! I just hope we come out alive.' Hooria's eyes widened. 'Enough people have been crushed to death because of the crowds.'

'Damn. Why did you have to say that??'

'Oops, sorry,' she replied sheepishly.

The air of unity soon began to warm and subdue my initial nervousness. For a brief moment, I had the corny urge to beckon everyone to outstretch their hands and walk together, hand in hand. Singing 'Hallelujah.' *No, maybe not. That'd be taking it too far.*

We trawled for another hour in silence, past the deserted shops and buildings and along windy, rocky roads. Most areas were not well lit and I found myself struggling to see where I was walking. That inevitably led to several knocks and stumbles. The additional discomfort caused by the drop in the temperature and rubble under my feet began to take its toll, as did the weight of the rucksack on my shoulders despite having packed very little.

'Only pack necessities ok? Simplicity and humility is the key to Hajj.' Layth had eyed the women in particular whilst giving this bit of advice at our earlier dinner.

Necessities were all I packed. One pair of sandals, one set of clothes, one Islamic robe, one headscarf, my glasses, contact lenses and my sleeping bag. Also, plenty of books on how to perform Hajj. My rucksack was as sparse as a man's night bag but now it felt like I was carrying a female's holiday bag.

'Should we stop for a break, I'm tired?' I complained to my two older friends – Daania and my mother – who were huffing and puffing, struggling to keep up.

'No.' They both replied together.

Raising my eyebrows, I intently watched their mouths. I had caught Daania piling Lucozade energy sweets into her bag earlier and I wondered whether they were both sucking on them. 'Hmmmm...'

'Oh Paiyaa!' A laughing man suddenly ran towards Layth, giving him a big bear hug, whilst fifteen other pilgrims scuttled behind him awkwardly. It was another group from England whose group leader was an old friend of Layth's. Out of the fifteen in this group, there was one white English woman, Hannah. Intrigued by the Arabian headscarf that framed her ice blue English eyes I made way to speak to her whilst they temporarily joined us on our ramble.

'What made you convert?' Hannah was in her thirties and I discovered that she was a new convert, from Atheism to Islam three years ago. She was one of a few converts that I had met in my life and their decisions always aroused some curiosity in me.

'Revert. Remember all kids are born Muslims and unaccountable until puberty,' she politely corrected me.

'Oh sorry' I laughed '*Revert*. What made you revert?'

'Ermmm, a lot of things. Life was a bit of a mess; drugs and ermmm other bodily abuse...'

'It's ok, you don't have to say.' I think she meant prostitution.

'Erm yeah. Just, stuff. Then I met that lovely guy.' She pointed to a tall, black man who was talking to a few others. 'We became friends, I ended up hearing about Islam through him and I somehow, over a period of months, ended up reverting. Then he asked me to marry him!' She grinned and flashed her wedding finger at me. It was empty.

'You've lost your ring.'

'Oh no. Ha. I can't wear the ring in ihram but if you look closely you can see the tan mark on my finger.'

I peered at her finger. 'Haha. That's really sweet. Any regrets?'

'Well, when he leaves his dirty socks lying on the bedroom floor then I do think twice.'

'Nooo, I mean with the convers... reversion?'

'Not at all. I feel beautiful and... clean again, like when I was little. And I'm respected and very well looked after by my husband.'

'Labbaik Allah humma labbaik.' Our conversation was broken by a bellowing chant. Swivelling around we saw a male pilgrim holding his hand up in the air, whilst thirty or so Chinese pilgrims followed him, repeating his words. The men wore their two sheets whilst the women wore long white robes with pink bands around their heads. They spurted with energy and scurried past us in a flash like squirrels.

'The passion of some Muslims is still difficult for me to understand.' Hannah remarked, having been startled too.

'And so is the compassion,' I said softly. By now I was watching a very old frail lady, covered from head to toe, being pushed in a wheelchair by a young lean man. There was another young woman who accompanied them but it was the one in the wheelchair that was the one to be admired. Her dedication and will to embark on this daunting journey despite her disability was unmatchable. The man who pushed her wheelchair was one to be cherished too. Selfless. Kind. His decision to be this woman's aid throughout the challenging feat ahead was heart-warming.

My gaze shifted to another group of passing pilgrims. Light brown skin, brown eyes, black moustaches, long black hair – they looked Mexican. My jaw dropped. One of the men was missing half a leg. He hopped forwards using a crooked and battered stick to support his body weight. Dripping face scrunched in pain. With each movement his arm shook arthritically.

'Good grief. How on earth will he get through this alive?' I asked no one in particular.

'Look at his eyes.' Aliyah, one of the Scottish women, spoke behind us. 'He will do this or die trying.'

Ashamed by my earlier complaints I gathered my courage together and ploughed on, reciting Labbaik. The rubble pierced my soles. I forced myself to think that each jab carried a therapeutic benefit. Like Chinese acupuncture.

Two and a half hours later, one o'clock in the morning, we had passed the crunchy, moonlit road and emerged onto a smooth plain. 'We're here!' Layth let out an almighty sigh of relief, as did the rest of us.

The terrain was brightly lit by lamps and encompassed rows and rows of camps packed closely together like houses in a city. The camps spread across the land that was visible to the naked eye and even ran over onto the nearby rocky mountains. These temporary homes were set up by the Saudi Authorities to accommodate the three million people expected to stay here for the next few days.

Mina. So we've reached our first stop. My feet and legs were battered and the dust that had accumulated on my body was in need of being washed off.

'Prophet Mohammad had spent his first night, first day and second night in Mina, in a tent, doing nothing but devoting the time to Allah in worship. We're here, to do the same; to live and breathe the worship of Allah.' Layth informed us again as we approached our designated camp.

On closer inspection, I saw that the camps were constructed of PVC and cotton and were held up by steel poles. Small, red, steel gates had been erected to form entrances and exits. The camps were sturdily and meticulously arranged alongside each other, each labelled with numbers followed by a letter. Nothing else distinguished these thousands of darkened rooms.

'This is ours.' Layth stopped outside 48B.

A man stood at the entrance, a Saudi official, and checked the identification badges that Layth had given to each of us before we set off. The green uniformed official led us through the entrance, along narrow pathways formed by fabric sectioned areas – mini tents. Taking several right and left turns, I realised that we were in some sort of intricate tent maze.

'Tent 116, 117, 118.' The little Arab man pointed to a row of three clothed sections that were marked in black pen. 'Woman here and man here.' He lifted the cloth of 117 and ushered the females in. Ducking under his arms, we crept inside.

The five square metres of the PVC and fabric tent were completely bare, bar the piece of patterned cloth that covered the sandy ground. Unlike an average tent, that would be lit by a romantic oil lamp, a fluorescent tube hung from the beams of the encampment, giving off a blinding clinical light. Hospital light. The fifteen of us were to occupy that space during the next day or so.

In silence, the rest of the women rushed with their companions to make their claim on the best spaces. In swift military action, they rolled out their sleeping bags in two rows, leaving a small narrow path in between. My mother and I were slow to claim our plots and were left with the unwanted patch alongside the make-shift entrance.

'We're finally here!' Noor, a petite and polite Indian lady, and my now sleeping neighbour, buzzed excitedly in the hush.

'Mina', I broke into a grin. 'First night of Hajj.'

***

The night prayer was yet to be made. The chubby Scottish, Iraj, had dragged me to the wash area, despite my reluctance to accompany her. She was outrageously bubbly for my liking. I had eavesdropped on a few of her previous conversations, which were predictably noisy, and knew that she was thirty eight years old, enjoyed eating cakes – would you believe – and had two children who were being looked after by the grandmother in Scotland.

The ladies washing area was located several paths away. The

modernity of the washing facilities — for desert standards — came as quite a surprise. I am not totally sure what I was expecting, but it was something along the lines of a hole in the yellow ground with a bucket besides a well. Instead, a row of ten individual toilet cubicles gleamed at me. Two contained seated toilets and the other eight had in fact holes in the ground but, sophisticated porcelain holes, with a flush. On either side of the stretch of cubicles sat two large sinks, spurting four taps of water.

Hygiene and cleanliness were as important to me as wearing underwear. Although I did not border on obsessive compulsive disorder, like some I know, the thought of sitting on toilets used by many others and not cleaned properly made me constipated. Much to my relief, the porcelain sparkled. Either Mr Muscle, the bathroom cleaner, had worked his magic here or we were one of the first ones to arrive at this camp.

Choosing the seated toilet, I shut the door to the cubicle but then ran back out. *No toilet tissue.* I peered into the adjacent cubicles. No toilet tissue there either. In the place where there should have been a tissue holder was a long, thin, plastic hosepipe that connected to a tap.

'There's no toilet tissue!' recoiling, I looked at Izzah, the girl from London.

'I guess it'd clog up the pipes.' She shrugged her shoulders. 'Hey, Prophet Mohammad didn't even have toilets or taps when he did Hajj. If water was good enough for him, then water is good enough for me.' With that, she cheerfully leapt into a cubicle and bolted the door.

Feeling my intestines tighten, I stepped back into the cubicle. Izzah was probably the same age as me. *If she can do it, I guess I should be able to too. Doesn't look like there's any other option.*

Having had a fight with the hosepipe, I moved over to the communal sink. Already surrounded by six women who splashed themselves like dolphins. I squeezed my skeleton through a small gap, stretched out my hands and gathered some water.

As most clean-freaks would be, I was glad that Islam was strict on bodily purity and cleanliness. Muslims are politely asked to be in a state of cleanliness at all times, but sternly told to wash before worship. It was obligatory. That was fine by me. I liked to be clean. I liked to be around people that were clean.

Ablution, washing before prayer, was an act that I was very used to. Continuing the ritual of ablution at the basin, having already washed myself down below, I washed my hands. Then, gargled thrice, cleaned my nose thrice – my little finger shoved up my nostrils – splashed my face with water thrice, washed my right and left arm thrice – up to my elbows – wiped my wet hands over my head, around my neck and in my ears, raised my feet to the basin and washed each foot three times. Ablution was done.

'Which way is back?' I asked Iraj, looking for something to dry myself with. *Damn, I didn't even pack a towel.* I blew on my arms.

'Erm I'm not sure,' she confessed looking in all directions of the maze.

'Oh heck.' I could not remember the number of our tent nor the route we had taken.

'Where's Izzah?'

'She's gone, I think.'

We wandered for a while, peering into tents hopelessly. Each one looked exactly the same as the other.

'I think we're lost,' turning around to face Iraj. My heart skipped. She was not there. I shot my eyes in all directions. *Where the hell's she gone??* Unfamiliar men, women, walked past me carrying on with their tasks, each a mirror image of the next. I had no idea how far I had come out from my tent. Nor did I know where exactly I was positioned in this maze.

'Shit.'

Hesitantly, I walked towards a red gate and poked my head out. It led outside, to the other camps. I quickly jumped back inside. Panic rose. Wherever my tent was, it was somewhere within this camp. Like a chicken, I weaved through the narrow passages, poked my head in some tents, out of others, back again in more. I passed new washing areas, a small kitchen, an information centre. *Information.* I stopped.

'I'm lost.' I said to the moustached man stood at the foot of the portable stand. Wrapped in a large belt, walkie-talkie in hand, he looked more like an idle Marks & Spencer's security guard.

'Huh?' the same bored, wandering look on his face as those who protect M&S.

'I - am – lost.'

He arched his eyebrows and looked down at my pink flip flops.

'Tut!' raising my hands in exasperation. 'Lost!'

He shrugged his shoulders. I was not sure whether that meant he did not understand English or he did not care. He carried the same look of insincerity and discourteousness that I had seen in many

Saudi officials. *Why are these Arabs so flaming rude?* Prophet Mohammad and his friends were Arab yet they were the sweetest people on the planet.

In frustration, I walked off after giving him a withering look; one that I hoped would haunt him for a long time.

Defeated, I stopped at a junction and resorted to standing there and biting my lip. The water from my wash had dried up. Beads of sweat now replaced it. Unfamiliar territory, alien people, alarm bells rang. *What if I never find my way? Never complete Hajj? What if I'm stuck here forever?* My irrationality seemed perfectly rational.

'Inna lilllahi wa inna illaihi raajiun.' The Arabic rolled off my tongue.

***

'Mum, I've lost Minxy!' I run into the kitchen, hysterical.

'Who's Minxy?'

'My Tamagotchi!' These electronic pets have been the latest craze at school for a couple of months now.

'Who's mamotchi?'

'Mum! My pet! You know, its small, yellow with four buttons on it. That electronic key ring thing I got when I went to town with Rebecca and her mum. I showed it to you!'

'Oh... I haven't seen it.' She slaps a chapatti on the stove. 'Where'd you put it?'

'If I knew where I put it I wouldn't be asking you!' I turn the kitchen drawers inside out. Hairbands. Felt tip pens. Tennis ball. Batteries. No Minxy.

'Don't worry I'm sure you'll find it.' She balls up another sticky chunk of dough in her hands. Minxy is the least of her worries. Her family need feeding.

'No mum! She'll die!' My hair is sticking up, like a woman who's lost her baby.

'Don't be silly.'

'She's been alive for forty-eight days! If I don't feed her dinner tonight she'll die and I'll have to start all over again.' Being a mother to a Tamagotchi is an exhausting process and I would have thought my own mother would understand.

'Stop being pagal [silly] if you lose something pray: inna lilllahi wa inna illaihi raajiun, It means, 'we belong to Allah and we shall return to him' and it's a way of surrendering to your misfortune,

taking that to be God's will.' You'll find Binky, inshallah [God-willing].'

'Inna lilllahi wa inna illaihi raajiun,' I continue saying for a few minutes.

I find Minxy at the bottom of my school bag.

***

'Inna lilllahi wa inna illaihi raajiun,' I repeated.

Minutes passed. I tried to let it work.

From the corner of my eye I spotted Iraj's husband. Bizarre coincidence or an answer. And miraculously I recognised him even though he looked like the hundreds of men I had crossed since being lost. *Thank the Lord for his tallness and long pointy nose.* I ran up to him. Flushed with relief.

'Brother! I'm lost.' I did not know his name. 'Can you take me back to the tent please?'

'We're not that far off,' he smirked. 'How can you get lost?'

It's your stupid wife's fault! 'My sense of direction is terrible.' It was. I could get lost around my own street at home and went nowhere without my TomTom.

Relief subsided and was replaced with sheepishness. *Lost forever. Is that what I really thought?*

As I entered the tent, to my disbelief, Iraj was casually tucking herself into her sleeping bag.

'You left me!' I accused.

'I blinked and you were gone... It took you a while to find your way back.' She cackled.

A fleeting thought of pulling her sleeping bag off her whilst she was fast asleep and hiding it somewhere in the wilderness gave me a jolt of dirty pleasure. 'Sigh.' *I doubt Hajj will allow it.* I gave her a withering look, the same one that was currently haunting the Saudi Information clerk, and decided to settle on that.

'This night is not to be wasted with sleep.' Iraj's companion, Aliyah, said to her. 'This night...,' whispering in a breathy romantic voice, '...each breath is just for Allah.' A calm silence slowly filled the air. Each person began to immerse themself into mental seclusion.

Having prayed my night prayer in the now dim light, I lay in my sleeping bag. It was quite a contrast. Lying on the rocky ground in Arabia calmly reflecting, as opposed to lying in my foam bed in

Lancashire wallowing in misery.

All that pain.

All that pain Allah, you gave me. To test me or to punish me? It was still difficult to comprehend. *Was that pain necessary?* A big part of me wanted to be angry with God. For testing me so relentlessly. Or punishing me for a crime that I was not really aware of.

Instead I sighed. Powerlessly. *What good is my anger? God's greater than me, his will is his will. He's the creator of this big world and I'm just a weedy girl with weedy arms.* I lifted one out of my sleeping bag to assess it.

I can't fight him. What choice do I have but to accept what's happened. Surrender. Endure more repercussions for shouting at my mum all the time, hurting people all the time. More repercussions. I wanted to crawl into the ground.

'O Allah, ease my difficulties… I am torn… I have lost the will to live…' Those words, that sorrow-drenched call, throttled my throat. I lifted my head off my sleeping bag. It was Zia, Mr Raul's frail wife. I could only make out her silhouette; she was huddled in the corner, her head bowed, hands raised. 'Please ease my difficulties, don't let me feel this pain anymore,' she whimpered, softly. An injured kitten.

Her pain clutched me in the gut.

I, in my twenties, she, in her eighties, yet it seemed that her pain was just as plaguing as mine. In silence, I cried for her and I cried for myself. 'Allah, she speaks the words that my heart wishes to speak,' I whisper to him inside my sleeping bag. *How many others sit on these plains tonight, crying out the same heartbroken words?* 'Allah, help me.' *Are we all beings of helplessness? All at the mercy of God?*

'All five days are just for Allah.' Aliyah continued with her subdued melodrama. 'After Hajj we will be like newborn babies!'

Newborn babies, the desire that drove these pilgrims to Hajj. Clinging onto the promise that they will be born again. Sin-free. Free from punishment. Loved, like an innocent child. Start afresh.

'Is that why you've called me?' I ask him. 'For me to do Hajj and become sin-free? To ask you for forgiveness? To be born again and start afresh?'

The thought that I may cry the same words as Zia sixty years from now sent an icicle down my back. I shook my head, shaking the shivering thought away, and took out my prayer beads. 'Forgive me for my sins Allah. Let me start again.'

That was the moment when I surrendered to the same desire as those around me.

12

THE CHAOS HAS DEFINITELY begun. Jaw dropped, I stared at the queue outside the toilets. 'Oh...,' dreading what was about to come. 'This is not what I need.'

Pain was at the forefront of my mind as soon as I had awoken. I had been dragged out of my sleep pitilessly at four o'clock in the morning by my mother. The sun was about to rise and we needed to wash and make the pre-dawn prayers. My eyes had opened to the sharp pierce of the fluorescent lighting. My first gulp had created a razor cut in my throat. A surge of pain had shot through my temples. My back was sore from the rocks that I had slept on. My legs ached from last night's trudging and my clothes, which I was advised not to change out of because of the ihram recommendations, were damp from a night of profuse sweating. I was ill.

To top it all off, I was faced with a queue of fiftyish women lining the toilets as though it was a queue for free Louis Vuitton handbags rather than a queue to pee. All kinds of bladder bursting women filtered out of both ends of the cubicles. Each one peering to the side impatiently, hoping the others would miraculously disappear.

The same preposterous scene was being played outside the men's area.

'Mum, let's try the other wash areas.' I remembered from my run around the place the night before that there were other facilities within the camp.

We hurried to the other wash areas, noting the route we took. The states of those were just as horrendous. 'I'm not waiting in these queues!' I protested. 'Let's go back to bed?' It was a futile suggestion. I knew it as soon as I uttered it. Could there be a bigger crime than deliberately missing one of the obligatory prayers whilst on *Hajj*?

'There'll be many struggles, but then there are no rewards

without struggle on Hajj'. Layth's advice resonated in my ear.

'Sigh...' Defeated, I slogged behind my mother as she led us to the back of a queue.

The stench coming from the toilets was nauseating. Falling into an open sewer in Pakistan was not much worse – and that had happened when I was 12. The state that the camp had gotten into in such a short amount of time was astounding. It was a mess.

Arms folded, breath sucked in, I sulkily watched the others. Little Chinese women, large bright-teethed African women, annoyed Asian women, impatient Caucasian women.

A full hour of watching passed before I reached the end of the queue. Getting hold of a seated toilet was wishful thinking. I knew I would have to make do with whichever cubicle was available next, be it a sophisticated hole in the ground.

Hands around my nose, I stared at the cubicle doors, anticipating the next squeak open – so did the white woman on the other end. She gathered the bottom of her cream robe with her hands and penetrated the doors with her stare – piercing blues eyes, mine brown; I felt she had an unfair advantage.

'Clank.' The bolt on one of the doors shifted. It was closest to me. I stepped forwards to claim it as mine. Lifting the bottom of my robe up, I looked down and penguin-style, flapped towards the cubicle, carefully minding the deep puddles and brown muck. Before having the chance to exhale, the blue-eyed woman, a bigger penguin, splashed towards the cubicle, brushed me aside with her flap and leapt inside, slamming the door shut.

'What the...,' startled by her audacious behaviour, my foot caught on a pipe on the ground and I stumbled backwards. I tried to break my fall onto the wall behind me but I missed it, tumbling to the ground.

Squelch.

'Ah! Arrgh!' My bottom had hit the stony rocks and the puddle water – I hoped it was just water – seeped through my robe and under trousers. 'Eugh!' Burnt by mortification, I shot up. The other women sniggered, watching me with glee. I was sure I heard the blue-eyed thief teehee-ing inside whilst she peed.

I craved again for toilet tissue. This time to ball some up, soak it in the mud at my feet and throw it over the cubicle door, onto her head.

Frustrated, angry, humiliated, tired, poorly and now wet; I wanted to storm off, run back to my sleeping bag and hide in there for the rest of the day.

I stayed put. Water dripped down the hem of my robe. *What would God think if I deliberately missed my prayer?* And I was desperate to pee.

'*Your patience will be tested to such a point that you will be on the brink of losing it. This journey is one of endurance and patience. You'll come across extremely pleasant people, but you'll also meet many rude people.*' Layth's words followed me as though he was stood on my right shoulder as a guardian angel. '*Don't be angry with the rude people. They've come from areas of the world that don't know the meaning of manners but only know the fight of survival. Be understanding. Allah is watching you now more than ever, remember that*'. I was tempted to swat him away.

Patience.

Patience.

Patience.

The three virtues spoken of most by my fellow Muslims. '*He who is deprived of patience and gentleness, is in fact, deprived of all good*', according to Prophet Mohammad.

'*What are your weaknesses?*' A partner of a law firm had asked me in a job interview. Classic interview question. '*I'm really impatient*', '*In what way?*', '*In every way*', '*Rrright*'. He scribbled something down. Probably should not have told him that. He never called.

I rushed important tasks; form-filling, assignments. Thirty seconds was the longest I would wait when picking a friend up, before honking the horn like a psychopath. I gave death threats under my breath to learner drivers who held me up on the roads. And worst of all, I fired up quicker than a blow torch on a petrol can: '*You called me stupid?? How dare you! You ******* ***** ****-****!!*' '*I don't care if you were joking!!!!*'

Either God had deprived me of patience or I had been taking too much heed in Hello! magazine. 'Impatience is a virtue', according to them.

Prophet Mohammad's patience through his extreme hardships was supposed to be taken as the perfect example; abuse, boycott, expulsion, violence – he was faced with it all yet he still remained gentle, considerate and sympathetic. *God knows how he did it.*

A door swung open. A sudden movement flashed past. The woman behind me leapt into the next cubicle.

'Oh for fu… don't get angry… don't get angry… don't get

angry,' growling, I paced my breaths, reining myself in from breaking the door down and demanding the upholding of my rights.

When I finally managed to get myself into a lavatory, I almost threw up a breakfast I never ate. The stench was unbearable. I stumbled backwards at the repulsive sight. A sight worse than the carcasses of fifty rats. The toilet – porcelain hole in the ground – had become unspeakably filthy. The sides were covered in a mixture of water, faeces and other unknown substances. The mini hosepipe had come loose and lay astray on the floor, amidst the mess. Piled in the corner of the cubicle, dirty white tissues, nappy-like material. It was horrendously revolting. Had this been a soap-opera, I would have passed out. But instead, my body seized, stared, shocked at how the toilet had turned into this in just a couple of hours.

A great proportion of the pilgrims had probably never used a toilet before and I judged that was the cause of this domestic anarchy. Africa, Asia, South America – house-keeping was probably of menial importance there in the daily quest to not sleep hungry.

'Yada!!!' shouted a woman from outside the cubicle as she furiously rattled the door. Letting out a meek animal whimper, I shuddered and proceeded to obey natures call.

The scrabble around the wash basin was just as unrelenting. I watched in dismay. Ten women struggled to perform ablution around the sink whilst forty others watched and waited. The biggest of women tried to squeeze into the smallest of spaces, between the ribs of one and hips of another. Others, who clearly did not understand the concept of queuing, went charging forwards past everyone until they were forced back by protesting pilgrims. Politer women waited patiently on the edges of the basin, mannequin smiles pasted on their faces. The majority nudged and shoved, desperate to draw drops of water toward themselves.

Another hour passed, the sun stirred, and I began to walk back, my body soaked by those splashing whales. More than just ablution. This was a full bath.

'My Lord, what an ordeal!' I complained to my group back inside the tent, shivering from my dampness and the traumas at the toilets. 'Argh!' Not wishing to be faced with the nightmare again, I resolved to eat nothing and drink nothing. That way my ablution would stay intact for days.

'Sigh.' *This indeed is going to be extremely testing.*

'Sigh.' *Must I be tested?*

***

'Women will eat first, men later.' Layth said decisively. It was breakfast time. There were food stalls nearby but they had not opened for service yet. Layth had brought some food with him, but there was only enough for half the group.

Blissfully sitting on top of my sleeping bag next to my neighbour, Noor, I drank a cup of hot tea and ate sweetened bread, consciously aware of the next trip to the toilets.

'*Right now*.' I smirked at Noor raising one eyebrow. 'I'm glad that I'm a woman.'

Noor laughed.

Then abruptly stopped. 'Right now?' she narrowed her eyes. 'Not all the time?'

I paused for a moment, remembering my earlier years. 'Well... I don't know.'

'You don't know what?'

'Well... When I was younger I always wished that I was a boy. Boys seemed to have an easier life than girls.'

'What do you mean?'

'As a girl I just had less freedom and fun. My brothers could wear jeans, I couldn't. They could swear, I couldn't. I had to be at home and learn how to cook and clean whilst they were out playing football or at the youth club. They were encouraged to study and so was I, but I had to be a domestic goddess too. You know, I've lived my life under the shadows of my brothers. I hated being a girl when I was younger. Absolutely hated it.'

***

'Can I play?' I ask my eldest brother.

I have been watching my three brothers and their friends play cricket on the street from my bedroom window. The fat boy with the snotty nose really did not know how to ball. He was getting no one out. I could have done so much of a better job with my spin balling.

Frustrated and envious of the cheers and hooting, I had swapped my sandals for my P.E trainers and had run out in my orange shalwar kameez.

'No you can't!' he shouts at me. Being five years older, and seventeen, he is the boss of everything and a complete bully.

'Pleeeease. I'll be on your team, I'll make you win!'

'No, get lost!'

'Ok, I won't be on your team, can I be on the other team?'

'No! Girls aren't allowed to play!' He yanks my pony tail, hits the tennis ball on my foot, and shoves me towards the door.

I run inside crying. 'Mum, they won't let me play!'

'Don't be baisharam! [shameless], girls don't play cricket. Come and help me chop these onions.' She hands me a bowl full of unpeeled onions.

I cut the onions and continue sniffling. Begging God to miraculously transform me into a boy.

***

'I hated it.'

Thankfully, albeit to the dismay of my parents, I had no interest in being a Nigella Lawson and spent years rebelling against their ideals. I fought for everything my brothers had and more. A tough battle, which led to a few smacks, groundings and threats of disownment. But eventually I won my freedom. Now, I had sympathy for those who had not been strong enough to break out of those old-fashioned cages. I still knew a lot of friends who were living under the shadow of men, simply because they were women. I knew men who argued that a woman's place is at home with the household chores and children and a man's place is outdoors, in the realms of work and play. The majority of these men that I knew who possessed these opinions seemed to be Asian Muslim. Often I wondered whether it was an opinion derived from Islam or an idea derived from Asian culture.

'Are we, Muslim women, not more...,' hesitating for a moment, not really wishing to say it, '... oppressed?' A strong word.

Noor's eyes turned to mere black lines and her lips pursed into pink ones.

A touchy subject. 'Ahem...,' shifting my gaze away from her and busying myself with inspecting my paper cup.

'Oppressed they are not!' She shouted out.

My tea spluttered out of my mouth, startled by her unpredictable and overly-defensive outburst.

'It frustrates me, when people like you can't understand and don't bother to understand that Islam rescued women not oppressed them!' her voice lowered a little.

'Rescued?' I willed myself not to provoke her. 'That's taking it a bit far Noor. Men, *Muslim* men, seem to have the upper hand in life. It's unfair!'

'Put your cup down,' she ordered, 'and listen.' A tone all too familiar to me.

Hoping to use my cup as some sort of protective shield from Noor, reluctantly, I gulped the last drop of tea and shoved the remaining piece of bread into my mouth, before setting it aside. Still chewing, I shuffled a few inches away from her, willing her not to notice.

'You know, women, before the time of Prophet Mohammad, fourteen hundred years ago, were treated very badly and without respect. Like objects. Used and abused by men. This was everywhere in the world not just in the Middle East. Men had hundreds of wives and they treated them like cattle, not people. They weren't able to work, just like in our country, England...'

'Oh yeah, I forget that' – something I had learnt in my history class at school.

'... Women weren't inheritors of property or money. In Greece they were seen as only good for three reasons; the pleasure of men, caring of men and as provider of children for men. Romans gave fathers and husbands the right to *sell* a woman! Arabs gave sons the right to inherit from the father and no rights for the wife. In Saudi, and I presume this happened in other places too, if a woman gave birth to a baby girl she'd be buried alive because she'd be seen as a creator of bad and no good.'

'WHAT??! Buried alive???' She now had my full attention.

'Yes! There's a small mountain in Mecca near the Al-Haram mosque where these baby girls were buried. You haven't had this pointed out to you?'

'No! Oh my God! That's disgusting!'

'Let me tell you something: once a man came to Prophet Mohammad to make a confession. He told him that his wife had given birth to a baby girl. He'd played with the girl and loved her until she was a toddler. The he thought, *'I cannot put up with having a daughter for the rest of my life'*. So he one day took her towards a well. The little girl thought her daddy was taking her to play. She skipped behind him, laughing. When reaching the well he picked her up whilst she was still laughing and threw her down the well...'

'No...'

'She screamed...' Noor paused for a moment, her eyes watering.

'She screamed, '*'oh abbeddah!'* which means 'oh father!' all the way down the well...'

'Oh God... No.'

'The man was unlike other men that had committed the crime, and was filled with a rare remorse. The Prophet looked at him in shock and he wept until he had no tears left to cry.'

'Oh God.' My eyes moistening for the little girl. An image of a young child falling down a well, echoes of her screams, ate me up. Pulling my head down to my hands, I willed the callous murder to disappear.

Clearing her throat, 'females were oppressed and exploited but didn't protest and continued to live in this demeaning manner. When Prophet Mohammad came he spoke for the women. He gave them their rights and equality.'

'How?' lifting my head up.

'The Prophet, following the revelation of the Quran, said women were just as equal as men were in the spiritual sense. In fact, for their worship of Allah they sometimes get more reward than men. Mothers have the *absolute highest* ranking in this world, heaven lies at the feet of mothers not fathers. He told fathers that, if their daughters spoke well of them on the Day of Judgment, they would enter paradise. That is how highly regarded women became.'

'Really?'

'Yes. The Quran gave women new inheritance rights. Women could work...'

'Erm, are you sure? That's not what I thought.'

'Yes they could work! Prophet Mohammad's wife, Khadija, was a shrewd businesswoman. All the money that a woman earned was hers only, not her husband's. No requirement for it to be shared with the family, whereas men are *ordered* to provide for their families. The Prophet also said that it was sinful for women to be treated inferior in any way. He urged men to treat their wives with gentleness and kindness.'

'Ok... But why do we have to wear the headscarf. The veil? Cover ourselves as though we're objects of shame?'

'Really! Is that what you think??'

'I love my hair. And my face, my face is the window to my personality. My smile, eyes, frown, expressions; they say a lot and are what make us human. So if we cover our faces, what does our worth become?'

'Hang on. Only the headscarf is compulsory, the veil is optional.

So you can show your pretty face.' Noor corrected. 'There were a lot of bad things going on before the Prophet's time: adultery, sex before marriage, unwanted pregnancies, rape, lewdness. It was realised that because of the dangerous magnetic attractions between men and women, to avoid further destruction, they'd need to be controlled as much as possible. How'd you that?

'Erm,' thinking for a moment. 'Lock men up,' not being serious.

'Haa haa,' sarcastically. Then said: 'well rules were created to make sure women and men are not put in situations where wrongful attractions are likely. The only differences noted of men and women were their physical differences. Men were strong, physically and emotionally, women were weaker and bearers of children.'

'No...' My feminism rose to protest.

'Come on! These differences are accepted by every single person on this planet, even the extreme feminists. Men are physically stronger than women. And women give birth to children. Do you deny that?' She challenged me.

'Ahem... so go on what were you saying?'

'Good,' smug. 'So as I was saying; in the old days the majority of work was manual labour. So men were advised to go out and work and provide for the family. Women were *advised*, not ordered, but advised to stay at home and look after the children. Make sense?'

'Yeah, so far. Go on.'

'*Both* men and women were asked to dress modestly to avoid being tempting for the opposite sex. But women were told to dress in a more modest manner when going out, for example wear a headscarf to hide the sensuality of their hair and wear robes to cover the shape of their body, because it was more convenient for them to do so than men, who needed to dress with ease when going about to work in fields etcetera. Also, men were more likely to chase attractive women rather than the other way around. So women covered themselves more.'

'Women chase men too!' Thinking of Sarah and her endless pursuits.

'I knew you were going to say that. Tell me, how many magazines are there of naked women in comparison to magazines of naked men?'

'Playboy, Nuts... the list goes on.' I rolled my eyes. 'We need more magazines for women.' I joked.

'Shush. It's so degrading for women. We're not respected when a man is lewd towards us. We're demeaned. Our sexuality should be guarded from unworthy eyes, since it should be your gift to the man who loves and respects you enough to marry you. '

'Aww yeah, that's nice, to give your body only to your husband,' smiling sweetly, liking the idea.

'So this was the separation of men and women to avoid evils, hence why we wear the headscarf. In those times the roles set for men and women had the most logic to them. There was never any intention to oppress women. Women didn't feel oppressed!'

'No?'

'Our country, England, for example, only recently accepted that women go out to work, wear trousers, mini-skirts. In the seventh century women had less rights in England than those given to Muslim women by Prophet Mohammad. That is fact.'

I tapped my cup at Iraj for a refill of tea.

'The west has now moved along with time. Islam has too but the fundamentals, such as modesty, still remain for obvious reasons; you know, to avoid pains of adultery, unwanted pregnancies, sex before marriage. I'd say these rules make for a more civilised society.'

I thought of Zameer and how his desire for me instigated the deepest and most crushing heartbreak I had ever felt. 'I still hate men.' *Zameer.*

'What?' Noor sent me a baffled look.

'Nothing.'

She has a point. As a feminist, I can deny and deny until I go blue in the face that women and men are unequal, but the truth is women and men are unequal. Men are stronger and women are mothers; we'll never be the same. Our bodies aren't the same. Thinking about the arm wrestles I had had with Danial whilst working at the Carphone Warehouse call centre. *'Grrrrrrr,'* I would use two hands, stand up, and throw my 7st 13lb body weight onto his single wrist. *'Look I'm not even trying and you can't make me move',* he would laugh. I once won an arm wrestle against Haroon but he was a sissy. He wore pink shirts.

I guess men were created as men and women as women for a reason. If we're to be true equals, then would God not have made us all into one? All male or all female? That would be boring.

Who am I kidding? Why fight the 'equality' battle when it's impossible to win?

'Then tell me why, Noor...,' *I might accept being an unequal but that doesn't mean I accept being an inferior,* '...why have I always felt inferior to my brothers? Why was I, along with many women today, encouraged to stay at home to cook and clean rather than, I don't know, join the football team? Answer that.'

Shaking her head, she sighed. 'That's your parents' fault honey.' She glanced over at my mother with mocking disdain. 'You should never have been brought up to feel inferior to a man, because you're not. You can enjoy all the things that they can. You can study, work. You don't need to learn how to cook or clean.'

'Don't I?'

'No. Islam sees that times are changing and adapts. You can do everything that a man can, so long as you stick within the key principles of modesty. Women to stay at home and men to work is not a strict rule of Islam. I think people in your parents' generation have simply not moved with the times and have got religion and culture mixed up. In the Pakistani and Indian culture women stay at home, in Islam they needn't.'

'So men don't have control over women, like my parents have always led me to believe?' needing reassurance.

'Listen, any man who treats a woman with inferiority and unfairness is a sinner. *A sinner.* Prophet Mohammad warned the married men saying that the best of you is that who is best to his wife.'

'So we Muslim women are not inferior?' The idea was too foreign to me, having spent my life with the view that I was of a lower-class than men.

'For the millionth time, no! Come on.' She poked my arm with her finger playfully, her facial expressions warming. 'More women convert to Islam than men because of the good treatment they get. If you were to ask any woman in the time of Prophet Mohammad's life, I can guarantee that she will tell you that the Prophet *saved* them, not *oppressed* them.'

'Did the Prophet save *you*, Noor?' smirking.

'Oi, cheeky bugger, I'm not that old!' She laughed.

'Hang on... why can't women in Saudi drive??' I remembered Layth mention it over dinner a few days ago.

'Erm. I don't know to be honest. Arabs make up their own rules sometimes.'

'It's stupid.'

'They can be.'

A short period of silence passed.

'Do you know what Noor? No one's ever explained the Islamic view on women to me as well as you've just done. I always thought that Islam gave men better rights. I always had this slight... resentment towards it. Why's no one ever told me this before?' I asked, feeling cheated. 'And why have people allowed me to grow up thinking I'm inferior and let me hate myself for being female?'

'I blame the older generation for this,' pointing at my mother. 'They confuse their cultures with religion and deceive others. Either that or they don't know how to communicate the principles properly.'

She stopped shaking her head and smiled. 'Well, at least now you know.'

Her grin widened. 'And if you ask me I think it's better to be a woman in Islam than a man, especially in today's times. At least we don't have to work if we don't want to, and if we do, we can keep our money and spend it on shoes and handbags and not bills and rent!'

'Yay!' I lightly punched the air.

'Our fathers, brothers, husbands, sons, have an *obligatory duty* to look after us. And look,' she raised her cup of tea, 'they treat us so delicately. Such gentlemen!'

'I like being treated like a fragile princess.' I giggled. Like a girl.

'Hey, Islam says that women are like diamonds; special and beautiful.' She winked, eyes sparkling. 'We are diamonds.'

I'm a diamond? Yes, I'm a diamond.

13

'SMILE, IT IS CHARITY.'

'Huh?' I looked at Zia.

She flashed her bright teeth – actually dentures – at me.

'You look glum. You know, Prophet Mohammad said that to smile is a good deed.' She flicked her prayer beads at a hypnotic speed, maintaining her Cheshire cat grin.

'Oh sorry,' absentmindedly. I did not feel like smiling but I smiled anyway. 'I was in a world of my own; thinking.' Wondering whether the sale of Mr Larkham's pesticide business had gone through. Hoping it had. Dreading going back to work and having to sift through hundreds of pages of due diligence documents again. And again.

Zia nodded and continued with her rapid meditation.

Meditation. That was all the first day of Hajj was for. That was all the three or so million pilgrims were doing in Mina at that moment. *Three million*. I leant against the pole in the tent. It did not seem like I was surrounded by that many people. It was too serene. Tranquil. Voices were hushed, shuffles were muffled.

Three million people.

Noor's lyrical whisperings added to the atmosphere. Momentarily, I was caught. 'Almighty Allah says,' she read breathlessly from something she had brought with her. 'I treat man according to his expectations from me, and I am with him when he remembers me. If he remembers me in his heart, I remember him in my heart; if he remembers me in a gathering, I remember him in a better and nobler gathering. If he comes closer to me by one span, I go towards him a cubit's length, if he comes towards me by a cubit's length, I go towards him an arm's length, and if he walks towards me, I run unto him.'

In the tent, for an unknown reason, I felt close to God. I wondered how close he was to me. Remembering what I had heard once, *'Allah is closer to a person than his jugular vein'*, I fingered my neck. *Is he that close to me?* A striking and consoling thought. Especially when I knew that I was on my best behaviour right then. Safe from his punishment, in the calm of the storm – I was sure – as I did not feel my usual bottomless depression.

I rolled my prayer beads in between my fingers, uttered words of supplication for him. There was not much else to do but remember him. Everywhere I turned I was faced with his reminder; worshippers, prayer beads, supplications, prayer mats, Mina.

Mina. I pondered over what Mina looked like right now from an eagle's eye. Sandy plains, thousands of red roofed camps, specks holding prayer beads, uttering the words 'Allahu akbar', 'alhamdullilah', 'subhanAllah, 'astagfirullah'?

'Pssst! Do you fancy taking a break, go outside for a bit?' Hooria crawled over to me eagerly.

'Ermmm...,' not really having the energy to get up. My eyes were heavy, my throat sore and my body ached. My fever appeared to have multiplied by the afternoon.

On second thoughts: 'well... I have been wondering what's going on outside and I guess the fresh air would do me good, so... ok.' I say.

This was not the uninhabited desert I imagined. Outside, a busy town was in action. The familiar sounds of hustle and bustle. Alongside our camp and the neighbouring camps, male and female traders had laid out mats on the ground in a long row, flogging prayer beads, ornaments, clothing, shoes and other knickknacks.

'Chippas? One riyal.' A sweating woman called out to us whilst she peeled potatoes on the ground, keeping an eye on chips that were frying in her big black pot.

I was bemused at the contrast of the mood outside the camps and inside. *It's so normal out here.* Pilgrims were bustling in and out of the camps, shopping at the mini stalls, drinking juices, soaking in the sun. *Are we still on Hajj?*

'Maybe later.' I smiled politely at the awaiting chip lady and her crackly brittle chips. Already with clippings of a cactus in my throat, I did not fancy any more.

Wandering a little further under the scorching heat, we came to a large track lined with larger more permanent stalls. Wooden stalls laid out drinks and food. Fruit, crisps, chocolate, bread and even Jaffa cakes.

'It can't have been like this in the time of Prophet Mohammad.'

I spoke to Hooria as she eyed an array of headscarves on the arms of a thin man stood like a scarecrow. 'He would've had to pack food, dates and water, and carry those with him for five days. He probably didn't have a camp either, nor washing facilities like we have. How times have changed...,' a bit disappointed. I would have liked to have slummed it as much as possible, like a real backpacker. Perform Hajj the way the Prophet did. Wash in the desert. Eat dates for breakfast, lunch and dinner. Ride on camels. That would have been a truly uplifting and spiritual experience. The modernity of civilisation would never have allowed it, unfortunately. In a few years' time, it would not surprise me if the authorities built hotels in Mina. That would be a sad day.

Hooria was not listening. I walked away from her and towards a large lorry that was parked up next to the stalls. I peered inside. It was half full of small brown boxes. Two men inside the lorry were handing the boxes to those passing by. One handed a box to me.

It contained a carton of juice, a date, two biscuits and a cake bar. *Free food.* Provided either by the Saudi authorities or rich sponsors of Hajj. It was nice of the Arabs to donate and make Hajj a little easier for the pilgrims. *I guess they do have hearts after all.*

'Jazakallah,' I thanked the truck man.

Hooria continued to browse the stalls.   The mini market interested me as much as a dry bone museum. I had not embarked on this five day journey to waste it on material indulgences. Just for these five days, I wanted to escape from the lure of consumerism, greed, pride, jealousy, pretentiousness and my other slaving desires. This rare chance had found me, to experience ultimate simplicity and search for my soul. An opportunity I doubted I would have again.

'Oh!' I hit the kerb of the road track as I took a step backwards. Looking down, a line of four rugs lay along the side. Curious, I took a closer look. Fabric sacks, thin brown blankets, a few dirty cups.

An old man walked towards the second rug, kneeled down, and rummaged through one of the small sacks. Old, skinny and washed-out. Rugged and frail. Underneath the thick wrinkles that encompassed his eyelids, peeped a glimpse of grey tired eyes. His two sheets were no longer white but stained in creams and browns. His appearance was unnerving. He finished fiddling with his sack, lifted the flap of the brown blanket and crawled underneath it.

My mouth opened. *Surely he's not staying here? In all this rubbish? Can he not get a tent? I thought everyone was given a tent?* I gawked at him unabashed. Willing him to make eye contact with me.

'Assalaamualaikum.' I smiled at him when he finally looked up.

'Waalaikumuslaam.' He returned the greeting of peace with a stutter.

'Ermmmm… do you sleep here?'

He looked at me blankly. His eyes so dead and lifeless.

'Do you sleep here?'

The blank expression on his face did not change. He did not understand.

I clapped my hands together and put them to the side of my tilted face, making a sleeping gesture, and pointed to where he lay.

'Haa haa,' he nodded, now understanding.

This is his camp. My mouth dropped with sympathy as I watched him unreservedly. Already, other peoples' trash had accumulated on the sides of his temporary home. *Is this man that poor that he cannot stay in a camp? Or has he struggled to find his way here and hadn't registered as a pilgrim with the authorities?* Either way it was clear that he had had an extremely bumpy ride and very little money in his pocket.

'Good?' I made an OK sign with my fingers.

He shrugged his shoulders – surrendered – raised his hands in the air, looked up to the sky, 'Alhamdulillah.' *All thanks is to Allah.*

'Wow.' This man had almost nothing yet was still grateful to Allah for being here. I dreaded to think what my attitude would have been had I been in his position. *Would I be grateful for my scraps or would I be bitter at my misfortune?* Already sour about my menial bad luck, I knew the answer.

'Where are you from?' I asked.

He responded with a confused look.

'Morocco, France, India, Africa, Afghanistan?'

'Ah. Palestine,' he said.

Palestine. I should have guessed from his face. A life of hardship was inevitable.

'You must be a witness of relentless trauma? Young, innocent children mercilessly mutilated by Israeli bombers. Right before your eyes.' I dreaded to think who he might have lost. 'Being here must be nicer, in comparison to being in Palestine,' rambling on, but of course he did not understand me.

His pained eyes just watched me.

Smiling again, 'Yes.' I nodded encouragingly. 'Alhamdulillah.'

A stone in my throat, I turned my head away.

Feeling the brown box in my hand I held it out, ushering him to take it. His bony hand advanced, taking it from me and lightly placing it on the side of his bed. *I should have brought some money with me.* I made a mental note to visit him again and give him a donation.

'May Allah make it easy for you.' I gave him a prayer and smiled at him, charitably.

He did not smile back.

Perhaps this man was too poor to give me the charity of a smile. Or perhaps he simply did not know what it was like to smile.

I never did remember to go back to him.

***

'Let me tell you of the most beautiful love story of all time.' Zia, being the eldest and seemingly wisest, had summoned all the women in our tent to gather around her sleeping bag after late lunch.

The bond between us – sisters – was growing, especially after food. We ate lunch together. A long scrap of paper had been laid across the middle of the tent in between the two rows of sleeping bags and we huddled together, tucking into our chicken curry and naan bread whilst making idle chit-chat. We were fast becoming friends and now it was story time.

Despite it shooting a jolt into my feverish head, I still raised my eyebrows – which I had not plucked for over a week. *A love story?*

'Love', it was taboo in my household. Never openly spoken about when in the company of my mother, father, aunties, grandparents or any other person who was older than forty. My upbringing was not an affectionate one and 'love' was certainly never mentioned at home. My family never kissed or hugged. Each of us would rather have eaten raw mice than have a group hug. They did not even know that I liked men. They knew nothing about Zameer and my other fancies.

I covertly glanced at my mother and felt my face warm. Awkward with embarrassment. *For goodness sake.* I scratched my ear and did my best to look disinterested. I stared up at the PVC roof.

'The woman was one of the noblest around. She came from a very prominent and rich family. She was beautiful. A rich and successful businesswoman.' Zia began. 'At the age of forty, she was a widow. Many men, a lot of whom were high up in society, had asked for her hand in marriage but she rejected them. She'd lost the desire to marry again...'

I stopped scratching my red ear and turned my head towards Zia with intrigue. Through the layers of denial on my heart, I admit that once peeled, a dreamy romantic is exposed. I love, love stories.

'One day, the woman decided she needed an honest person to help do business for her, because in that male chauvinistic society it was difficult to do it herself. A young man of twenty five years old came into her life. He was from a very noble family but he didn't have much money. He made a meagre living tending sheep in the surrounding hills. But... he was said to be a man of the most impeccable and moral character. She accepted on this basis and the young man began to conduct her business for her.'

My mother coughed.

'After his first business trip, the older woman asked the servant who had accompanied him, what he thought of him. With amazement he said that this young man was the gentlest and most remarkable man he had ever met. And as they travelled in the heat of the desert, the servant noticed that a cloud had followed them the entire time, protecting them from the sun. He had also come back with more profit than expected.

'The flame in the woman's heart, that had been extinguished so long ago, re-kindled. And just like that she said... this man is for me.'

The hairs on my arms stirred.

'They both got married. It became one of the most amazing and beautiful marriages of all time...'

Zia paused.

'Why?' She continued in her breathy voice. 'Because that woman was... Khadija. And that man... was the would-be, Prophet Mohammad.'

'Oh...' I whispered with surprise.

'Their love was unbreakable; they loved in sickness, in torture, in pain and in banishment.'

Khadija and Prophet Mohammad?

'Khadija became the Prophet's pillar on the most important night of his life; the night Angel Gabriel came to him in Cave Hira and revealed to him that he was to be a Prophet. On that night Prophet Mohammad was so distressed by this that he went running into Khadija's arms for comfort weeping and imploring *'Hide me!*

Hide me! I need you!' She gave him all the strength, love and support he needed. She was the first person to believe in him when no other person would. Besides every great man is a great woman; she walked by his side wherever he went.

'She sacrificed all her wealth to support her husband's mission; all of it. She suffered through the torture that her husband was put through by his enemies. When the Prophet was banished from Mecca she went with him and they lived in extreme hardship and deprivation for three years.' She stopped.

We were hooked.

Then continued. 'This hardship eventually led to her death. She died after twenty five years of being married to the Prophet. She loved him till... death did them part.'

'Prophet Mohammad mourned her death deeply. He remembered her all the time and his love for her never died. He had once said *'She believed in me when no one else did; she accepted Islam when people rejected me; and she helped and comforted me when there was no one else to lend me a helping hand'*. What love story is more beautiful than this?'

My heart rustled in its warm recesses of longing. I took in a deep breath. Blinked several times. *Don't cry*, I pleaded with myself. Someone sniffled behind me. It was enough to trigger a lonely tear which yearningly trickled down my cheek.

'It beats the story of Romeo and Juliet, doesn't it?' Iraj whispered aloud.

All the younger women who were familiar with Romeo and Juliet nodded unanimously.

But this was not a fairytale. It was not Shakespeare. It was real. And it was halal. *It's ok to have a Romeo and Juliet love story in Islam?*

'Prophet Mohammad only married again after Khadija's death.' Zia added for our interest. 'He did marry a handful of women in the time after. His reason not being for pleasure but because these women were widows and the Prophet married them to help them or because they were the daughters of prominent Arab chiefs and a marriage to them would have formed better Islamic relations between hostile tribes.'

The thought of Khadija and Prophet Mohammad made me bitterly compare what Zameer and I had had.

***

Akbars Restaurant. The waiter takes our plates away and hands us the dessert menu.

My stomach rumbles. I have hardly been able to eat, despite my eyes craving that grilled lamb and chicken korma. Zameer has that power. The power to make me forget about my hunger and think only of him. Thankfully, he has been more than willing to eat my share of food.

He pushes the menu away and reaches out for my hand. The candle flame pulsates as does my heart. His fingers on my skin send a shooting tingle up my arm.

He looks me straight in the eyes.

I catch my breath.

'I love you,' he whispers. His silver hair glints under the dim lighting.

My eyes water. I have never known happiness like this. 'Oh my God... really?'

He laughs. A deep, schmoozing laugh. 'Yes, ever since I first saw you.'

***

Cheating turd! Thinking about his hands on mine now sickened me. I furiously rubbed them. *Blatant lies. How could he have lived such a twisted double life?* I did not miss him nor did I long for him. The thought of the saga made me nauseous. Prophet Mohammad's and Khadija's love was not like that. Theirs was enchanting and, with it being within an Islamic marriage and not a sinful relationship, it was abundantly blessed by Allah.

Is that what helped make it 'the greatest love story' of all time; the fact that it was sin-free? Is that where I went wrong? Maybe that's what I need; love, lust and laughs only with the blessing of Allah, through a lawful marriage. After all, didn't Joanna Francis say; 'only in the safe haven of marriage can a woman's body and heart, be safe to love'?

I yearned to have that dreamy and exotic love in my life. The one that sent a flutter into my stomach. Carried my heart to the clouds. The kind of love that I thought only ever existed in fairytales. I longed for a man to love me the way Prophet Mohammad loved Khadija. I longed to love a man the way Khadija loved Prophet Mohammad.

***

A dreamer; day and night, I always dream the same dream...

A charming young man of royalty gallops towards me on his white horse. Tall, steely and perfectly carved; the epitome of man. He outstretches his arm and holds out his hand. 'I have come to rescue you,' he says, 'take my hand.' Mesmerised, I reach out my delicate fingers and lightly touch his... The stars twinkle, the moon witnesses and love casts its magical spell... He clasps my hand with a perfect strength, gazes into me with his deep and soulful eyes and raises me up to his horse. He smiles and says, 'my diamond.' I hold tightly onto his waist as he leads us out of the dark wilderness... We travel the world, we heal the sick, we feed the poor and we fight the evil... Together we live, together we laugh and together we love... Together... we become great.

***

I sighed. A wistful, aching sigh. *A girl can dream can she not?* And so a girl can wish too.

'Allah,' softly, 'write me a great love story.'

14

'THIS WORLD!'

THE SKY was deepening on the first day. Having discovered a secluded area away from the camps, I sat on a rock and gazed at it in awe. Blue, yellow, orange, red, purple, navy blue; it transformed before my very eyes. In my dusty robe, sweaty headscarf and scuffed flip flops I was truly miniscule under its vastness and beauty. Like a breath of raw air in a sauna, I welcomed this new unrefined earthiness.

The silent breeze kissed my fever filled cheeks as I looked out at the mountains and the encroaching moon. *Are these the same mountains that Prophet Mohammad saw?* Large, sandy hills, littered with amateur, flimsy tents perilously set up on the steep slopes. Some pilgrims sat on elevated ridges, around glimmering campfires, gazing out. I was envious of the fabulous view they must have had.

'This world!' I breathed again from my rock. 'How amazing and beautiful! And all created in six days?!' laughing in disbelief. 'Engrossed in the promise of study, the dollar, sparkly dresses, boys, parties and all along I missed this magnificent beauty?? I never had time to look up?? I come aaaaalllllll this way to search for peace and *now* I decide to look up??! I'm crazy…,' concluding with subtle irony.

'And how beautiful are you Allah?' I called out deliriously. My fever making me noticeably light headed. 'I think I must have missed your beauty too!'

Zia's earlier words came back to me. *'It's funny how people become fans of models because of their beauty, or actors and Elvis Presleys because of their talent without expecting anything in return. Allah is infinitely more beautiful, talented and magnificent than any of these famous people. He is Lord of the Worlds! For that reason alone we should be fans of him much more and worship him endlessly. And he created all of this!'* She had flung her short arms out as far as they would go, in an attempt to encompass the whole world. *'This beauty! This life! For us!'*

'What do you look like Allah...?' I remembered hearing that even a glimpse of a tiny part of Allah would throw a person into unconsciousness. I only knew that he did not look anything like a person and was the *'most beautiful'*. Squeezing my eyes shut I willed my imagination to conjure an image of him. A blank black page, I did not know where to even begin to place my pen. *He must be of remarkable and unfathomable beauty if he managed to create other objects of beauty so easily. Butterflies. The moon. Scandinavian models. Roses. This universe.*

'Allah,' earnest, submissive and fatigued, 'you are my creator. I'd like to worship you for the beauties you have given me that I never paid attention to. If it pleases you when I remember you and worship you, then I will. If I only exist to serve you, then I will serve you...,' rambling on like a lover drunk from a day of non-stop meditating.

'...If it warms you when I am kind to others, then I will be kind. If all this means that you will make life easier for me then I will continue. If, when I worship you, your love for me will blossom then I will continue. I will, I will, I will!'

'Allahu akbar!' I bellowed out. 'Allah you are the greatest!' I willed every cell in my body to believe with conviction that Allah was the greatest. Forcing my mind to submit completely and faultlessly, 'Allahu akbar!' *No, that's not enough.* I clenched my eyes shut, tensed my whole body and shouted out with all my strength 'ALLAHU AKBAR!!' My throat tore with the force. My entire body vibrated like a spring.

'You are the One!'

'The First!'

'The Last!'

'The Truth!'

'The Everlasting!'

'The Most Holy!'

'The Most Strong!'

'The Compellor!'

'The Most Generous!'

With a deep, worrying intensity, I rattled off some of Allah's ninety nine names and virtues, forcing my mind out of human consciousness. Into the realms of absolute devotion.

'The Protector! Protect me from harm...'

'The All Peaceful! Don't let me leave this place without peace in my heart!' Scrunched eyes, a speck of water escaped.

'Al Khaliq!' Eyes now wide open, staring wildly at the moon, as if a UFO. 'You are The Creator of all things!'

'The Causer of Death!' Heart drummed rhythmically in my chest.

'The Judge! Please judge me kindly. I fear your wrath!' Hairs on my arms stood on end. The breeze dropped in temperature.

'You are The Most Compassionate!'

'The Most Merciful!'

'The Most Kind!'

'The Forgiver!' I paused for a moment. My past flashed in my mind. 'Give me your mercy and forgive me, for I have sinned.' Dropping my head into my lap with shame, I pressed my hands to my head and unleashed feverish wails. 'I am ashamed of my bad deeds, please, I beg you to forgive me, please, you're the forgiver, al Tawaab! Accepter of Repentance, accept my repentance and do not punish me for my sins. Stop the punishment, stop the pain!'

The louder I screamed, the more my throat ripped, the more likely he was to hear me; I was sure.

'Al Alim! The Knower, please see what it is in my heart and understand what I need!' imploringly.

'You are The All-Seeing! The All-Hearing! The Withholder! Guide me away from the mines in life that I am blind to. Guide me away from imbeciles like Zameer!!'

'The Just! The Equitable! This world and this life on earth is so unjust. Let justice be done one day! Let the poor and innocent one day become rich and happy. Let the evil be punished!' Angry now. 'You are Ash-Shaheed, witness to everything!'

'The Responsive! Hear my prayers. Accept my wishes!' Louder, rocking back and forth.

Reality and sanity jumped off the cliff. Sick of what was real, I wanted to escape.

'The Most Glorious! Surely there's nothing more Glorious than you! Surely there's nothing more Glorious than you!' A rare passion.

'The Glorified!'

'You are The Guide! I am lost! Help me! Show me the right way! Walk with me!' My head filled with bricks of exhaustion, my zeal unyielding.

'An Noor, you are The Light!' I raised my hands, intent on reaching complete submission. 'An Noor! As Prophet Mohammad had asked you, I ask you too, to; place light in my heart, light in my tongue, light in my hearing, light in my sight, light behind me, light in front of me, light on my right, light on my left,' breathless I continued frantically, 'light above me and light below me; place light in my sinew, in my flesh, in my blood, in my hair and in my skin; place light in my soul and make light abundant for me; make me light and grant me light! Light, light, light!'

'Al Wadood!' Loud sobs. 'The Loving...'

Speech evaded me.

'Al Wadood, look at my broken heart,' prodding my chest. 'Al Wadood! I need only your love, love me please' I whispered. Pitifully. 'Love me!' Screaming out hysterically. An impassioned lover. 'Love me!' My chest heaved with need.

On the moon or in my bedroom; I could have been anywhere in the world and not have known.

My heart drummed only for Allah.

I breathed only for him.

Not caring for anything else.

Escaping from reality.

Entering an indescribable medium.

I pushed my mind deeper into the universe of submission.

My head span like a merry-go-round and longed for release.

I refused to let go.

I could not let go.

'Al Aziz! The Mighty!'

Yelling at the darkened, magnanimous sky.

'The Majestic!'

I was superhuman.

'The Exalted!'

Alive in this bubble of ecstasy.

Flashes of light danced in front of my eyes. Teasing my lucidity. White flashes. Shapes of human figures. Bending down in prostration. Now turning to shapes of figures standing in front of a cube. *The Kaba?*

'Al Azeem!'

My fervour, uncontrollable.

Irrational.

An inflamed bull.

'The Most Exalted!'

Simmering mind; a flame approaching a pool of hydrogen peroxide.

'The Most Great!'

I shrieked with ferocity.

'The Sublime!'

Body vibrating, wildly.

'The Omnipotent!'

My throat throttled.

'The Powerful!'

Elated, I was about to take off into space.

'Al Hameed! You are worthy of worship for these reasons alone! The praiseworthy! Your messenger was right; we cannot praise you the way you deserve to be praised! AL HAMEED!!'

'AL HAMEEEEEEEED!!!!'

My body froze.

Heartbeat, silenced.

Hands stopped shaking.

Eyes clasped shut.

Breathing ceased.

At the pinnacle of faith.

I waited for a bang.

An explosion.

Hydrogen peroxide to meet the blaze.

I waited.

The lake of time stilled.

I waited.

Nothing.

'Haaa-aah...,' gasping. Suddenly resuscitated, I lunged for breath.

My heart pounded ferociously, blood gushed to my head. The mountains appeared again, the jaggedness of the rock underneath me. My body unclenched. I pried my aching eyes open, seeing the world for the first time. I had not exploded.

'Malik ul Mulk, the Owner of the Kingdom... Al Malik.' I whispered numbly.

I bowed my head down, weighted by the power of gravity.

'You are my King and I am your servant.' And with that, exhausted, shaken, dazed, confused, I dropped to the hard ground on my knees.

I wept and I laughed.

15

'TODAY WE ARE RETURNING to God... This is the very land where every person to have ever walked this earth will be raised and be gathered... on the Last Day.'

With a light thud I stepped off the coach and placed my right foot onto the silky, soft sand. Immediately, I knew that this land was like no other. Untouched and pure. It was already mourning for the bloodshed to come.

'Arafat,' I whispered.

'Here every soul will be raised from the dead on the Day of Judgment where Allah will decide whether we will spend an eternity in hell or heaven.' Layth repeated in a hushed voice as the rest of our group got off the coach.

Shading my eyes with my hands from the blinding afternoon sun, I looked on at the vast plain. The surrounding sandy mountains loomed threateningly yet gently over the exposed but bashful, plainer land. The sun had lowered itself to beautify us with its light and scald us with its savage heat. Perspiration evaporated from our skins and forced its way into our suffocated lungs. Not a creature crawled the earth and not a bird flew in the sky. Only pilgrims stood awkwardly. The horizon flickered ominously. Silent and bright; it revealed little of the perils it was to be witness of.

It was the next day and we had arrived at Arafat, a few miles away from Mina, to spend the afternoon here as was the custom ritual. The day of Arafat was the all-important day of mercy. The essence of Hajj. Millions of pilgrims were here to seek Allah's forgiveness. Millions. Yet I barely heard a soul.

Hundreds of mismatched fabric tents stood dubiously on the flatter areas of the terrain. The rags and wooden sticks that made up the disordered tents were erected to shade the pilgrims from the unrelenting sun. A few pilgrims dared to hover outside, but most hid inside. Other than that, the land was faraway, desolate and untouched by modernism. No shops, no satellite dishes, no market traders, no fast cars, no buildings. A far cry from even the villages of Britain. A far cry from even Mecca. It was just a desert.

The Day of Judgement here? An eerie chill, like the slimy body of a lizard, slithered up my back. Terror sunk my feet into the ground, unable to move. Imagining the movie of all my dark secrets being projected into the canvas of the sky for the whole world to see. For God to judge me on. The blood drained from my face. *What if he's so angry with me and resolves to send me to hell? Right* here. *Is this the place where I will meet my end?*

'Why are you just stood there? Move on.' Daania pushed me forward.

'This way.' A Saudi official ushered us away from the coach and beckoned us to follow him. The tents were packed tightly together making the paths that they formed extremely narrow. A feeling of claustrophobia settled beside us. The sandy, rocky land sloped upwards and downwards haphazardly.

We followed him along the snaky paths with heavy and laboured steps; the only thing I seemed to be able to hear. That, along with my wheezing and choking.

I had awoken that morning to a fit of chesty coughing and a grinding pain in my head. *'You have a chest infection'*, Noor had given me her unqualified diagnosis. I responded with my best dying look, to which she said, *'Be brave. It's said that the more you suffer during the times of Hajj the more Allah is forgiving you. Apparently, whenever a Muslim suffers, even from the prick of a thorn, Allah is allowing his sins to fall away from him like leaves off a tree. See it as a blessing'.* I had tried my best to be optimistic, until I threw up my breakfast into the incessantly filthy toilets.

Peering through the passing tents, pilgrims sat themselves on mats, wedged together like blades of dead grass. No one interacted with their neighbour. Instead they sat in silence. A look of deep mourning on their faces. The sombreness of the site reminded me of the funeral of my sister.

A hundred or so men and women, half of whom I did not know, had sat on a large piece of cream cloth laid on the floor of my living room and front room. Quietly, they had flicked prayer beads, mourning Nafeesa's death, praying for her to go to heaven. The men had been in one room, the women in another. Shoes were off, heads hung low, not a sound uttered but that of beads and sniffles.

This was darker than the funeral of my sister. Here I was in a different time zone, uncomfortable surroundings and with a whole desert full of foreign mourners, mourning for a fate that had not yet arrived.

In all my time away I had not felt home sick, but now I did. I wanted to run away from this place. This place that harboured so much unknown terror. I was scared and I wanted to go home.

'Ladies, ahh! Men, ahh!' The official stopped and made a gesture to two tents opposite each other. Women and men segregated once more. I doubted there was any need for it. Given the circumstances, no man or woman was going to behave indecently here.

'Shoes off!' A woman inside the tent hissed at me before I had even managed to lift the flap of the tent up. The light inside was dim, bar the sunlight that filtered through the small gaps of the colourful mismatched pieces of cloth that formed the covering. The humidity was impeding. I lumbered through it towards an unoccupied corner of the tent. As I sat, the rubble underneath the cloth that lay over it penetrated my shins and feet. Not wishing to cut through the tense mood, I stifled my yelps.

Still unable to embrace the desert I was in, I just sat and stared.

Sixty or so women, on the clothed ground, each shrouded in their white robes and headscarves, occupying only the space of a prayer mat and facing the same direction; the direction of the Kaba. They had glanced up briefly at our entrance but then shot their heads back down and continued with the furious flicking of their prayer beads. The common whispering I had heard amongst women in Mina did not take place here. Here they were all alone. Grieving over their pasts and future.

'Astagfirullah. Astagfirullah. Astagfirullah', *forgive me Allah*, were the continuous hushed whisperings of the women. The woman beside me, shrouded in white, rocked backwards and forth, her lips quivering. Her trance-like state sent a chilling sensation up my arms. Silent tears fell down the cheeks of others. Tears of fear, worry, remorse.

What had these people done to feel such a cumbersome regret? I wondered. Had that woman, who scrunched her face in quiet pain, had an affair? Had Zia, who shook her head regretfully, beat her grandchildren? Iraj, who threw her face on the ground for what seemed like an hour, had she got pregnant by mistake and had an abortion? That young girl, with the faraway look, had she had sex before marriage? Shoplifted? Killed somebody? Or was she an alcoholic? A drug addict? And what had my own good mother done? Why did she hang her head down in shame?

Whatever shady secrets they had, I was certain that none of them would tell me. But God knew what guilt they hid in the crevices of their underarms. That is why they looked so shaken. Shaken by the realisation that, on that reckoning day, Allah would replay every scene of their lives in front of everyone, revealing every dark secret and ask them why they had insolently disobeyed him. These people were terrified. Terrified that Allah would decide for them, an eternity in hell. They were desperate to seek his forgiveness now before it was too late.

I fingered the palm of my left hand.

And what about me? Won't Allah replay the sooty scenes of my life? The scenes of me stealing money from dad's wallet to buy Craig David's album, carelessly sipping that Vodka and Coke in the Leeds nightclub, sitting on the benches of Houghton park, smoking to get high, laughing when girls were pulling Samantha's hair in the school playground, not going up to Joel to say hello because I think he's too ugly and fat for me to associate myself with, dancing and flashing my flesh in the R'n'B club knowing that it was making God angry, pretending to make my prayers but instead sitting on my mat reading Cosmopolitan, and...

I shook my head as though I was seeing my house collapse, brick by brick, because of my own punches. Thousands of guilty scenes to play back, each one made me want to claw my way deep into the ground.

Superseding the feelings of remorse were the feelings of a crashing fear. The fear that Allah would, on the Day of Judgment, ask me about each of my actions. Each and every one. And I would not know what to say but 'sorry'. The fear that he would reply, 'it is too late to say sorry. You had your chances on earth to say sorry when I gave you so many warnings'. The fear that he would send me to hell, an agony infinitely worse than a thousand breaks of my heart, a thousand breaks of my neck. A pain that would be unrelenting. For an eternity. I could barely tolerate the pain of one heart break, one stone under my foot; what hope was there for me in hell?

'Oh God...,' physically immobilised. Closed in by the bricks of my sins. 'What have I done...'

...Stamping on that innocent spider in the bathroom repeatedly until it became a black smudge, throwing a shoe at my father for not

giving me the TV remote when Home and Away was on, lying to Sarah when she asked me why I hadn't returned her phone calls, walking past the poor man at the London tube station who begged me for 30p...

A woman behind me let out a profoundly poignant cry. A cry burdened with sacks of guilt, shame, fright. A tear drop, channelling the same burdens, instinctively trickled from my eye.

...screaming at mum, shoving her out of the way – she only asked me why I'd not eaten dinner – throwing pebbles at the pigeons at the docklands and laughing, punching my brother in the face for not giving me a ride on his new bike...

'I am sorry,' came out of my strangled throat, hanging my heavy head low, covering my face with my hands in shame.

I wanted to go home.

But I could not escape it. I could not escape this terrifying place. I could not escape God.

I felt so alone.

A soft touch on my arm. I jumped. It was Zia, my neighbour.

I gaped at her with wide and petrified eyes.

'*'Have faith in the mercy of Allah. Surely, only the disbelievers lose hope in the mercy of Allah.'* Those are words of the Quran.' She nodded at me as if to confirm its truth and then rummaged through her bag and picked out a green tattered book. I glimpsed at the title; 'Mercy'. She opened up a page and pointed her finger to a paragraph. 'Read this.'

Taking the book from her hands I read the passage out. '*Prophet Mohammad, peace be upon him, had said that Allah says to the people 'O son of Adam, so long as you call upon Me, and hope in Me, I will forgive you for all that comes from you, and I do not care. O son of Adam, if your sins were to reach even the farthest heights, clouds, in the sky, and you asked for My forgiveness, I shall forgive you."*

'He will forgive me?' questioning, eager, hoping for her to say yes.

'Only Allah knows that my dear.'

Slumping my head back down, I handed the book back to her.

'The point is, that it might be that a person reaches the age of ninety having committed the gravest of sins like murder, adultery and idol worshipping, but if on his death bed he says, just once, 'Allah forgive me', with sincerity and remorse, it may be that Allah forgives him and sends him to heaven. That is how great Allah's compassion and mercy is for his people.'

'Wow. Really?' A jolting hope straightened my neck.

'Yes, really!' She exclaimed.

A voice inside me whispered. *It'd be ok to live as you please. Go on a rampage of sex, drugs and rock n' roll. Ask God to forgive you when you're dying.* I fought against the grin emerging on my face.

She narrowed her eyes, reading my mind. 'But we cannot be sure. He may still send someone like that to hell. He might send us all to hell. So don't go around living like a devil thinking he'll forgive you.'

'Oh...,' disappointed, perplexed. 'I don't understand. Should I hope or should I despair?'

'These two emotions you must balance. A person is best to have hope in God's mercy but also fear his wrath. It's difficult to do, yes, but it's the only way. They say that on this day, today, Allah forgives all the pilgrims when they seek his sincere forgiveness. It's on this day that all the sins of our past are wiped away. Ask him to forgive you... sincerely.' With that she turned away from me and bowed her head, continuing with her supplications.

'Allah, forgive me.' I uttered.

Reaching out my hand, I scooped up some sand, letting my fingers run through it. *The sand of Arafat. The sand that would witness the gravest day ever.* I raised it to my nose and smelt it; earthy, raw, rugged. 'What cries have you already witnessed? What cries are you yet to witness?'

***

'Oh Lord of the worlds... Forgive us!' Imam Isa's cries were soft.

The sun was due to begin to set. Hundreds of us were called out of our individual prayers, hours later, to gather in one of the larger tents to make a prayer together with an Imam. The Imam, an old man with a long white beard, sat at the far end of the tent with his back to us. The men sat behind him and the women sat behind the men. Each pilgrim had their heads bowed and hands cupped in front of them. The atmosphere was strained. Heavy. Really heavy. The largest of bulldozers would not have stirred it.

'Ameen,' we all uttered after him; *amen.*

'Oh Allah!' His voice strengthened with our needs. 'We people are sat here on this holy ground where so many millions of people have also sat, where Prophet Mohammad, peace be upon him, sat.

We, like him and the rest, have come here today to ask for your forgiveness. O Allah…,' his voice trembled.

I shivered.

'I do not know what problems my dear sisters, my dear brothers have left behind.'

His fresh cries instigated the cries in others. Each person recalled sorrows and miseries of their past. The unconditional love in his voice shot right through my heart. My lips trembled. A rope noosed around my neck. *If only you knew. If only you knew the endless days and nights I spent distraught. If only you knew, the way my heart was ripped out my chest. If only you knew, how I have longed for the ground to swallow me up and take me away from the sorrows of my life. If only you knew. If only you knew, how I crawled to this place, desperate, wounded, on the brink of losing my mind forever, in a final attempt to save myself. If only you knew…* The haunting tears emerged. A hundred worms of memory squirmed in my stomach.

'But please my Lord, our Lord, you are the most compassionate please show compassion to us. We have suffered enough, please don't punish us anymore.' He paused, unable to control his sobs. Chests heaved. 'Please stop the pain. It hurts Allah!' Cries amplified with his screams.

'Ameen.'

I watched in disbelief as every back vibrated erratically. The cries of both the men and women, piercing and surreal. Men were crying like helpless children. My father, his head pressed down on his hands, clenched in a ball, his back trembling. My mum wailed out loud, face streaming with perspiration, tears. No one cared for emotional restraint. The desires to seek forgiveness were as free as rain in a storm. If the world had split in two, there and then, I doubted these people would have broken from their repentance.

'We have done so much wrong,' he sniffled. He could not contain himself. 'Your messenger knew. He knew we would disappoint you. He tried to warn us but we still strayed. He cried and cried for his people and yet we remained ignorant!'

The shooting of his howls reverberated in between my ribs.

'Oh Allah, please forgive us for all our sins, we have committed so much sin! Years and years of it! Our hearts are black with them! Oh Allah we are ashamed. We come to you beaten and bruised. We come to you with nothing left, but the blackness of our sins and the shame in our hearts!'

Remorse streamed down my face; liberated and wild to roam the breadths of my cheeks.

'O Allah!' wailing, 'O Allah! We are so, so ashamed! We do not deserve to be here, we deserve hell! O Allah! WE DESERVE THE HELLFIRE!'

I froze with alarm at his open words of suicide. 'No...' I shook my head urging him to prevent this mass killing. *No you crazy man, no, why are you saying that?*

'But no Allah,' he whimpered softly. 'Please don't send us to hell. Please not hell. We fear your wrath, but Allah we have hope in your mercy. We come here with hope, the hope that your love instils in us. You are the most merciful. Please show us your compassion. O ALLAH! PLEASE!!' His voice rattled the tent. It tore through the camp site.

'AMEEN!' I cried with the rest; sharing their pain, guilt, terror. This was worse than mourning for our own deaths. We were not crying for our lives. This was mourning for the death of our afterlife. We were crying for our afterlives.

'O Lord of the Worlds! We are your servants! Your small servants. And you are our master. We raise our hands to you and beg you! O Allah, see these hands?? They *beg* you, they plead with you! Have mercy on our souls! Do not punish us!'

He abruptly stopped.

A moment passed.

'ASTAGFIRUALLAAAAAAAHH!!!!' His final wail, before he crumbled into his lap.

***

'His last message to the people was made up there.'

Moments after Imam Isa's prayer, I ploughed my way out of the sludge of intensity inside the tent. I needed air.

But it was not much better outside. The potency of the atmosphere now spread outwards and closed in on my head in all directions, threatening a crushing. Like meat in an oven, my red and blotchy face was scorched by the heat. The light of the sun, which had now moved to the west, sent shooting laser rays into my bleary eyes. Dazed from emotional and feverish exhaustion, I faintly looked at what Hooria was pointing at.

A mountainous area on the east side of the land came to view. Surprisingly, I had not noticed these enormous sandy mountains before but they now glared at me as though they had been watching me the whole time. Specks of white dots peppered the nearest one. Pilgrims had ventured up the perilous slopes. Most had gathered around the large, long piece of white-grey rock that she was referring to. The 'Jabal Rehmat'.

'Prophet Mohammad made his last plea to his people there, his last plea to us.' Hooria croaked, the emotion rising again.

'What did he say?' still staring upwards.

'Not much but a lot at the same time. It was a speech of urgency and final desperateness. It was so poetic… *'O People, lend me an attentive ear, for I know not whether after this year, I shall ever be amongst you again. Therefore listen to what I am saying to you very carefully and take these words to those who could not be present here today."*

'You know it off by heart? Did he know he was going to die?'

'I don't know. It seems that way doesn't it? He told people not to hurt anyone. Beware of the devil. Told men to be good with their wives. Advised people not to discriminate against race and colour, saying we are all children of Adam and Eve. He said that he would leave the Quran and his legacy and we only need follow them to be successful. And…' She paused and showed me her bloodshot eyes. '…And he warned of the Day of Judgment and our meeting with Allah.'

'Meeting with Allah…' My stomach somersaulted.

'His last words were his most poignant words.' Whispering, she looked up at the distant Jabal Rehmat again. 'They make me feel sad.'

'What did he say?'

'He ended by saying *'All those who listen to me shall pass on my words to others and those to others again; and may the last ones understand my words better than those who listen to me directly. Be my witness, O God, that I have conveyed your message to your people…'* And then he left us…'

'The man that we need the most left us.' I matched her melancholy and grief.

Hooria cleared her throat. 'Yes he left us, but his message has passed fourteen hundred years and still touches millions of us today. A billion in fact. It's touched us. It's as though he said those words today. Just like he wanted.'

'His legacy remains.' I continued gazing up at the tall rock that was less than a kilometre away from me. Envisaging Prophet Mohammad standing there, making his final plea to a crowd of people. I imagined myself being in that crowd, listening as though they were the wisest words I would ever hear.

'Did you know that is where Adam was first put when he was banished from heaven? They say he spent years in prostration to Allah, and Allah finally forgave him.' Hooria informed.

'Really? Wow. It must be the best spot to repent on...'

'Yeah... The sun's setting. We'd better make our last prayers of forgiveness before we leave.'

'I want to go up there,' looking at Hooria for encouragement. Then gazing back at the rock.

'Don't be crazy...'

She barely finished her sentence. A woman of impulse; I succumbed to my urges once more and ran for the mountain.

I have to go up there.

Time was short, there was approximately twenty minutes to sunset.

I have to go up there and stand where Prophet Mohammad made his final plea. I need to see what he saw.

With the envy of Nigerian Olympians, I sprinted towards the mountain in my slippers, weaving through pilgrims and passing countless tents.

I need to go up there and seek Allah's forgiveness just like Prophet Adam did. He'll surely forgive me if I stand there.

My legs had found a new spirit; a cheetah catching its prey.

My heart thundered. My breathing quickened.

I made my race against time.

Reaching the foot of the mountain, with dread, I saw how steep and rocky it actually was. The Jabal Rehmat was less than half a kilometre away but not without ninety degree slopes and jagged ridges in its path. With dismay I looked down at my bare slippers and the pilgrims that loitered at the foot of the mountain.

Adrenaline got the better of me. I pounced onto the first ridge despite the dangers. Bending forwards, I used my hands and feet to crawl up like a four-legged animal. Pebbles, rocks, stones, caught between my slippers and the soles of my feet. I gritted my teeth at the sharp pangs but carried on nonetheless.

A mad woman.

I had climbed half way up until I was forced to stop at a steep slope. My slippers did not have the grip to carry me up any further. Refusing to give up, I ignored the pleas of my tattered pink soles. I reached out for a jagged edged rock high above. Lifted my leg.

Placed my foot along the slope. Heaved myself up. Before I could make my next move, in a sharp flash, the rock that I had a hold of suddenly snapped.

In that split second I envisaged myself tumbling down the mountain and meeting a traumatic end.

'AAARGH!!!' A digging sensation in my back, legs, hands, 'AAAAARGH!!'

But the fall was short. I had stumbled back to the area where I had just tried to haul myself up from.

The blood rushed back to my face. My senses returned. I realised with disappointment that I was not Tarzan nor was I Rocky. This was no action movie. Half-shut eyes, I stared down at my dusty robe, frazzled slippers and weeping limbs. I resigned to surrender. Perspiration dribbled from my nose onto my lips. My lungs shook under my ribcage, gasping for oxygen. I was not going to make it to Jabal Rehmat.

Still facing the mountain I noticed the quiet cries of pilgrims above me, in the grooves and on the ledges. White sheets, brown sandals, a mountain and in the middle of nowhere; it took me a moment to believe with conviction that I was definitely in the twenty first century and had not travelled back in time into 560CE.

The colour of the sky had rapidly changed from its baby blue. Realising that I had not turned around yet to face the sun and the direction of the Kaba as the others had, I inched myself onto my feet and slowly moved my body around.

I gasped.

My eyes misted.

My knees buckled.

I was faced with the most overwhelming scene I had ever witnessed.

The innocent cloudless sky streaked with spectacular colours of indigo, red, purple and orange. Painted by the artist of the world. Across the horizon, the mountains of Arafat positioned themselves deep into the ground, for another eerie night. There in the middle of this striking art floated the perfectly shaped golden sun; a real and surreal magnificent ball of blazing fire.

On the sandy uneven grounds, below, ahead, to the side, stood all three million pilgrims facing the direction of the sun, the direction of the Kaba. The buffest of men, the oldest of women stood humbly in their white rags of cloth, with their heads lowered in shame, hands raised like beggars, weeping like children. The yellow plains of Arafat were filtered with the servants of Allah. Each one of them made their last pleas of forgiveness before the day of mercy ended and the sun disappeared.

It was the most heart rendering scene I had ever beheld.

It is the Day of Judgment.

I'm seeing the Day of Judgment.

The scene seemed to follow the descriptions of the Last Day, as set out in Islamic literature. Pilgrims stood on this land as though it was the Day of Judgment. The sun burned ominously in preparation of that day when it would be brought as close as a mile away from the earth. The faces of people darkened as though the darkest time ever known to man was already here. They screamed as though to deafen the blowing of the trumpet; the signal for the arrival of that day. They took their positions like they would on that day. The day that is said to be 50,000 years long. They trembled as though God, as promised, was about to make his appearance. They shrieked with franticness, terror, confusion, just as it was said they would do on that day. Mothers and fathers did not even glance at their pleading children, just like it was said they would not do on that day. My own mother did not worry whether I was still alive just like it was said she would not worry on that day.

Every man was for himself.

Dressed in minimal rags, they hung their heads down in shame, in fear, just like they would on that day. They wailed in remorse as though the movie of their life was being played out in front of them, as already warned. They raised their trembling hands and begged Allah to give them another chance, just like they would beg on that day, when they would ask Allah to send them back to earth to try again. They cried out like dying animals as though they had just been told that there were no more second chances and they were going to hell. Just as they would on that day, they only uttered 'Allah, forgive me'.

The hairs on my body erect. Cold blood ran through my veins as I watched on with terror. I stood stunned and paralysed for what seemed like an eternity.

This is a glimpse of the Day of Judgment.

'No...,' sheer fear. The sun was descending. The day of forgiveness was fading.

'No!' I cried out again. Willing it not to go and leave me in darkness.

Visions of me on the Last Day consumed my mind like a ditch

full of scorpions on a flea. Visions of the unavoidable and inescapable carnage and chaos that had been described to me. Visions of this plain being filled with a bizarre darkness yet with the burning heat of the sun sizzling my flesh. Visions of me standing, just like this, on that dark day saying the same words on this same spot. Visions of my shadiest secrets and deeds being replayed as I try to turn away from them with shame. Visions of me crying, just like I cried now, begging Allah to forgive me; my eternal life depending on it. Visions of me offering a leg and an arm in return for being put back on earth and given another chance to be a good Muslim. Visions of my ears popping from the loud shrieks of people I loved, as they are lead away to hell fire. Visions of my mother ignoring me, too consumed in her own fear, as I stand in front of her begging her to comfort me. Visions of me clenching my jaw and squeezing my eyes shut so tightly in horror, that my jaw breaks and eyes pop out. Visions of my terror when Allah is about to decide my fate.

'O Allah, I'm sorry!' Frantic desperation superseded. I howled out as loud as I could. Hoping my shattering sounds would vibrate through the skies and reach him.

'Save me from hell! FORGIVE ME!'

I felt so alone.

'Don't go… FORGIVE ME!!' I shrieked again. It is all I could say amongst my mammal cries. I no longer cared about the pain that I had come to Mecca with. All that meant nothing to me. My heartbreak, my career, my dreams were as meaningful as the dust on the ground. Only the possible pain of my afterlife as a result of the sins of my past mattered.

I was desperate to erase everything, turn back time, start all over again. Only to be a better Muslim. I felt like a crazy fool for wasting my twenty four years on music, dance, TV, friends, shopping and making futile plans for the future rather than seeking God's mercy and thinking about the bigger life. The afterlife.

I willed my body to rip open, let the floods of tears, the torrents of blood gush out of me immediately as an act of regret.

'FORGIVE ME ALLAH!! I promise not to sin again!' It was an impossible promise to keep. Desperate. The intensity of my terror pushed me to my knees in exhaustion and left me sobbing helplessly.

I felt so alone.

'Laaaaaa-aaaaa ilaaaaa ha illallaaaaaaaa-aaaah…' A nearby pilgrim began to sing 'there is no God but Allah', in an eerie and poignant harmony.

My cries muted. I gazed out. 'I will not move until you have forgiven me,' whimpering. A thousand wild horses could not have dragged me away at that moment.

Time stood still.

There I was.

On the sacred mountain of Arafat, the most spiritual day of my life, I watched the flickering sun begin to descend amidst the magnificent horizon. Never had I seen the beauty of such a sunset. I knelt on the land the first Prophet walked his first steps, where the last Prophet uttered his last plea. I watched on as a live scene of the terror-filled Last Day played before my very eyes. Alone, on my knees, in my tattered rags, with tears in my eyes, I raised my hands, like a true servant and did what the first man, Adam, did here; I cried 'Oh Allah… forgive me.'

There I was; desperate to save my soul from an eternal misery.

Time stood still.

There are no other words for it.

It was the most moving moment of my life.

16

SHE HUGGED ME.

SEVEN years old. I must have been seven years old when my mother last hugged me. She had even failed to take me into her arms on the mournful day that my sister passed away. But on this momentous day in Arafat, the day of forgiveness, she hugged me.

In the darkness I had slithered down the mountain and run to her. Taking one look at my tear streaked face and dust stained robe, she maternally opened her arms and pulled me into her comforting embrace. I closed my eyes and for a moment, I pretended it was the same embrace as that when I was a little girl. The one that protected me from the Goblins under the bed and assured me everything was going to be ok. For that moment, wrapped in her warm arms, I was safe again.

'We need to get going quick. Dusk prayers need to be made in Muzdalifah.' My father wiped his face and regained control.

Muzdalifah was our next stop. As with all the rites of Hajj, I did not know what to expect from Muzdalifah. It was in between Arafat and Mina, a few miles away, and was the place where Prophet Mohammad had stopped for the night and engaged himself in rest and the worship of God. It was there he collected forty nine pebbles for the stoning ritual that was to take place during the next three days.

In the darkness, Arafat now uncovered an urgent energy. Pilgrims hurried to pack their bags and make way for Muzdalifah. We picked up our own bags from the tent and hurriedly followed Layth out. He shoved us onto the nearest bus and seconds later it sped off.

In the haste I did not get a chance to bid farewell to the land that had gifted me with the most moving moment of my life. I looked out of the dusty window of the bus and gazed at the now ghost-like terrain. It would remain unoccupied for another year, until the next

Hajj. Or until the Last Day. Intermingling waves of sadness and relief washed over me. Sadness that the precious day of forgiveness had evaporated with my perspiration, relief that I could take respite from the imminent day of terror for a little while longer.

Not a pilgrim said a word.

All that could be heard was the racket of the bus engine and rumbling of its wheels as it drove along the rocky, windy desert tracks. They were either reflecting on their personal experiences in Arafat or simply recuperating from the mental exhaustion of the day. My mind was sapped of all its energy to reflect. I was glad to blankly stare out of the window watching the mountains and sky as they became darker and darker until everything became black and I was faced with my own reflection.

***

'I bet Prophet Mohammad didn't have this problem when he was coming into Muzdalifah!' Mikaeel exclaimed as he peered out of the bus window.

Mikaeel had a good point. Muzdalifah was only six kilometres away from Arafat, yet two ragged hours later, we were still stuck in the traffic. Wedged, bumper to bumper, between hundreds of buses lining the road of this land. Prophet Mohammad would have travelled to this place on a camel and with a lot fewer people. He certainly would not have had this problem.

Muzdalifah was seemingly nothing but a vast area of plain desert land surrounded by large, dark, thundering mountains. The few lamps dotted around the field went only a little way in numbing the blackness of the night. Illuminated signposts etched with numbers had been erected in certain places. They appeared to correlate with the numbers of the camps in Mina.

Pilgrims that had already been dropped off at their stops walked past our stalled bus. In the lit areas I saw others creeping towards the open camp sites or, having already reached the sites, settling themselves on the ground – rummaging through rucksacks, laying mats and sleeping bags or sitting to take a breather. In the more distant dark areas, silhouettes stirred covertly and mysteriously.

A further hour passed when we finally reached our campsite and were able to step off the bus.

The immediate cold and murkiness sent an uncomfortable shiver through my limbs. Raven black mountains stared conspicuously at the hundreds of thousands of pilgrims invading their plains. *'Jinns loiter in desert areas'.* The tour guide's words brushed past my ears. I clung onto the nearest sleeve, Hooria's. There were no tents here and the night was to be spent exposed to the dark sky, ominous mountains and lurking jinns.

'Quick,' Layth ushered us forwards. 'The plots fill up quickly so let's grab a space.'

Weaving past rugs and sleeping bags, the ad-hoc camping style reminded me a little of Glastonbury music festivals. Except the festival goers have tents. We did not. We passed a washing area that facilitated portable toilets and water taps jutting out of walls. I dryly noted how queues were already forming outside those. Queues were also branching out of small food carts that sold small snacks and hot tea and coffee.

We found a vacant spot directly in the middle of the camp site and laid our sleeping bags on the sandy, pebbly ground, claiming the space as ours for the night. I ensured that my mother and father would be sleeping on either side of me. *If the jinns come they'd get them first.*

***

'Why are we picking pebbles and not bricks??' I called out to my mother.

Having prayed our dusk prayers and eaten the cold chicken Layth had carried with him for who-knows-how-long, my mother and I ventured towards the frightening mountains to collect our forty nine pebbles. The stoning ritual would involve throwing pebbles, over the following three days, at three large pillars that represented the devil.

'If we're stoning the *devil*, whom I'm guessing we hate so much, then why are we using these measly pebbles? This is hardly going to cause any harm?' I fingered a pebble the size of a peanut.

'It's the way Prophet Mohammad had done things. Would you be able to carry forty nine bricks with you?' She was quite a distance from me and I could not see her face in the dark but I imagined her pulling her infamous look of incredulity.

'Hey! I'm strong enough,' mocking disbelief. 'I spend two hours a week at the gym lifting iron!'

'I'd like to see your matchstick arms carry even *three* bricks.' She remarked, laughing.

The mood at Muzdalifah was very much unlike the mood in Arafat. We were here to relax, and relaxed was the atmosphere indeed. Other pilgrims crouched and picked pebbles in the distance as though they were picking shells on a beach; inspecting, throwing or keeping. I leisurely wandered towards the foot of the mountains, an area that was heavily scattered with pebbles. The mountains did not appear so terrorising anymore and I ventured under their dark shadows mindlessly, singing Westlife's 'you raise me up so I can stand on mountains' in a melody that probably sent the jinns running for the hills.

A couple of young women hovered nearby. I stopped my singing, not wishing to cause anyone unnecessary discomfort whilst on Hajj.

They were speaking English amongst themselves. English with a rich African accent. In the thickened darkness I could barely see their silhouettes.

'It's difficult to see up here isn't it?' I said to the silhouette closest to me.

'Yes,' replied the other one. 'It is difficult to find pointy stones!' chuckling.

'Ha! Where are you from? Africa?'

'Yes. You know? Zimbabwe. That is my sister.' She approached a little closer, pointing to the other dark figure next to her.

I feel a familiar dull pang in my heart. Fourteen years on and the pain still throbs every time I see two sisters together. Laughing over ice cream. Sharing secrets about boys. Trying dresses on at the shops. How I longed for Nafeesa to be here, picking pebbles with me.

'So how has it been so far? Have you enjoyed it?' I had to fill the silence.

'Yes it's been very good experience. We lucky to be here. We see this in pictures all the time. And now we are here!'

'Yes.'

'It does not feel real. It is like a dream.' Her hushed voice filled with the emotion of a young woman whose dream had come true.

'It is,' recalling the surreal events. 'It is indeed.'

Hovering around each other for a few minutes, we busied ourselves with our pebble search as she elaborated on her experience.

'I am a teacher.'

'Oh yeah?'

'My dad is just farm worker but he has worked very hard to take me and my sister to school. I am now a teacher because of him...' She paused for a reflective moment before continuing. 'My father, my mother and my grandfather, they dream of doing Hajj before they die. When I was a little girl papa would show me a picture of the land of dreams and cry. I promised I would grow up and work hard and take him.'

My eyes dampened.

'For years I saved money for tickets and we all come...'

'Just tickets?' I interrupted.

'Yes. All thanks is to Allah.'

'Do you have a hotel?' I stopped picking my pebbles and stared at her shadow.

'No hotel. We sleep where there is space. All the grounds of this land are holy. We are happy. We eat once a day and walk wherever we go. We are happy.'

'But it cannot be easy?'

'It has not been easy. My grandfather has been to hospital four times here but he is happy. I just pray...,' her voice lowered, tinged with forlornness. 'I pray that we get through it all. I want their dreams to come true before they die.'

Minutes passed. I said nothing. Just watched her and her sister bend down in the darkness, meekly scrounge for stones. The love for her parents and grandfather was extraordinary. Nothing I had ever encountered. As a powerless woman in Africa, I admired her devotion to fulfil her parents' ambitions above everything else. The way she spoke of her struggles, with not a hint of complaint or bitterness but only a brave smile. Astounding. It laced my own ingratitude with shame.

'I sincerely hope that Allah makes your mission easy for you and your family.' I wished her before she left at the call of her father. 'And you... you are beautiful. May Allah gift you for the warmness of your heart.' In the dark, I had not seen her face once, but I knew, I just knew, it was beautiful.

***

With our pouch full of pebbles, my mother and I walked up the slope of the nearest mountain and sat on a flat ledge. Immersed in darkness, away from the hustle and bustle of the campsite, we were plummeted into a peaceful silence. Silence that would crack with the drop of feather.

The view was fascinating.

The vast night sky sparkled with tiny stars and the white sensational moon floated above us with serenity. A cool breeze brushed my face and with prayer beads in my hand, I watched the three million campers, or as many as my eyes would allow me to see, in muteness.

They sat cross legged on their rugs and chatted amongst their companions. They lay gazing at the stars with prayer beads in their hands. They ate cold dinners without complaint. Followed by hot tea. They picked pebbles as they strolled with a rare leisure. They washed their bodies paying attention to their cleanliness. They spoke to God in silence. Or they sat as I sat and watched on at Mudzalifah. They brought this solitary desert to life – a life that was born only one night a year – whilst the mountains, the sky, the stars and the moon marvelled. Whilst I marvelled.

Whites, blacks and browns; so many races yet they all rested together on this one plain.

The words of Malcolm X came to mind. He disliked white people and did not agree with integrating with them. A human activist, he spoke for non-whites, as one of the most influential African-American men in history. Similar to Martin Luther King. Years after he converted to Islam, a life changing event in his life altered his dogmatic views; Hajj.

The infamous letter he wrote about the Hajj in 1964, before his assassination, now came back to me. As a non-white living in a pre-dominantly white country, I had always found the letter compelling and inspiring, no matter how many times I read it or had it read to me. But now, on the second day of my Hajj, it did more than it usually did. This time it struck a deep chord and expressed my truest sentiments of the moment.

'Never have I witnessed such sincere hospitality and overwhelming spirit of true brotherhood as is practiced by people of all colors and races here in this Ancient Holy Land... For the past week, I have been utterly speechless and spellbound by the graciousness I see displayed all around me by people of all colors... There were tens of thousands of pilgrims, from all over the world. They were of all colors, from blue-eyed blonds to black-skinned Africans. But we were all participating in the same ritual, displaying a spirit

of unity and brotherhood that my experiences in America had led me to believe never could exist between the white and non-white... this is the one religion that erases from its society the race problem.

I have never before seen sincere and true brotherhood practiced by all colors together, irrespective of their color... You may be shocked by these words coming from me. But on this pilgrimage, what I have seen, and experienced, has forced me to re-arrange much of my thought-patterns previously held...

During the past eleven days here in the Muslim world, I have eaten from the same plate, drunk from the same glass, and slept on the same rug, while praying to the same God, with fellow Muslims, whose eyes were the bluest of blue, whose hair was the blondest of blond, and whose skin was the whitest of white. And in the words and in the actions in the deeds of the 'white' Muslims, I felt the same sincerity that I felt among the black African Muslims of Nigeria, Sudan, and Ghana. I could see from this, that perhaps if white Americans could accept the Oneness of God, then perhaps, too, they could accept in reality the Oneness of Man and cease to measure, and hinder, and harm others in terms of their 'differences' in color... Never have I been so highly honored. Never have I been made to feel more humble and unworthy.'

As a fellow pilgrim, his words articulated my thoughts. In fact, dare I say it, they did not speak enough.

Malcolm X's letter spoke only of race. What I now witnessed, whilst sat on the mountain, was far beyond equality within races. I witnessed wealthy and poor; young and old, pretty and not so pretty, crippled and healthy, male and female, educated and illiterate, elite and common. I witnessed them all rest as one, on the plains of Muzdalifah. I saw an absolute end to discrimination of all kinds.

Rich privileged men who had never in their lives slept below bed height, now slept on the rough ground. They slept amongst those poor men who only ever knew how to sleep on the floor. Female divas that had always turned their noses up at the thought of lying on dust now lay on it for the night. They slept on the same rubble as those women that would on a normal day scrub their shoes.

It would not have mattered whether a pilgrim was a Cindy Crawford, George Bush, David Beckham, Tom Cruise, Queen Elizabeth, Einstein or Aishwaraya Rai. There was no raised pedestal for such people. No red carpets. No golden beds. They shared the same bed as those of the hungry from Africa and used the same toilets as those of the grieving of Palestine. Each man wore two simple sheets of white cloth. Each woman wore plain robes. That was it. No Rolex watches. No Tiffany jewellery. No Prada dresses.

Truly extraordinary.

How are the elitists coping? How are they coping wearing rags? Sleeping alongside the poverty stricken? On the dirt. How do they feel when nudged out of the way by the cleaners of the world? How do they find standing in the queue for the toilets, behind a man who has only ever used fields for release? Do they cope, knowing that no paparazzi will chase them begging for a photograph? Do they cope when not a head turns their way in recognition? How does it feel to be brought right down to the same level as the other three million people?

'Where are the Kings? The celebrities? The presidents?' I mockingly raised my hand to my forehead as if to gaze out in search. Rich. Poor. With no tell-tale signs, I could not have told them apart.

Incredible.

And what about me? How am I coping, as an average lawyer, standing on the same peg as the lower class street sweeper and the upper class yacht owner? If it is possible to feel worthy and unworthy at once, then I felt it. I saw that I was nothing special to those less fortunate than me. That reined in my pride. It was humbling. But what delighted me the most was when I saw that I was worthy enough to be in the company of Kings and Queens. It was as stark as the jut of the ledge I sat on. *I am not better than anyone and no one is better than me.*

'Does it matter where the kings are?' My mother responded to my rhetorical question after a long silence. 'The only thing that distinguishes one person from the next is good deeds. Not good money or good looks or good brains. Allah doesn't care about that. In Allah's eyes we are all equal except for our piety. Those that carry more piety are superior to those that carry little, as we will see on the Day of Judgment.'

'Mmmm.'

'So flick those prayer beads and rise above the rest,' she winked.

I flicked.

'Is there any place in the world like this? Is there any place where a King of Arabia and a peasant of Ethiopia would lie side by side on the same rough plain, wearing the same clothes, standing in the same queue for the same toilet? Even if it is just for one night? Is there any place on earth where such remarkable equality amongst humans exists?'

'Ermmm...' My mother stopped to think with me.

'Think about it.'

'Well...'

'No, mum. No. Only here.'

Only at this place could three million people from all over the world become one and be seemingly happy about it. We mixed together like pots of hundreds of different coloured, textured, quality paints and became united as one race. One pot of paint.

Malcolm X is right. If the rest of the world was like this and embraced equality then there'd have been no World War I and II. There'd be no war between Palestine and Israel. Perhaps, if everyone united as one, like here, there'd be an end to all the injustices of the world...

As I lay that night on the stony ground, gazing up at the sky, searching for a shooting star, I could not help but wonder which one of my neighbours was a prince and which one of my neighbours was a pauper. *Who is prince? Who is pauper? Who am I?*

Finally I gave up and closed my eyes.

It doesn't matter. Allah doesn't care about that, so why should I?

Prince of Arabia or pauper of Ethiopia; for that night we were all equal.

We were all one.

17

I DO NOT KNOW what the voice of an angel sounds like. But as this voice gently kissed my ears and caressed my soul whilst I lay, I was sure it was the voice of an angel.

'Allaaaa-aaaaaaaaaah hu akbarrr... Allaaaaaaaaaa-aaaah hu akbar....'

The most seraphic, the most melodious voice I had ever heard called out to me for prayer. The singing oozed warmth into my blood, like thick, sweet honey in my veins. My admiration for the voices of Mariah Carey and Katherine Jenkins could not have been victorious over this voice. This was much more than just a ballad or an opera.

Is this the sound of heaven? Or am I dreaming?

With reluctance and desire I opened my eyes. If it was a dream I did not want it to leave and if it was heaven, I wanted to see.

'Ash hadu allaaaaaa-aaaaaaah ilaaaaaaaa-aaaha ill lalaaaaaaaaaaaaah...'

My body tingled with a current travelling from head to foot, as I gazed at the still starry sky of Muzdalifah. It was real. Not a dream. Not heaven.

'Ash-hadu anna Muhammadan rasulullaaaaaaaaaaaaaaaaaaaaaah... Ash-hadu anna Muhammadan rasulullaaaaaaaaaaaaaaaaaaaaaah...'

My soul stirred from its slumber and the hairs on my arms rose in preparation for a standing ovation. I lay spellbound for a long enchanting moment. It was a harmony that was as pure and soft as silk. It was without violins, pianos or flutes. Untouched; it was just a human voice. A human voice that sung with incomparable euphony, melancholy, devotion and velvet passion. In those moments it sung as though it was telling a story of years of love, heartbreak, joy, sorrow. Its music spoke where a lifetime of words would fail. This voice seeped through the air. The ground. The skies. It roused the mountains, kindled the sun and touched the hearts of all; I was sure.

It was just a human voice, but it had captivated my soul and hypnotised my mind. A tear from my eye sacrificed itself. A sacrifice in the name of this striking beauty.

'Hayya   ala-salaaaaaaaaaaaaaaaaaaaah...   Hayya   ala-salaaaaaaaaaaaa-aaaaaaaaaaaaaaaaah...'

Where is it coming from? I had to know. I had to see who possessed this entrancing gift. Jolting upright, not breaking from the spell, I straightened my headscarf and swivelled around.

Amidst the morning darkness, a luminous light shone over one man. The young man had his hands raised to his ears. His arms forming the shape of wings. He made the call to pre-dawn prayer, azaan, whilst pilgrims formed dark silhouettes around him. His beguiled audience listened to him. They watched him in awe amidst the surrounding darkness as he released the music on his tongue with an extraordinary elegance.

'Hayya   alal   falaaaaaaaa-aaaaaaaaaaaaah...   Hayya   alal falaaaaaaaaaaaaaaaa-aaaaaaaaaaaah...'

I almost stumbled over the Moroccan lady by my side as I moved towards him in a robotic trance. My eyes transfixed on him, restraining any blinks lest he disappear. The strength of his tall and slim body resembled strength in his will and his faith. A radiance of pearly white graced his exquisite face. His eyes were the greenest of green, perfectly framed by his dark brown eyebrows. Full of soul, these sparkling beads gazed upwards with a mysterious yearning. The expression of sorrow and love marked his face as if from birth. An aura of extraordinary humility cushioned him from the evils of the dirty world.

'Allaaaa-aaaaaaaaaah hu akbarrr... Allaaaaaaaaaaaaaaaa-aaaah hu akbar....'

Truly mesmerised. I stared. I listened.

'Laaaaaaaaaaaaaaaa   illaaaaaa   ha   ill   allaaaaaaaa-aaaaaaa-aaaaaaah'

The final note. Like a puff of smoke he disappeared. My eyes had not dared blink, but the rising pilgrims carried him away back into the mysteries of the darkness. He became one with the crowd again. The angelic man with the incredible voice, the incredible beauty had vanished.

Having been dumped into reality with an unwelcome abruptness, a rising ball of sadness caught me in the gut. I longed to find him, to take him home with me, so he could bless me with his beauty and sweet singing of holy Arabic lyrics all day long. I longed to wake up to his charming symphony every morning, be hypnotised out of sleep with this deep pleasantness. But immersed in these countless pilgrims and nowhere in sight, I knew it was a futile desire.

If I walk through the doors of heaven, I will ask Allah to bring this man to me.

***

'Today is going to be the most difficult day for you all...' Layth warned us. His tone uncomfortably serious.

We huddled closer to one another on our sleeping bags as we drank hot tea and ate flat bread for breakfast. Muzdalifah had risen from its sleep and prayers, and now basked under the bright morning sun.

'You need to make sure you stay strong and remain patient throughout the hardships you might suffer.'

I shot my eyes up at him. It is not what I wanted to hear, especially with my debilitating illness. I was just about coping with the grogginess, burning fever, bunged up nose, the razor blades in my throat, the pounding mallet on my head and the shooting pain in my limbs every time I coughed; especially my back, having slept on a bed of rocks. And my patience had already been given away in the forty minutes I spent queuing to use that nauseating toilet.

'What are we to expect?' not hiding my anxiety.

'A lot, including the stoning of Satan.' His two bushy eyebrows joining to form one grey stroke. 'You all know about the purpose behind the stoning, yeah?'

Most of us shook our heads.

'Ok, very quickly then. The stoning ritual comes from an event that took place in Prophet Abraham's life. Allah had ordered him to sacrifice his son, Ishmail, as a test of his devotion to Allah. Prophet Abraham plucked up the courage to do this, and as he and his son went to carry this out, Satan appeared before him urging him not to do it. Prophet Abraham threw seven stones at him which made him disappear. As Prophet Abraham walked a few metres further, Satan reappeared whispering the same discouragement. Prophet Abraham threw seven stones at him again until he disappeared. He walked on a few metres and Satan appeared one final time. Prophet Abraham threw seven stones at him again until he disappeared. He didn't return after that...'

'So why do we do it?' interrupted Mikaeel. I would have thought this intelligent man knew the answer to that. *I bet he's testing Layth.*

'I was getting to that. The place where this event took place is a couple of miles away from Mina. There are three pillars that are in place to represent Satan. Today we'll stone the third, largest pillar, and the following two days we'll stone all three. We throw these pebbles at these pillars to commemorate Prophet Abraham's triumph over Satan but more importantly for us to feel triumph over the Satan in our own lives. Do you see?'

'So are we just stoning today?' asked Noor.

'I'm afraid not. We'll now go back to Mina to put our luggage back at the camps, as we can't take anything with us during the stoning ritual. The crowds are too severe for us to be carrying rucksacks. We'll then go to the Jamarat, the place where the three pillars are, for the stoning. Then we'll arrange for a lamb to be sacrificed for each of us. Shave or cut our hair. And from there we'll walk straight back to Mecca, where we'll have to circulate the Kaba seven times and walk the mountains of Safa and Marwa, just as we did when we first arrived in Mecca. Then we'll head back to Mina for the night!'

'Uffff! All that in one day???' exclaimed Iraj. 'Hai Allahhh, how will we cope??' raising a tissue to her forehead and dabbing at the sweat.

The crowds are too severe', he had said. I had stopped listening at that point, my toes had curled and the cup of tea in my hand had turned cold. Many horror stories had been told about this ritual and I had heard them with the same shock each year.

The pillars were apparently small pillars, only between five and ten metres wide, and the recommended time for the pilgrims to throw these stones was from sunrise to noon. This left most of three million people six or so hours to throw their pebbles at the pillars. The chaos that had been created in the past was fatal.

With terror churning in the pit of my stomach, I remembered watching BBC and SKY news report over the years how the crowds had been so colossal that people had been trampled to death as a result. In 1990 almost 1500 pilgrims had been killed in a stampede during the stoning. In recent years hundreds had been killed and thousands badly injured. I had tried not to think about this during my journey so far, but now I had no choice but to come face-to-face with the realities.

'Severe. What do you mean by severe crowds?' I asked Layth, pressing my head to soothe the magnifying ache.

'The crowds are pretty bad, but don't worry, the system is not as bad as it was in the past. It's now a one-way system, and the pillars have been extended. We'll look after you, don't worry.'

Don't worry? I was not convinced. The dreadful stories about the uncontrollable chaos and how even the authorities did not dare venture near the area of the pillars due to the perils, poisoned my mind.

'Mum, I'm scared,' whispering to her.

'So am I... But Allah is with us. Put your trust in him,' her eye bags suddenly swollen.

I nodded, but worried for our lives.

***

'Oh crap...,' the first words I instinctively uttered whenever Layth revealed that we would be getting on a bus to our next destination.

The panic and anxiety that came with getting on a bus raised my blood pressure a few notches, to say the least. Nervousness would simmer during our usual one or two hour wait for a bus. It would heighten when I turned around to see thousands of pilgrims waiting for the same forty-seater. Backpacks hoisted, feet ready to sprint. We would wait and wait, looking out for the vehicle, eyeing each other furtively. When the bus was spotted from a distance, within seconds, hundreds would clamber to the front of the queue, knocking their neighbours out of the way with their heavy rucksacks. Layth would sprint forwards, urging us to do the impossible task of hurtling over the others too. When we miraculously got onto the bus, he would never check to see that we were all on, like a good guide would, but instead would breathe a sigh of relief as the bus sped off, assuming that all of us had fought through the hungry pack of herds.

In Muzdalifah it was no different.

Except, numerous rails had been erected at each bus waiting area, forcing pilgrims to queue up. Huge, locked gates barricaded the pilgrims from the bus track. Behind the gates peered Saudi Officials, attempting to maintain order with, well, just their eyes.

'Please let my dad come on,' I pleaded with the official as he slammed the gate shut. He had allowed half of our group to scramble through for the next bus. We knew this free bus would stop in only one place in Mina but neither of us had any idea where we would be dropped off or which one our camp was amongst the tens of thousands of others. Alone, we were sure to get lost. 'Look its only one more person.' I made a one sign with my finger as my father peered through the gate like an abandoned puppy in a dog home. 'Come onnn, don't be mean!'

The puppy dog eyes worked. He relented and, with a reluctant sigh, opened the gates to momentary freedom.

The churning in my stomach began as soon the bus began to churn its own wheels into the rough road tracks. It started with a moderate discomfort but very rapidly switched to an excruciating wringing pain.

It must have been the cold chicken of last night, which Layth had been carrying with him for two days, the bread I had eaten in the morning bought at the food carts or something related to my illness. I dug my finger nails into my belly as the pain shot in and out of my abdomen like a ferret high on cocaine. The contents of my insides were desperately looking for a way out and were relentless in their search. I tightly squeezed my eyes shut and bit my lip until it bled – pain on top of pain. I rocked backwards and forwards, willing the agony to hush and sleep. The sun beat down on me, penetrating my intestines.

I endured the pain for a few minutes. But I could not take any more. I called out for Layth. This was no time to feel embarrassed about my digestion problems.

'I... need the... oooh... toilet...' I managed to croak out a sentence amidst groans and moans.

'We can't stop.' He shook his head resolutely. 'We're in the middle of nowhere. The bus driver won't stop. You'll have to wait till we get back to Mina.'

'No... please,' my breathing laboured, like a woman giving birth.

'I'm sorry, we're only half an hour away,' apologetically.

'Aaaaaargh...' *Half an hour!* The conversations the rest were making blurred into a hum in my head. The buzzing of a wasp. I tensed myself with all the energy I had, fighting against the powerful natural urges to just let go. Just let go. Throwing my head into my lap I bit into my knee, unable to bear the pain. Excessive blood lingered in my head. An explosion of stars danced before my clenched eyes. The sweat from my efforts drenched my clothes. Sudden stop of my heart. Sudden start again. Pounding. The churning pain in my stomach, hitting every nerve in my body. My insides being repeatedly punched by Mike Tyson. I wanted to scream out as loud as I could. Release the pain or at least let out the coughs that were itching at my throat. *Keep control. Keep control. If I don't die from a brain haemorrhage from this, I'm going to pass out right now.*

It was, by far, the most excruciating and ruthless stomach pain I have ever had and it was the longest bus ride ever. I silently prayed that the unbearable agony would end or the bus would stop or even crash and put an end to it all.

Amid my prolonged deafness, I faintly heard my mother tell me that we had arrived. Raising my glazed eyes I saw the haze of the white and red camps of Mina. I would have cried for joy if my bowel would not have given way.

'We're nowhere near our camp. Don't drop us off here!' Layth protested to the bus driver.

I don't give a crap if this is our camp or not! I hopped to the front of the bus, jumped off and ran into a random tent.

The flesh of Hooria ran past me. 'I'm dying!' She screamed out.

Like lunatics on the hunt for crack, we frantically searched for the toilets. Once found, we tore past the queuing women and rattled the doors of the cubicles until someone came out. Inside, I slammed the door shut and let out a quiet whimper. The whimper of a battered kitten that had eaten a plagued fish.

***

'We're lost.' Layth admitted once I re-joined them.

'Great...' *You're a guide, how can you say that??*

We had been dropped off at camp number 126K. Logic would say that to get to camp 43B, our camp, we would have to walk past 126J and keep following in the descending order. But that would be logic. There was no logic here. The camps, seemingly, had no particular order in which they had been numbered. To the immediate left of us was camp 12R, to the immediate right of was camp 114B, and behind us were camps 56C-58K. The camps were scattered as though a five-year old had been the architect.

At first it was puzzling. Then absurd. And soon it became downright annoying.

We trotted laboriously in the squelching heat around the vast and incessant maze. Sometimes we walked in circles, sometimes we walked in straight lines and other times we walked backwards.

Hooria, I and now a couple of others, including my mother, gate crashed many camp toilets in between our trek to answer the cries of our food poisoning.

An hour passed when we spotted a loitering Saudi official, who directed us to our camp. There was a large, red balloon that floated in the sky, above our camp that had apparently been set there for our recognition purposes. No one had bothered to mention this to us before.

***

'Take only what you need, nothing too valuable as your backpacks might be ripped off by the crowds.' It was time for the stoning ritual and Layth was giving us a quick pep talk.

I gaped at him, shocked by his unabashed choice of words.

'Here, wear this,' urged Iraj. She handed me a pink flower-print scarf.

'Erm are we allowed to swap headscarves? I thought when in ihram we have to wear the same clothes unless they got dirty?' I had not changed out of my clothes for almost three days now, despite the buckets of sweat they had soaked in and the spades of rubble they had rolled in. But I did not feel unclean. I had performed ablution almost ten times within that period.

'Shush. We're gonna need to distinguish ourselves from the crowds. Look your mum is doing it too, I gave her that blue one.' My mother had swapped her white headscarf for a blue printed one. Iraj and Aliyah wore red printed scarves. The men had no choice but to remain in their two white sheets. I was not sure that we were permitted to change into such colourful cloths on our heads either.

But I took it from her without any further questions and made the swap. I would rather have worn this distasteful granny scarf than be lost amongst millions of pilgrims in the middle of nowhere.

I also took my bright pink backpack and filled it with water bottles, Arabian energy bars and my Hajj guide book. My pouch full of pebbles was wrapped around my wrist.

'Are we ready to do this?' Layth spoke to us all but looked at me directly.

My fight and flight psyches roused. My mind told me to run. To run as fast as I could away from the life-threatening perils that were imminent and into the safety of my feather-filled duvet. *'Take the next flight back to England!'* But my heart prodded me like an irritating 'good-advice' friend urging me to do this or live forever in regret of my cowardliness. *Are you a coward??* It taunted me, dared me.

No, I'm not ready for this…

…But I'm not a coward either.

Always a follower of my intuitive heart; I gritted my chattering teeth and sucked in the deepest of breaths. 'Let's do this.'

18

'I DON'T WANT TO die.'

The scene outside the camp instantly tinged with heavy darkness. As though looking through brown shades. We walked past camps as pilgrims filtered out and joined the rapidly growing pack that was marching towards the Jamarat; the place of the pillars. The more that joined the pilgrim river, the faster the current became.

'Be brave!' Layth shouted above the growing rumble. Layth, although a small man, was as macho as they came. Taking giant, splitting strides, puffing his chest out as much as his torso allowed him to and holding his head high above his shoulders. I, on the other hand, with my rattling chest, walked tentatively behind him; eyes darting in all directions, like a squirrel looking out for foxes.

There were only fifteen of us who followed him. The rest, who had not caught the same bus as us, had not yet arrived in Mina. Layth reassured us that they would find their way and cope on their own – his guide skills to be debated once more.

Five minutes and not yet out of the campsite – my clothes had become totally drenched in sweat. The heat of the sun scorched my skin, my apprehension simmered underneath it.

'Keep reciting Labbaik!' shouted Layth over his shoulder. Labbaik was actually supposed to be recited throughout the whole journey of Hajj but I do not think many remembered this. I certainly did not amidst the drama of each day.

Once we had scuttled out of the camp site we found ourselves heading towards a wide and open dusty track, lined with small buildings. These marbled buildings were protected from the crowds by waist-high steel bollards on either side of the track. The rails sickeningly reminded me of those that farmers erected to reign in their cattle and sheep. The existence of these barricades spoke clear words.

I reeled in dismay at the enormity of the crowds ahead.

Thousands upon thousands of pilgrims appeared out of nowhere. White sheets, white robes, brown, black, white faces, coloured headscarves, blue headbands. Barely dots in the scene. Some leaders raised flags in the air for identification purposes. Small groups clung onto to each other like leeches – for dear life. They wore only sandals or slippers to walk on the sandy track but each step caused the rumbling of an earthquake. The roars of 'LABBAIK ALLAH HUMMAH LABBAIK!!' were fierce, making the chants during a Manchester United and Liverpool football match seem like meek whispers.

These were not the same pilgrims I saw in Mina, Mudzalifah or Mecca. These were frightening, seemingly possessed pilgrims whom I no longer recognised. Dangerous, uncontrollable and worst of all, unpredictable. Their passion was as ferocious as the burning sun above us. Their fear, erratic as the movement of their eyes.

Needing immediate comfort, I reached out for my mother's hand. Her widened eyes flickered, left to right. *Fear.* She had the same fear in her eyes as I had. I turned to find my father's hand. His brown face was dripping with streams of perspiration. His expression did nothing to ease my anxiety.

'LABBAIK!!!'

The thudding grew heavier with every second. The chanting wilder. Streams upon streams of pilgrims joined to form one thick consuming river. The space between our neighbours became tighter and we were soon packed closer than the teeth on a nit comb. Hundreds of thousands behind us pressured us into quickening our pace as the steel banks rattled precariously. All three million pilgrims were now out. And they were all out to stone one small pillar.

The air humid with both tension and passion. A smell lingered above us, raw sand, mammal odour. Blood.

'Hold onto each other!' shouted Layth.

We formed our train.

This no longer felt like reality. It was more of an imminent nightmare. I turned around and saw an endless mass of crowds behind me. There was no turning back. I had jumped the cliff and was about to plunge into the sea. Whether I would swim or drown; only time would tell.

'LABBAIK!!'

We marched.

How much longer to walk, I dared not stop to wonder. My

headscarf began to slip off but I did not venture to free my hands for a second to uphold my modesty. I sinned to save my life.

'Everyone hold on to each other!' bellowed Layth. The crowds surged abruptly. My body was thrown from side to side by the ferocious ripples.

'LABBAIK ALLAH HUMMA LABBAIK!' A group of four young, middle-eastern men came charging from behind. Shouting with one hand raised in the air and the other firmly on their companion's shoulder. They stormed past like horses on a race track, fuelled by zeal and fervour. Running on adrenaline, one bumped me with his elbow recklessly.

A powerful jolt. It knocked my grip off Daania's shoulder.

Like a slow motion movie the surge of crowds washed past me as I momentarily stilled.

Nails dug into my shoulder. I spun around and saw that it was just me and my parents left. We had lost the rest.

'Amee! Where are they amee, where are they??' Amee means 'mother' in Punjabi and I only ever used the word when I was petrified. Usually during nightmares.

Frantically, I searched for the group amongst the indistinguishable bobbing heads trooping forwards.

'DAD! Find them!' crying out.

'LABBAIK!!'

He shot me a worried look. Without the guidance of Layth we knew we would not be able to complete the remaining tasks.

'ALLAH HUMMA LABBAIK!'

'INNAL HAMDAH!'

'Over there!' shouted my father. On his toes, he pointed his hand to a place ahead of us, a few yards away. I inhaled and stepped on my toes too. Iraj's and Aliyah's red heads bobbed up and down. They did not turn around once. They probably had not noticed us gone. Or, more likely, resorted to the philosophy of 'eat or be eaten'.

If we lose sight of them I doubt we'll ever see them again.

The thought of tearing through this unruly and thick crowd to get to them was as despairing as considering the possibility of running through a metal fence. My father took control and pulled me and my mother by our hands. I yelped as I was dragged forwards. His hold reminding me of the time when I was eight years old and almost slipped down the stairs of a shopping centre.

'WA NIH MATA!'

He pulled us diagonally through the crowd with such determination that had the rest not had the same determination they would have jumped out of the way and opened a pathway for him. But they did not. So instead we broke through the hard bodies, shoved others out of the way, and squeezed through the tightest of channels.

'LAKA WUL MULK!!'

'LA SHAREEEKA LA!'

A big group of African women were trooping forwards at our left. We were slightly ahead of them. *Oh crap.* I knew my father was going to try and cut past them before they reached us. The look of stone on these large footed, big boned women made me cower in dread.

My father managed to move past them avoiding a collision. My mother got through too. I wavered a little. Cringing when I saw that they were charging faster, relentlessly. My father's arm outstretched on one end, mine outstretched on the other, as the African tribe met us and attempted to break our hold.

'LABBAIK!!!' One of the women screamed in a wild passion that rattled my ears. My arm stretched longer than it physically was as my father tried to yank me through the, now closed, gap between the black woman and the person in front of her.

'AAAARGH!!!!!' My elbow popped. A sharp pain shot through my arm.

The African was sturdy and unyielding. She would not let me through.

'DAD! LET GO!' My ligaments stretched to a gruelling degree. The pain unbearable. If he did not let go of my hand right then, it would rip it off my wrist.

'LABBAIK!!'

'LET GO!' screaming again. Tears of pain bled from my eyes. He could not hear me. *Is he out of his mind?!*

'MY ARM!!' I shrieked, rupturing my throat.

'AAAAARGH!!! LET ME THROUUUGGHHHHH!!!!' Squeezing my eyes shut I punched the busty woman with all the energy I had. She staggered to the side for a brief second and I ran through the gap. Almost toppling to the ground, my father caught me.

'My arm! Dad! My frigging arm!' shoving his hand off me, I blew on my limb before bursting into tears. Frustration, pain, stress.

'ALLAH HUMA!!'

'Shush! Keep moving!' The herd was not going to stop for us. He took hold of my elbow and pushed us through the crowds again. I succumbed in surrender and allowed my resigned body to be manoeuvred by him. He carried us through human trains, broke through groups, squeezed through gaps. Our robes ripped, our feet trodden on, our ribs jabbed.

Breathless, sweaty, exhausted and feeling as though I had been trampled on by twenty elephants, we finally reached our group. Layth had not realised we were missing.

I pulled Daania's shoulder towards me using my good hand and clawed my nails into her flesh. Determined not to be parted again. I winced, as my mother in turn dug her fingers into mine.

'Another thirty minutes or so to the pillar!' Layth shouted. *Thirty minutes!* Almost an hour had already passed. The hair under my scarf dripped in perspiration like wet laundry. In contrast my tongue felt like tree bark. My eyes abutted from their sockets aspiring towards pivotal vision. Meanwhile, the chants of 'LABBAIK' boomed in my ears unrelentingly. All this on top of my fever-filled chest infection.

We approached a tunnel and my heart plummeted upon seeing the width of it. A semi-circle construction of grey concrete narrower than the breadth of the track we were on. Inside, a gloomy dark grey, lit by harsh fluorescent lights and air conditioned by reverberating fans. Pilgrims were compressed as they forced themselves through the entrance of the tunnel.

'ALLAH HUMMA!!!'

Layth led us to the edges of the pilgrim river before he charged through the opening. The swell of crowds pushed me to the right. My hand declawed from Daania's shoulder and my mother's hand kicked off mine. In a blink the strangers surrounding me swept past. I saw my mother turn around and gape at me in silence as they engulfed her and I lost her.

'LABBAIK!!'

A group of pilgrims gushed from behind and threw me forwards. I yelped in pain as my foot was crushed by a giant man.

In sweeping devastation, I was dragged into the channel by the rest of the pilgrims.

Inside, I span around in all directions looking for someone remotely familiar. The sound of each footstep, each chant, magnified ten times with the echoes. My head whirled like a tornado carrying with it anxiety and panic. Immersed in an overflowing river of complete strangers who were determinedly reciting 'LABBAIK!' Unpredictable, madly chanting, fixated strangers. Chinese, Black, African, Arabian, Asian, White; all foreigners.

The blood drained from my face.

I'm lost.

Oh my Lord, silently crying, walking forwards, *I'm lost. I am lost! I've no idea where I am. No phone. Money. Can't speak Arabic. I'll never complete Hajj. Forget that, I'll never return home. I'll never see my family again. These people will crush me. Will mum mourn for me? Oh my God, what if mum is killed here!*

'AMEEE!! DAD!!!!!!!!!' I screamed and ran forwards, not caring if my ribs were bashed or toes trodden on.

A man with a beard. A grey beard, just like my fathers. I gasped. I ran towards him. Then stopped. He was larger than my father. It was not him. With hope I looked on at the back of a lady, a white robe, a flowery coloured scarf, like my mothers. I ran. And stopped, crestfallen. She was not as chubby as my mother. I saw a little lady to the left of me. She wore a blue back pack and a white robe just like Hooria. I stared at her with hopeful eyes. It was not her. Grey beards like my father's, bald heads like Layth's, women wearing robes like my mother, women wearing backpacks like Hooria; but all of them transpired to be complete strangers.

'Oh Lord, no! Please no!' searching in vain. *Are they looking for me? Will they wait for me? Have they all been separated?* My mother's final panic stricken face flashed in my mind before she had been taken away by the crowds. *She's weak. Has she fallen? Has she been crushed?*

'LABBAIK! ALLAH HUMA!!'

As more and more strangers surrounded me and the more I searched, the more hysterical I became. The more I feared a tragic and traumatic end to this. For all of us.

'Oh God.' Fear. Dehydration. Even my tears had dried up. 'Oh Allah! Please reunite me with my family.' I pleaded. I remembered the prayer I prayed when I was lost in Mina. 'Inna lillahi wa ina illayhi raajiun,' whispering in a voice that was drowned out by the grumble of the air-conditioning fans above me.

'Inna lillahi wa ina illayhi raajiun.' I repeated, wavering. I had never felt so lost. It felt worse than the time when I had got lost at the Birmingham carnival at the age of three.

'Have trust in Allah', my mother had said.

'To you we belong Allah and to you we will return.' I said again with more determination.

God, for goodness sake, I'm here for you so please don't do this to me! I stared out, ignoring the reverberations, chants, prods.

Moments passed.

No sign.

I watched a small hand bobbing in the air a few metres ahead of me. I gazed down and saw the back of a short podgy lady. She wore a blue flowery headscarf. She turned around with her mouth opened wide. Her face glistening.

Mum!

My heart skipped a beat. Relief surged through my legs. She was with the rest of the group.

A current of electricity lifted me off the ground and I sprinted with an almighty power. I tore through the hundreds of pilgrims between me and her. I pushed through huge fat men, without fear. Shoved through the tight little Filipino trains without a moment of hesitancy. Stepped on toes recklessly, without shifting my gaze away from my companions.

'Amee!!' I threw myself onto her.

'Thank you Allah, thank you Allah,' she panted, raising her lustreless face upwards to the ceiling of the tunnel. She squeezed my arm and gave me an angry look as she paced forwards. 'Why did you leave us?!'

'I didn't mum, I didn't!' shouting. 'I want to go home!' I really wanted to go home. I could not take the stress of this ritual, which had not even begun. I just wanted to sit in my living room, in front of the TV, with a cup of hot chocolate and watch Friends. *Oh, how I miss such normal pleasures.*

'LABBAIK!!!'

'Keep hold of each other!' Layth scolded. 'Don't let anyone push you apart! Be strong!'

Be strong. I wrapped the end of Daania's long headscarf around my wrist for extra security and vowed not to let go of anyone now, even if was at the risk of having my hands hacked off.

'LA SHAREEKA LA!!'

My legs craved for rest. I realised that we had not stopped moving for even a second throughout. Had we stopped, the consequences would have been grave; a trampling. The more we walked, the louder and fiercer the crowds became. The fiercer they became, the edgier I became and the more I struggled to stay upright.

'LABBAIK!!'

Why are these people so bloody scary? And they're all scared of each other!

The other men in my group, which did not include Mikaeel, let the sweat stream down their faces and did nothing to hide their anxious expressions. They ran after Layth erratically, shoved each other mindlessly. These were men. Big men.

Bravely, I took quick glances at the faces of other pilgrims. They all had the alertness and apprehension about them as I had. But some possessed something else.

Excitement.

They bellowed 'LABBAIK' and marched with a passion for the coming task. Thrilled at the prospect of stoning Satan. Eager to hurt him with their pebbles. Satan – man's biggest enemy.

Is it some sort of revenge?

A line of men surged past us, on their toes, holding up a white flag, yelling 'LABBAIK!!!' in unison. Their leader, a broad white man, had his fist in the air. His stubbly face dripped with large globules of sweat. A high-voltage charge in his eyes – anxiety, passion. Anger. *Anger?*

Anger.

Fuelled with rage. These people stomped harder than they should, shouted louder than they normally would, punched the air unnecessarily.

They were angry at Satan.

Satan; who had vowed to lead everyone astray and drag them to hell with him. Satan; the most evil of kinds. More wicked than Hitler. More contemptible than a serial killer. More sinister than a paedophile. More malicious than that person who has committed the most horrendous crime in the world.

'LA SHAREEKA LA!!'

I had never thought of it in this way, but now it kind of made sense. They saw him as the most evil because he was the one that drove people to commit evil. The leader. The one who whispers in the ears of murderers and lures them into killing. Tempts paedophiles into carrying out sickening acts. These marching people were angry with him for making them commit sin and leading them to hell. Angrier with him than they would be with the killer of their daughter or mother.

He's tried to take me to hell too. Gritting my teeth, my blood temperature hit boil. *He's made me do all those bad things that God is now punishing me for. It wasn't my fault, it was his. Bastard!*

'LABBAIK, ALLAH HUMMA LABBAIK!'

He took me to that piece of turd, Zameer! Satan played tricks on me. Told me Allah was nasty and led me to sin promising me happiness. There was no flaming happiness! Just misery! Bastard!

'LA SHAREEKA LA!!'

He made me suffer God's punishment. Caused this depression. Destroyed me. Made me cry all those nights. Made me feel like I couldn't go on. And he'll continue to give me more misery, until I die, and after I die! Bastard!

'INNAL HAMDAH! WAH NIH MATA! LAKA WUL MULK!'

How dare he! Who does he think he is??

'LA SHAREEKA LA!'

Fuming, I clenched my jaw. Tightened my grip on the pouch containing the stones. 'LABBAIK ALLAH HUMMA LABBAIK!!' I shouted out. My breaths became heavier with contempt. My nostrils flared with fury. My heart beat with wrath. Red splashed my vision. I wanted his blood.

I was nudged again. But I remained calm. These people were not the ones to be angry at. They were like me. Wanted to beat Satan. They did not intend malice or hurt; I was sure. We all had the same purpose. Satan was the one to be angry at. We were part of a team. United. On a mission to fight the same evil. These were my friends. He was the enemy.

'I hate him... he will not take me down with him, never!' shouting out aloud. *I will throw these stones at him and hear him cry.* I stomped my feet rocking the earth and quickened my pace. Now desperate to get at him, becoming impatient. The longer I had to wait the more my anger rose. I was burning so much that I wanted to run. I wanted to run past all these people, leave my group and push through to get to the pillar and throw my stones at the devil. *'He screams every time a stone is thrown at the pillars',* Layth had said. I wanted to hear him shriek like a dying witch.

'We're here! The pillars are in there!' Layth pointed to another, larger tunnel metres away from us. This grey industrial channel had two entrances, separated by huge concrete blocks.

We entered the tunnel. Each footstep echoed tenfold. The roar of the pilgrims created the sound of hundreds of electricity generators clashing together. The tension grinded. Paces quickened. Nerves heightened.

My fear, my excitement, my anger, had climbed the mountain of emotions and reached the peak. Adrenaline drummed my heart but dread laboured my breaths.

'Get your stones ready in your hands!' shouted Layth as he slowed down a little. 'There is one pillar to hit today! The third one! The furthest! Throw seven pebbles at it with your right hand and say Allahu akbar each time you throw! After you've thrown seven then come to the side, raise your hands, make a prayer and wait for me! Is everyone clear?'

Breathless, we nodded.

'Come out as quickly as possible, don't hang around in the crowds or you'll be crushed! Ok?!'

'God, help me.' I whispered earnestly.

Layth made a 'follow me' gesture with his hands and we scurried behind him closely, tightly holding onto each other.

'LABBAIK!!'

Thousands upon thousands of pilgrims rushed towards a large block of concrete, past two other concrete blocks on the right. It was the third pillar. It did not look like the pillar I imagined it to be. It was a block of white and grey stone, a few metres wider than it was taller and with little depth. A few short metres from this pillar was a large circular wall that surrounded it, shoulder's length high and acting as a barrier.

A blur of crowds had gathered around the wall throwing stones at it with an intimidating fury. They scrambled on top of each other to get a good shot. Or even just a shot.

'Oh God...' I cried out meekly. Hundreds of thousands at the back of the mass plummeted forwards, pushing relentlessly through gaps that did not exist whilst others who had thrown their stones pushed in the other direction, struggling to get out. Ladies, old weak ladies, were squashed by herds of people around them, as they tried to get further inside to stone or to get out of the chaos.

This is the death trap.

A thought infiltrated my mind and I became paralysed in horror. *It is right here that so many people have died as they went to throw their stones.* Crushed by the very same people who had the same fear as those that were about to meet their death.

Unwillingly, my imagination conjured a horrific scene in my mind. Influenced by the horror stories I had heard from witnesses and the media on the tragedies of this place. More influenced by Daania's graphic story-telling the night before.

***

An old lady of the age of sixty. Maria. It is her first Hajj. Her life-long Hajj ambition is finally becoming a reality. She goes in on the third day to do the obligatory; to throw her stones at the pillar.

She feels a sudden squeeze as bodies from behind her and in front collide and press into her remorselessly. She screams out loud. Uses all her might to push the pressing figures away. But the force of thousands of frantic, confused, scared people is too great. She feels a snap. Then several snaps. Her ribs break one by one from the weight of pilgrims. She screeches in pain as her ribs are pushed into her lungs. Pebbles fall out of her hand. She screams again, a terrifying gut wrenching scream as she sees her life flash before her eyes. Her heart tightens. Then stops. Maria is dead.

Her lifeless body is pushed from one person to the next. No one perhaps knows she is dead, or if they do, they realise they cannot do anything without being crushed too. Maria's headscarf is dragged off her head. Her face, limp. Her eyes bulge out. Her mouth and nose seep with blood. Then her heavy body finally finds a space to fall and as it is shoved from one person to the next and as knees knock into her face, it finally hits the ground. Hundreds of thousands of people trample on her body. On her face. On her stomach. On her chest.

Her son is frantically looking for her. He knew he should have held on to her hand tighter. Should have protected her with his body. He cannot find her. He keeps looking, swept with panic.

She is found five hours later when the crowds have dispersed. Half naked and unrecognisable amongst the others that lay strewn on the floor.

***

Traumatised. A tear rolled down my cheek and a painful lump of terror emerged in my throat.

'Stop!' I shouted. My imagination would not stop.

Why am I doing this to myself??

I wanted to slap my face. Slap it so hard and get these shocking thoughts out of my head. I regretted reading those witness accounts on the internet and listening to Daania's ghastly stories the night before. My mind consumed with those thoughts, leaving me motionless with terror. I could not move.

Is this what awaits me? Will this happen to mum? Dad?

'Come on!' My father pushed me forward when he saw I had stopped. My legs would not move. I whimpered as I resisted his push.

No.

I wanted to run back. I wanted to run, run, run three thousand miles all the way home. I shot my head around and saw a stampede surging towards me. I would have met my death if I ran back. There was no turning back.

'LABBAIK!!'

Recalling the feeling when I had been pressured into sitting on the Oblivion at Alton Towers by my friends. Strapped in with the 'start' button pressed, I wanted to jump off the ride and leap for the exit, but I had no choice but to meet the 90 degree drop.

'Oh God please help me.' That scenario was different. That theme park ride was over with in an instant and I was pretty sure that I would not die.

I clung tightly onto my mother and father and entered the tumult. My group was still close but not everyone held onto each other anymore. That was now impossible. The anger I had felt towards Satan disappeared and was replaced with an intensely crumbling fear of death.

'LABBAIK!!'

I fumbled for my seven stones and got them ready in my wet hand.

We edged closer to the pillar. I felt the squeeze of the bodies. People thrust past, knocking us with their elbows and hands desperate to get the frenzied moment out of the way.

'ALLAH HUMMA!!'

Ten metres away. I took a deep breath and took the plunge into the core of the crowds.

The noise drowned out and the scene blurred as I became immersed in this moment of madness. The crush of torsos immediately took my breath away. Some came outwards from the pillar having thrown their stones. Others pushed inwards, stones clutched in their hands. A huge collision of bodies. I used all my strength to fight the powerful currents.

Miraculously, I neared the edge of the circular wall. I did not turn around to see if my parents were with me but only hoped that they were. There were a couple of rows of people ahead of me but I was a sufficient distance from the pillar and got ready to throw my stones.

Body tensed to resist the squeeze, I stood still.

With my shaking hand I held one stone and raised my arm in the air.

A vision of a horned red devil standing at the pillar. Dancing. Taunting me. Laughing at what he had put me through.

The anger for him raced through my body, parallel with fear. With both these feelings at their peak, they threw me into a subliminal state of mind.

It was now just me and him.

'ALLAH HU AKBAR!' I shrieked and threw my first pebble. It hit the huge pillar. I imagined the devil yelping in pain as a part of him was kicked out of my heart. 'It is you who lead me astray!' muttering through clenched teeth.

'Allahu akbar!' I threw the second pebble. A bewildering ecstasy. 'It's because of you I've suffered so much pain!' I was blazing.

There was no time to pause.

Third stone thrown. More confidence. 'It is you who drove people to murder!' My body liberated of my rage towards him. It was remarkably satisfying. Better than throwing my fists at a punch bag during PMS.

Fourth stone. 'It is you who started paedophilia!' A stone knocked the side of my temple. Screaming, I lent forwards as the pain rattled through my head. Someone had a bad shot.

Quickly refocusing, fifth stone. I accidentally knocked the person ahead of me on the head with my hand and felt a pain shoot through my fingers.

Sixth stone, 'it is you who has made it your duty to send me to hell!'

Furious.

'IT IS YOU WHO HAS MADE IT YOUR DUTY TO SEND EVERYONE TO HELL!!' Letting out an angry screech, I lunged forwards and threw the last stone.

My chest heaved with fury. I wanted to throw more. I wanted to hurl my slippers and those sandals that lay strewn on the ground at him.

With a sadistic delight fuelled by psychotic adrenalin, I watched a few of the twenty one million pebbles smash against the pillar. Twenty one million. If Satan did indeed feel the force of each pebble then surely he would have died three million times over.

'GET OUT!' My father shouted from a distance.

'Shit...'

The moment of ecstasy, as with all moments of ecstasy, did not last long. My feet firmly back on the hard ground. The roars louder than ever. The crowd glared at me with the intensity of gigantic, thunderous clouds. Having turned around, my passion quickly abandoned me and was replaced with cowardliness. Thousands of fiery heads bobbed before me. I was not sure how to get out. I held my arms out to protect my body and pushed forwards.

'ALLAHU AKBAR!!' they screamed in my ear.

Somehow I ended up in the middle when I should have been on the side. Herds pushed me backwards. I looked around in despair. *Amee? Dad*?

My foot was trampled on repeatedly, I restrained the futile yells. A powerful wave of people suddenly threw me backwards. I instinctively screamed out as the weight of the gorilla bodies pressed onto me. I struggled to take in air.

'ALLAHU AKBAR!!'

'No, no, no...' I clenched my hands into fists and just as I was about to lethally push against the swarm, a hand wrapped around my arm and began to drag me sideward.

Dad!

It was when I was being tugged away by my father that I spotted an old man a few feet away from me on the floor. My face numbed. He was alive but trembling as he cowered, raising his arms over his face to shield it from the scrambling legs that were already over the rest of his body.

'DAD! PICK HIM UP! PICK HIM UP!!' I shouted hysterically, pulling back. *This man cannot die before my eyes.* In vain I outstretched my weak arm. But I did not move from my spot. If I went to him and knelt to pick him up then I will have created my own death trap. 'No!' whispering in despair. 'DAD!' I turned to my strong dad, pleading with him to help this man. More people climbed over him. My father had not seen him or heard me and drew me in the other direction.

It was only a few seconds but it had slowed down to a painful pace.

It was like watching someone drown whilst stood on the shore because you do not know how to swim.

His face remained obscure. Except for his eyes. His eyes

cowered, submissively. He had given up. I stared at him in horror. 'No.' *This old man will be crushed to death.* 'Oh Allah, make him alright!' was all I could say. Helpless, I could only give him a prayer.

In that wretched moment I was nudged, powerfully. The grip I had on my pouch released and I watched it fall to the floor.

I gasped.

I do not know why.

I panicked.

I do not know why.

There were only two or three spare pebbles in there and a small Hajj guide.

But panic I did and, with a hint of insanity, I bent down, jerking my arm from my father's grip.

I do not know why.

Perhaps it was a reflex action or perhaps it was because the Hajj guide contained the names of Allah and I had always been told that the name of Allah requires so much respect that nothing that contains those words should be put on the floor. Maybe I did not want millions of people treading on his name.

I do not know.

Whatever it was, recklessly, I reached down to pick it up.

It was right beside me and I managed to grasp it with my fingers. Before I had the chance to straighten up, I was knocked from behind.

This time I fell to the ground.

My knees cracked like a glass vase. My hands grazed, painfully.

A turbulent whirling roar gushed into my ears. Hundreds upon hundreds of feet, legs, lost sandals consumed my sight. I whimpered as I was kicked in all directions. I tried to scream. Feet trod on my hands. I squeezed my eyes shut, in pain. I willed myself to try and get up.

But I could not move.

My body froze.

I'm going to die.

I'm going to die right here.

***

Death. The most avoided topic. But the only inevitable event for every person. The topic that I hate to think about, hate to talk about.

Yet, ironically, if there is only one thing in life that is certain, it is death.

No one could tell me what death felt like. No dead person could describe death for me. There were no real life accounts. Only descriptions of it in the Quran and other books.

They say that Angel Izrael, a huge terrifying angel, will come to extract my soul from my body. The angels of mercy and punishment will surround me in those final moments. If I had lived my life as a good Muslim, my soul will be extracted with ease and taken away respectfully by the angels of mercy. If I had lived my life as a bad Muslim then my soul will be ripped out of me agonisingly and the angels of punishment will take my soul away in disgrace.

And my body – my dead body will be washed by my family, just like I had seen the body of my grandma being washed.

I was twenty one years old and my mother, a couple of my aunties and I, had gone to the mosque where her body had been placed temporarily. I was curious. In the back yard of the mosque under the grim night sky, my mother and aunties stripped off her shalwar kameez, removed all her gold jewellery and placed her naked body in a cold metal tub. They poured chilled water over her colourless skin and washed her with their hands in the deadly silence. They washed her long, grey hair whilst she lay like a mannequin. A dead person. Only the splashes of water were heard. And the odd sniffle. I watched in shock and terror as my grandma, who only days ago smiled and laughed with me over custard cake, was now suddenly nothing but a cold dead body. Her seventy six years of life had now come to this; three women exposing her and cleansing her one final time. Did she feel them washing her? Was the water too cold? Was she embarrassed at these younger women looking at her? Or was she someplace else?

I lay awake for nights after that. Shaken.

What shook me more was knowing that this is what will happen to my body. That is if I was lucky enough to have a respectable death, unlike some whose bodies lay in dirty ditches or in mutilated scraps. This body, which I valued so much, will soon be washed, by God knows who, with freezing cold water. And then I will be shrouded in strips of white cloth, revealing only my face. Just like my sister was.

'Nooooooo!!! Please noo!!!!' I scream hysterically. I have just seen Nafeesa's body in her coffin. Her face tightly bound in a white

shroud. Her whole body wrapped like an Egyptian mummy.

She lies there, in the middle of my living room, lifeless. Grey face. Sunken eyes. I do not recognise her amidst my shrieks.

It cannot be real.

Only yesterday she twirled me around on this spot.

I heave uncontrollably and try to reach her. To shake her. Tell her to wake up. To stop this.

The others attempt to pull me back.

I go to climb into her coffin. I will go with her. Without her I am alone. I have no one.

'Please tell her to wake up... please. I beg you all.'

My aunty covers my eyes and drags me away.

The screams of a wild animal ring in my ear as the image of her skeletal face implants itself in my memory.

I need her to tell me it is all a nightmare. For her to wrap her arms around me in our bed and tell me to go back to sleep.

Without her, I am alone. Without me, she is alone.

That would be me one day. My family will mourn my death. Gather around my coffin and cry. Pray that I go to heaven. Just like we prayed for Nafeesa – she would go to heaven anyway as she was still an unaccountable child.

My body will be carried to the graveyard in the cold night. Perhaps by my father, brothers, future sons. And then I will be buried six feet underground whilst those who loved me mourn.

Would I feel the heavy, wet soil be thrown onto my coffin until it completely covers it? Would I feel the darkness? Would I beg them not to leave me alone as I hear their footsteps walk away from me?

Alone.

For months following Nafeesa's death I worried for her loneliness. They would not let me go to her grave again because of the last screeching incident. I was convinced that she was still alive in her grave. Hungry. Thirsty. Several times I did not eat my Snickers bars during school lunch and instead saved them and put them in her purple coat pocket – which still hung in the garage – when I got home. Just in case she got hungry. And her favourite sweets too, strawberry Chewits, which I specifically bought for her. She had always spent her money too quickly, so I put 70p in her pocket too. She would never get home without money. I worried for her. My mother eventually took the coat away.

All alone in my grave I would be too. But they say that would not be it. Death would be no respite. That is where the real events of my existence would begin.

Shortly after my loved ones leave me, two angels will then rip through the earth. Black in colour and made of fire. More frightening than death, they will shake and rattle me to awaken. They will ask me three questions.

Who is your Lord? What is your religion? And who is your prophet?

If I had been an abiding Muslim I will be able to answer those questions with confidence. If I do, then Allah will say to the angels, *'My servant has said the truth. Lay the tablecloth of Paradise for her. Give her clothes from Paradise to wear and open the doors of Paradise for her'.* The cool air and the sweet fragrance of heaven will tantalise my senses and my grave will be made wide and large. The angels will say, *'sleep like a queen sleeps'.*

If I was not a good Muslim then I will be unable to answer those three questions, even if I knew the answers in my lifetime. Allah will say, *'she has not said the truth! Lay the table-cloth of fire for her, and give her clothes of fire to wear and open the doors of Hell for her, from which the heat of Hell will reach her'.* My grave would crush me with such intensity that my bones on the right side of me will end up on my left side and the bones on my left side will end up on the right. There will be two Angels who will give me relentless punishment with hard objects, scorpions, snakes, until the horrors of the Day of Judgment arrive – which might be an hour away or a trillion years away. Who is to know?

***

'I DON'T WANT TO DIE!!!!!' I screamed out, unexpectedly finding my voice.

A desire no one could fulfil. Ever.

'AAAHH!' letting out another scream, I was jerked backwards. I felt my robe rip on the shoulders. My head shot upwards and I was lifted off the ground.

Dad! He wrapped his arms around me whilst I rested limp with my pouch clutched in my hand, and pulled us out of the savage sea of pilgrims.

'TAKE ME HOME! THIS IS CRAZY!!' sobbing, I pleaded with my father. My mother put her arms around me as I hopped from the pain of my flattened toes. My headscarf had come undone and she wrapped it around my face again.

'Come on! Hurry! Raise your hands and make a prayer of forgiveness for being a slave to Satan.' Layth gathered us in a less congested area.

Raising my quivering hands up in the air obediently, I snivelled 'oh Allah, I have beaten Satan out of my heart and mind, please forgive me for my sins.' This was no place for reflection.

***

Motionless and numb I sat on the quiet edges inside the tunnel and looked out blankly. Two tears lay still in my eyes. My robe was tattered as though I had just fought fifty lions. My feet bled having gone through all kinds of torture. And my arms lay numb and limp.

Traumatised, was a word that did no justice. I could not even cry with relief. Or scream in frustration. Or laugh with exhilaration. Or thank God for getting me out alive. I just stared at the chaos in the distance with no emotion whatsoever.

Layth was telling the others of the reasons why the stoning was so difficult. They had the same look on their faces as I had. I doubted anyone was listening to him except his wife.

'The authorities have made it a hell of a lot easier now. Five to ten years ago, the pillars were a lot smaller. About the size of a door and the system was a two way system. Do you see how people are throwing their pillars and walking to the left in one direction? Well, this system has only been introduced recently. Allah willing, they are intending to improve it further. They have spent billions of dollars already and have restricted the number of people allowed in the country to perform Hajj. How do you try to organise millions of people in this small area?? Impossible! Prophet Mohammad couldn't have envisaged this.'

I wonder what happened to that old man I saw.

'The risks are just something we have to put up with if we really want to do Hajj. Older people and women can now do the pelting later on, after noon or sunset when it's quieter. I don't know why most choose to do it at this time...'

Why didn't you tell me this before??

'In previous years, people would throw their stones and walk back the way they came, colliding with all those that were coming into the tunnel. Imagine the chaos! So many people died in those years, so many people were trampled to death. Once someone fell then that was it for them. The old and the weak did not stand a chance. When I did Hajj in those earlier years I would see dead bodies being dragged, people covered in blood, clothing being pulled off...'

Please stop.

The only movement that now came from me was the occasional shuddering as I watched the pillar.

If extreme anger, fear, excitement and nervousness are mixed together and multiplied by three million people from all kinds of countries and cultures then uncontrollable anarchy was inevitable. The violence and the tragedy that had taken place here over past years and what potentially might have happened here today was unfathomable.

Layth cleared his throat. 'But those people are very lucky,' he said.

I shot him an appalled look. I could not have imagined anything more terrifying and more tragic than such a death for that person and his or her family. It would be one horrible nightmare.

The eyes of that old man flashed in my mind again. *Did he come out alive? Or did he die? Was I the last person he saw before his soul was taken out of his chest?* The chill in my back, despite the heat, returned like a haunting plague.

'These people have died in such a way striving for Allah and have committed a form of jihad.' Layth continued. 'The more brutal the death, the more they have strived for Allah. They have also died whilst in the state of purity, ihram, and only a day after the day of Arafat, the big day of forgiveness. They will surely go straight to heaven. I am sure of it. I imagine these people will be transported to the highest platform of heaven. I imagine they will not suffer the pains of death and the grave as we may suffer.'

I guess everyone has to die one day. Better this way?
Death.

I had come so close to death.

Willingly.

Have I just risked my life for God?

I had never risked my life for anything or anyone, nor did I think I ever would. I had had no idea that this was what I would go through. *Allah had better repay me for this.*

But then, if he'd written for me to die today, there is nothing I could've done to stop it.

'Think of death all the time. Think of death all the time. Think of death all the time', were the repeated words of the pious people I had come across – which were not many, I must admit. But these few had a point.

In the hospital a few months ago, I had had a heart scan. Watching my heart on the monitor beat, like a small pump, with seeping amazement and slow chilling terror. *'This heart'*, I had said to the nurse. *'This heart, this delicate little ball of flesh and blood, is what keeps me alive. And if it stopped pumping I would instantly be dead'*. I realised then that if that little thing on the screen stopped beating I would be dead in an instant. That could be tomorrow.

And now I had a graver realisation.

I could die tomorrow and be full of regret. Realise the worthlessness of my short life and forever regret being a defiant Muslim.

Death, my dark grave, the Day of Judgment and an eternal hell were as close to me as my feet.

'Think of death all the time'. They have a point.

But how? How can I live my life with a reasonable degree of happiness if I thought about death all the time? How morbid. My friends would hate me. How do I get up in the morning? What would be the point of going to work if I'm thinking this could be my last day? Should I not spend my last day on a prayer mat?

'They are blessed,' said Layth. I had momentarily lost myself in my thoughts and looked at him with confusion until I remembered he was talking about those that had died besides the pillars.

I shook the questions from my head like I always did and avoided trying to answer the unanswerable.

I could not face it and I could not run away from it.

But I could pray. So I prayed that Allah, when he did decide it was time for me to die, ticked me off in the 'good Muslim' category and saved me from the pains of the grave, Judgment Day and hell.

I looked down at my feet.

One thing was for sure. I was hell scared of dying.

19

THE CONTRAST AT THE opposite end of the tunnel was bewildering. The number of pilgrims present remained the same but the chaos had disappeared.

People now walked leisurely as though the carnage that took place in the tunnel had never happened. Strangers to those hurried, blood thirsty mammals I saw only a few moments ago, they strolled like they had not a care in the world. The fire in their bodies, extinguished with exhaustion. The fear in their eyes turned to thoughtfulness. Angry expressions, now expressions of relief.

'We're going to have to walk to Mecca.' Layth told us shortly after we had offered our noon prayers on borrowed bin liners.

'And how far is that?' The muscles in my legs cried out.

'A few miles. Then we'll have to circulate the Kaba and walk the mountains of Safa and Marwa. Phew! We'll have walked twenty miles by the end of this!'

Twenty blistering miles in this blistering heat.

There was slight respite. The roads appeared to be wider and there was enough space to outstretch my arms. There was no chance of being elbowed in the ribs here. No bollards were erected to rein the crowds in either. There was even a parked truck containing free bottles of water for passing pilgrims.

Water was not enough for me. I needed medication for my chest infection, a cool shower, a soft bed and a toilet by my side for my reawakened stomach bug.

'Come on! Pull your strength together!' Layth barked at us all. We were dragging our feet as though marble rocks were attached to them.

Moments passed before I heard Layth bellow 'start the sacrifice!' down his mobile phone.

'What's he doing?' I asked Daania.

'He's calling the slaughter house now and asking them to

sacrifice an animal for each of us.'

'Oh, we aren't making the sacrifice ourselves?'

'Ha. Imagine that!'

A brief image of me bearing a knife and a blood-splattered white apron whilst I chased a lamb entered my mind. Shamefully disappointed at missing out on the fun, but then relieved and somewhat surprised that we were not required to take part in the slaughtering. I imagined three million lambs running around Mecca with pilgrims running after them brandishing knives would have caused too much of a stir.

'You know why we make the sacrifice?' Daania asked.

'Yeah. Prophet Abraham.'

'What kind of answer is that? 'Prophet Abraham'. We do it to celebrate the triumph over his test of faith. When he was commanded to kill his son by Allah as a test of his faith, he was prepared to do it and just as he was about to, Allah told him that his 'sacrifice' had already been fulfilled as he had shown that his love for Allah superseded his love for all others.'

'So we sacrifice an animal.'

'Yeah, usually lamb in the name of Allah. Some of the meat will be eaten by us, the sacrificers…'

'No. I don't want to please.' Never a lover of red meat, the thought of eating my own killing did not sit well.

'…or friends, but the majority of the millions of carcasses will be shipped out to the poor in other countries. This sacrifice is supposed to symbolise our willingness to give up things that are of benefit to us or close to our hearts, in order to follow Allah's commands. It also strengthens friendship and helps those who are in need.'

'Makes sense.'

Daania began to lag behind in silence for a while.

'Ah!' I felt a yank on my hair.

Swivelling around, I saw Daania with a pair of scissors in one hand and the other wrapped around my hair.

'What are you doing??' jerking my head back.

'Sacrifice has been made. You're supposed to clip your hair.' She swiftly took my hair back into her hands.

'Ok, but hey watch it! I paid forty two pounds for this layered style. Try not to ruin it!' Taking huge chunks of my hair, she clipped haphazardly whilst we walked, as though a hairdresser in a mental asylum.

'After all this,' spreading her arms out to our surroundings, 'do you even still care about your hair?!'

'Well...'

'Well you shouldn't.'

'I think I'm just too tired to care about anything. Go wild. Be the hairdresser you've always wanted to be,' handing her my hair again.

Over an hour had passed before we approached Ibrahim al-khalil road, leading to the Al-Haram mosque. The masses jammed together again at this meeting point. Packed with devotees. All the shops and stalls had closed to prevent their destruction.

Our leisurely pace now slowed almost to a standstill.

'How on earth are these millions of people going to circulate the Kaba all together!?' I asked my companions. It was absurd and incomprehensible. *Surely, that's impossible?* With dread, I knew what was about to come.

Anarchy.

'Labbaik Allah humma labbaik!' The chanting started all over again. Picking up in decibels the further we shuffled towards the centre. Passion swelled. Hunched shoulders straightened up. Tired eyes widened. And groupies clung onto each other for the love of life once more.

My mother crushed my hand.

'Here we go again.' I muttered.

Layth weaved through fleeting gaps whilst Daania, my parents and I jumped after him. The rest of the group had dispersed. They did not need Layth anymore, having reached familiar territory and knowing how to perform the next rituals. It also would have been too stressful for them to spend the next moments attempting to stick together.   My parents and I lacked the competence and needed Layth. Although I had circulated the Kaba during Umrah only a few days ago, I had already forgotten the specifics of the ritual.

After another half hour of trudging went by, we finally reached the courtyard of the Al-Haram mosque. Upon seeing the mosque I instinctively broke into a grin. How I had missed its familiarity and joyous beauty after those two days in unfamiliar dry deserts. Its radiance soothed me for a brief moment until I was jabbed in my ribs by an elbow.

By the time we had laboriously waded our way into the mosque we were faced with an unbroken standstill.   Pilgrims, like us, attempted to force themselves through the doors despite the Saudi police ordering them not to with their 'Yalla!'s.

As soon as I got the opportunity I threw my slippers into my backpack and took respite in the coolness of the marble floor on the soles of my feet. Notwithstanding the chaos at the foot of the mosque and within my failing body I could not be held back from indulging in the beauty of this world famous mosque once more. Without effort, the desire to see the Kaba again soared above every other feeling. Tiptoeing, I peered over the tall heads in front of me.

'Labbaik' I whispered. Golden lyrics upon black silk. It had not changed since the first time I had seen it.

Paddling further, I caught sight of the thick circulating pilgrims and sunk with dread. The inner courtyard was completely taken over by one gigantic, revolving cluster of heads. The movement was so slow that unless I watched it intently, I would have thought these people were standing still. Never had I seen this place so populated.

Layth coerced us through the sardine crowd and we managed to latch onto the wheel. Daania held on to her husband, I held on to her, my mother held onto me and my father held on to my mother. Our little train had been formed and we began our circulation ritual just as we did when we first arrived into Mecca, only this time many metres out from the centre.

'ALLAHU AKBAR!!'

A quick glance upwards told me that pilgrims were performing the circulation on the other two floors too and would soon be circulating on every inch of the mosque, turning the mosque with them. I briefly noted how I had not been able to venture onto the other storeys in all my time at Mecca, blaming the relentlessly back-breaking traffic.

Body tensed at all times I assured that the sweaty torsos in front and behind did not catch me off guard and fall onto me.

'ALLAHU AKBAR!!'

Each round trip seemingly took forever. Several times I questioned whether we were moving at all but that would soon be answered by a sudden jerk in the crowd that would send us all into frenzy.

But those were not the most obtrusive thoughts of the moment.

Another perilous thought slowly bled into my mind until it infected my every thought, like ink in water, and insisted that I do something. I wanted to touch the Kaba. No, it was beyond a want, it was a need.

I have to touch it.
Why?

There was no logical reason behind this sudden desire. God would not have favoured me more if I placed my hands on it.

It was those people. The envy, as I watched the hundreds besides it, stroking its cloth, crying, laughing. The longing within me simmered. I wanted to touch this beauty. This beauty that millions had travelled for. This beauty that billions upon billions had bowed towards.

I could have waited. Waited until the next day and try to place my hands on it when there would be less people.

'I have to touch it now,' telling myself resolutely. It had been decided. My impulse had spoken, my heart had stamped its desire and my brain was already forming a plan. A wild elephant could not have pulled me away from this nagging desire. Seeing that in fact, the crowds were wilder than elephants, I began to fear myself.

I have to touch it.

I became obsessed.

Twenty or so tight rings of pilgrims separated me from the Kaba. To get to it, I would have to break through these layers of moving human walls that stuck together like cemented bricks. The final barrier consisted of a chunky spreading of pilgrims that put their hands up in the air as they thrust themselves forwards attempting to graze the cloth with their fingers. It seemed virtually impossible to get to without suffering from consequences. A crushing, an injury or worse, a failure.

A gust of invincibility blew into my body.

I'm on Hajj. On the holiest ground in the world. At the peak of purity. Surely nothing can hurt me? Am I not surrounded by thousands of Angels? Isn't Allah watching me? He'll look after me.

We had almost completed our final lap when I turned to my mother. My face soaked in sweat, heart pounding in my chest, I told her, 'Mum, I'm going to touch the Kaba. Let go of me.'

'Don't be silly,' squeezing my shoulder tighter, not believing that I would do such a crazy thing.

'Wait for me there.' Calmly I pointed to a distant pillar directly in line with the black stone.

'No you can't! Are you crazy??! You'll be crushed!'

'Allahu akbar!' We raised our hands in the air as we reached the black stone, marking the end of our circulation.

'Right, let's get out this way!' yelled Layth.

My mother pulled at my wrist.

It's now or never. I have to touch it.

I looked down at my hands until the voices of the supplicating pilgrims around me drowned out of my ears. Until my body became numb to the shoves. Until the faces around me were just a blur.

'Aaargh!!' I tore my hand out of my mother's, and pushed through the crowds.

Wedged in the cement of this moving wall, I thrust myself inwards as pilgrims resisted and dragged me along in their orbit. My headscarf began to fall off my head and I scrambled to put it back on. My robe got caught in between knees, feeling another sharp tear.

Fuelled on adrenaline, indestructability, I found a superhuman strength and attacked the wall. Pilgrims shouted out objections ordering me to turn away but I ignored them.

I pushed and I pushed.

I emerged at the final wall.

In dismay, I watched people climbing each other as though rocks on a mountain. Just to get a feel. There was not a visible centimetre gap here.

I tried to jab my way through two women who were reaching out to touch the black silk but even with my new herculean strength I could not spread them apart. Breathing became a struggle. Women began to clamber over me from behind.

Why am I doing this?

'Allah, help me! Aargh!' gritting my teeth, tearing in with more strength. I wedged the two women apart enough for me to get in between. My torso was squeezed tighter and tighter. There was still someone in front of me but I spotted a gap above her head. And stretched out my hand.

'Oh!' My fingers were not long enough. I could not reach it.

I tiptoed and almost grazed the cloth of the Kaba before I was pushed to the side.

'Oh... ARGH!' On my toes again, I reached out once more. I lost my balance and threw my weight onto the large woman in front of me.

In that moment the fingertips of my right hand grazed the black velvety cloth.

Soft.

So soft.

Softer than the emerald silk in which my mother wrapped the gold ring my grandmother had given her.

A fleeting tingle buzzed through my fingers. Through my arm. Into the rest of my body.

I touched it.

I touched the Kaba!

Screaming laughter, I closed my eyes, oblivious to those around me clambering to feel the same magic.

Intensifying exhilaration, elation gushed from below my feet.

More screaming laughter.

I had become that woman who I had witnessed on the second day in Mecca. The one who had run to touch the Kaba with her child. The one I had called crazy.

***

'So what do you call this again?' I ask Ibzy as he lines the brown muddy substance in the white paper and rolls it up.

'Rizla paper,' he mutters as he fumbles for a lighter.

'Right, rizla...,' intrigued.

He takes a puff and hands it to me. 'Right here you go.'

'It smells awful.' I say, gagging.

'It tastes worse,' he laughs. 'Take it deeeeep into your lungs. Take a puff. Suck in. And don't breathe out until I say.'

I wrap the rolled paper in my lips, suck and breathe in.

'M m nnn,' urging him to let me breathe out.

He waits. 'Ok now.'

I breathe out. 'Whoooooooooooooo!' laughing.

A few moments in the dark park later, we head out into the city centre. My mind is whirling. I feel dizzy. Each step feels unreal. Each sound, from a different time. 'Am I dreaming or is this real?' I call out. 'Only one way to find out!' A blast of invincibility and I run out into the middle of the road.

Car horns blare. A skid. More horns. A red Honda stops in front of me. I hear shouts.

Ibzy jerks me back. 'What the hell are you doing??'

'Get off me!' I wrestle out of his arms.

'Come here!' He pulls me to the side. 'Calm down!!'

'Get off me, you bastard!' I screech at him, slapping him.

'Listen, just calm... What... www... why are you crying??'

I heave uncontrollably.

He watches, not quite sure what to do.

Fifteen minutes pass.

'I hate you all.' I finally whisper.

***

That was a different type of crazy.

'Stop laughing!! It's not funny!! You could've died!' My mother scolded.

Uncontrollable giggles, I spluttered my Zamzam water out of my mouth.

The reprimand I got from all of them was totally worth it.

'Ok stop it now. Offer your two nafils here,' said Layth.

The next step of offering two bows and prostrations was upon us. According to Layth, the nearer to the Kaba we did this the better. So he led us to a perilously populated area which flashed unendingly with the swift movements of pilgrims.

'I'm going to put my forehead on this marble ground, whilst these people walk on me?' I asked him. Incredulous. There was no room to bow or prostrate without being knocked by knees and stamped on the head by feet.

'Impossible! Look at all these people! Impossible!' My father's nostrils flared at Layth – who was trying to kill us.

'Come on, quick! We'll cover you. Quick. The rewards are great!' He was insistent and urged Daania, my mother and I to offer our two nafils right there. In the flapping pit of danger.

'Oh no you don't. Come on let's go!' My father pulled on my mother's arm.

'This is crazy Layth?' I quizzed.

On my side a woman was attempting to face down unsuccessfully, bearing the knocks on her head by passersby.

'We're making a wall around you. Come on!'

Layth was adamant, and in the frenzy of the moment we accepted his urges. The three of us, with great dread, stood in line and began to offer our two nafils whilst my protesting father and the guide outstretched their arms around us, forming a barrier.

My first bow, someone knocked my head and I nearly toppled sideward onto Daania. I would have yelled out but would only have had to start the prayer all over again. The two men were doing a terrible job with their wall.

I got ready to kneel into prostration crying out, *when is this craziness going to end!?* I closed my eyes, took a deep breath and lunged forwards to place my forehead on the hard floor, bracing myself for someone to stamp on my head and mangle my nose. Body tensed, I hurriedly recited 'subhana rabiyaal ala' three times and shot back up. Inhaled. Plunged down again to repeat the prostration. I went to raise myself when a limb kicked the side of my head. The blow threw me off guard. I almost screamed in pain. Almost. Persevering, not wishing to break the prayer, I gritted my teeth and, with wet eyes, continued until the end.

'Now, you three make a wall around us as we pray.' Layth insisted.

'I'm not praying here! I'm going to find a space where I won't have my skull cracked!' Huffing, my father stomped off.

My mother and Daania covered Layth with their arms as he whizzed through his two nafils, bearing the knocks and whacks.

'Next. The walk between Mount Safa and Marwa.' Layth said and led us to Mount Safa as he had done during Umrah.

On our first lap we passed an old man who had fallen onto the floor. He looked like he had collapsed from exhaustion. Surprisingly, there was enough room and time for a handful of pilgrims to stop and lend a caring hand. I watched with concern before the floods of crowds behind me forced me to move on.

The constant rush was taking its toll on my limbs. My legs screeched out that they could not go on anymore. They were ready to leave me. Scrunching my face, I willed them to continue. Just a little more. Every movement was more excruciating than the last but I persisted.

The final lap was the worst. Each step on the hard marble ground sent an agonising drill through my heels, into my calves. Stamina and perseverance were words I loathed.

By the end I was ready to hack off my blistered feet and swollen legs and throw them away to save myself from the horrendous punishment they were giving.

I crawled away from the Mounts like a tortured puppy.

'It's Eid today you know?' said Daania, wiping her brow.

'Oh is it?' letting out a dry laugh, kneading my legs. I had forgotten that Muslims all over the world were celebrating the festival of Eid.

Christmas was never celebrated by us, unlike the kids in my school. Christmas for me, was just another day. Toast for breakfast, noodles for lunch and a bit of Scrooge on TV.

It was Eid that was my Christmas. Actually I got two Eids in a year. Eid-ul-fitr and Eid-ul-Adha. Each year, each Eid, I was adorned in traditional Asian clothes; sparkly pinks and glittery reds. I opened presents, ate a banquet of spicy food and hung out with my family. Eid was never the same once my sister passed away and it eventually got to the point when I was receiving less presents and having to give more because I had grown older. Becoming older also meant slaving away in the kitchen and helping my mother with the preparation of the enormous feast she always insisted on making. Still, Eid was a happy day because it gathered the family and extended family together and I got the chance to get the latest gossip and have a laugh with my cute baby cousins.

'Why do you get two Christmas's?' I was always asked that question at school by the other kids. The freckle faced boy, Shaun I think his name was, asked me this very same question with the same scrunched expression, every single year. Twice each year.

'I don't know. Because ermmm... I'm Muslim?'

I dug up a better answer than that in my later years. Eid-ul-fitr, I found, was the day of celebration of having completed the thirty days of fasting in Ramadan. Ramadan being the special month each year where people renew goodness in their hearts and Allah is said to shower his blessings, accept prayers and forgive sins.

Eid-ul-adha, which was on this day, is a day that Muslims commemorate and celebrate the trials and triumphs of Prophet Abraham. More particularly the sacrifice of his son he was about to make.

'Eid eh?' I looked down at myself. Here I was, having just escaped death, in my dusty, ripped robe, clothes that I had sweated in for three days, with my blistered, cut feet, scratty hair, lying on hard marble, on the brink of collapsing, whilst other Muslims in the world wore their best dresses, ate delicious dinners and opened presents. 'Ironic...,' laughing. A dry, bitter-sweet laugh. 'Could there be a starker contrast than this?'

***

'Oh my God... I can't breathe...'

In our hotel room, I had managed to lie down for a couple of minutes having removed my ihram attire, had a shower and stepped into a fresh robe. But respite was not to be mine. A sudden coughing fit shot me off my bed and straight into the bathroom to vomit. In the calmness of the hotel room, the magnitude of the symptoms of my chest infection crept out of the shadows, glaring their ugly faces. I wheezed like a dying woman. My head cracked each time I spluttered.

'Hospital... Take me to the hospital.' I croaked at my mother. I was losing my voice.

The timing was not bad. We were still in Mecca and the hospital was apparently only round the corner.

Layth waited outside for us as my mother and I entered the grim building. We were immediately met by a silent, dark lady. Black robe, black veil. She ushered us to the reception area. Not saying a word. The receptionist, another woman completely veiled in black, stared at me through her cloth slits.

'Erm, I'd like to see a doctor please?' I said nervously.

'Name?' in a strong Arabian accent.

I gave her my ID card. She wrote the details down and waved her hand ushering me to follow another fully veiled woman who had slithered out of an unknown corner.

We followed the woman down a narrow, dark corridor, lined with doors and empty chairs. We stopped outside one of the doors and she signalled for us to sit down on the waiting chairs. Sitting down, we watched her disappear down the shady corridor until we were left alone in the haunting silence. I tried to figure out whether these mysterious and stealthy women were nurses. They certainly did not make an ill person feel welcome or at ease. *And why don't they speak?*

Confused and apprehensive, we waited for a few, long minutes until the door opposite us creaked open. Another dark, veiled woman beckoned me in. Sat at a desk was a lady in a white headscarf and a white lab coat. Relieved that she was not dressed in black. Not so relieved when I saw her furiously scribbling in a book with her head down, like a mad professor.

'Name?' she finally asked without looking up.

Sitting myself down, I handed her my ID card. I had little voice left in me to spend on repeating my name ten times in vain.

'Problem?' still writing.

'Chesty cough... sore throat... headache... fever...' Without warning she pushed a stick into my mouth and put her cold hand down my robe with her stethoscope.

I shuddered.

She sat back down, wrote something on a piece of paper and handed it to me. After a few minutes of staring at her whilst she continued to write her plans to take over the world, I realised that the appointment was over and she was expecting me to leave.

'Erm, so what is it? Chest infection?' I wheezed, puzzled by her behaviour. Surprised that she was not going to tell me.

'Haa,' she nodded, clearly annoyed.

'Is this a prescription?'

'Haa,' nodding again and waving her arm, signalling for me to get lost.

Appalled by her rudeness and lack of sympathy, I came out feeling worse than I did before I went in.

'Good luck.' I muttered to my mother as she went in next. She too had been suffering from similar symptoms as mine.

In the darkness, we then silently followed the corridor, only hearing the hurried scrapes of our slippers on the marble floor. Eventually ending up in front of a room with a glass window, behind which, a veiled woman sat. The pharmacist, I presumed. Handing her my prescription, she flicked a couple of bottles towards me and turned around. End of service.

'Hey, these bottles are labelled in Arabic, how do I take this medication?' I sounded like a ninety year old man.

'Sigh... one, three times day,' she said without turning around.

'Bloody hell. As flawed as it is, I miss the NHS back home.' I rasped my complaint to Layth as we emerged out of the Addam's-family hospital. 'Saudis are so rude and uncompassionate! Why?'

'I don't know. Give them the benefit of the doubt and remember they have three or so million pilgrims from all over the world to deal with over these five days every year. Maybe they don't have time to be all smiley and caring?'

'Hmph!'

'Or maybe they're just arrogant oil diggers!' He joked. 'Hey, but you've got free medicine, so something positive. Make sure you take it asap. We're going back to Mina tonight and have two more days of stoning, and that's all three pillars on each day. So it's going be difficult.'

I stopped and vomited in the street.

Two more days of stoning.

20

'SO THIS IS *BETTER* than finding a cure for cancer? Or giving bread to the poor? Or adopting an orphan? Or erm... ending a war?' I ask.

'Well... this is the best of *any* deed a Muslim can do, so I guess so.' Hooria shrugged her shoulders.

We were back in Mina, the fourth day, and were lounging in our tent.

'Like, better than absolutely *anything*?'

'Absolutely anything!' nodding affirmatively. Her emerald eyes wide with surprise too.

'Oh my God, but it's so easy to do?' I was not quite sure whether to believe her.

'Well yeah, it is isn't it? But he said it, Prophet Mohammad. It says here.' She pointed to a paragraph in the book she was reading. 'He told his companions often; *'shall I tell you about the best of deeds, the most pure in the sight of your Lord, about the one that is of the highest order and is far better for you than spending gold or silver? The remembrance of Allah."*

'Let me see...' I took the book from her and read the paragraph. She was right. It was the remembrance of Allah. I turned the book over to see whether it was authentic. 'The Sealed Nectar. Biography of the Prophet, written by professors of the Islamic University of Medina. Ok, that looks reliable.'

'Apparently, a man had come up to the Prophet and said, *'the laws of Islam are too heavy for me so tell me something that I can easily follow'*. The Prophet told him to simply keep his tongue busy with the remembrance of Allah.'

'That's too easy. Look I can do that now whilst talking to you.' I picked up my white prayer beads and flicked each one. 'Alhamdullilah, All praise be to Allah, Subhanallah, Glory be to Allah, Allahu akbar, Allah is the greatest. As easy as that?'

'Erm... yeah?'

'Well I can do that anywhere, whilst driving, getting ready for work in the morning, eating, whilst at the gym. And that would be the best of all deeds?!'

'Yes! Ok, will you please shut up now? You've asked me the same question like, fifteen times!' Hooria gave me a withering look.

'Hmph!' turning away from her, I continued to roll my prayer beads in between my fingers.

And that is all we did for the next two days of Hajj. We busied ourselves with the remembrance of Allah. We did not save polar bears, end wars, march for peace or travel the world in the name of God. No. We simply sat in our tents, basked under the sun, chatted amongst ourselves whilst we flicked our prayer beads and remembered Allah.

We did the best of all deeds.

***

Oh, and there was the stoning ritual.

The stoning ritual on the fourth and fifth day was not as bad as the third day despite there being more pillars to stone. Pilgrims were out of their ihrams and their appetite for vengeance was slightly subdued. The fear, and thus the mayhem, was brought down a notch. A tiny notch. There were still three million pilgrims who aspired to stone the three pillars during the day which meant the shoves, the stampings, the elbowing and the near-death falls made their loyal appearances.

On the fifth day, the final throw of my stone at the third pillar was to mark the completion of my Hajj journey.

I marched to the final pillar with an astounding and fearless determination. The coughing, the trodden foot, the sore rib, the rupturing headache; I placed them to the side. The sound of the other pilgrims disappeared. Each thud of my steps resonated through my will. I was a seething woman on a bloodthirsty mission. A woman who was out to take her final revenge on the one who almost destroyed her. Satan. This woman was not going to leave until she was sure that he was completely dead.

'AAARGH!' teeth gritted, face twisted, pure hatred. I threw the first stone in a mad fury.

'No!' I imagined him crying out.

'YOU CAUSED ME SO MUCH PAIN!!' Second incensed

stone thrown. The pillar was not grey, it was red.

'No! Please stop!' I imagined him pleading.

'YOU MADE ME CRY EVERY NIGHT!!' Third enraged stone thrown. The blood in my veins bubbled, popping out over my skin.

'Aaaghhh!!!' he screamed.

'YOU TAKE PLEASURE IN MY MISERY? WELL LET ME TAKE PLEASURE IN YOURS!' rasping as I hurled the fourth stone.

'I gave you pleasures! Why are you doing this to me??' He was desperate.

'SINFUL PLEASURES! YOU ONLY WANT TO TAKE ME TO HELL! HOW DARE YOU!!' Fifth stone flung like a burning ball of fire.

'Aargh!' He was dying.

'YOU TRIED TO TAKE ME AWAY FROM MY ALLAH. ALLAH LOVES ME!!' Sixth stone thrown with a maddened force.

'I love you!' He was grovelling now. Grovelling to save himself.

'I HATE YOUUUUUUUUUU!!!!!' The seventh rock was his final cry. The seventh rock was his death.

It still was not enough, I wanted to leap over the wall and run to him, kicking and punching the pillar until his ghost died over and over and over again. Until there was nothing left of him.

'Come on. Out!' My father dragged me away.

He tried to take me to hell.

Well, Satan. Hell hath no fury like a woman scorned.

***

Their hug completed my Hajj.

My mother and father's tight embrace around me, amongst those millions of noisy strangers at the foot of the third pillar in the perils of Jamarat, completed my Hajj.

In the moment of the hug, my story flashed before me. The flickers of memories and images poured into my mind like a DVD on fast forward.

A young me scribbling in my Maths class hoping to finish my times table before everybody else. The round of applause by the audience as I am presented with the 'Best in the Year' award in my final term at high school. The look on Mr Gregg's face, my school teacher, when he says 'the world is your oyster'. The blue of my prayer mat I sit on, asking God to give me a first class degree. The graduation hat as it is thrown up in the air and lands straight back into my hands. The joyous scream when I am offered a job as a trainee solicitor at my first choice law firm. My first smile back at Zameer as he grins at me. The warm feeling that fills me when I tell my friends 'he's the one'.

The images flooded in as my mother whispers in my ear, 'we've done it.'

The despair in my hands when I see that I would spend the rest of my life in an office, working without real meaning. Tears in my eyes when Zameer's fiancée lunges at me. My smashed up phone after he refuses to answer my calls to explain. My scrunched up prayer mat in the bin. My mother's face when I scream at her 'I hate you all!' The flicking and flicking of Ibzy's lighter. The winks from the sleazy bouncers at the club. My cold response when I am asked, 'are you using me?' My wet pillow as I cry all night long, too weak to dry my tears. The moments I want to end my life. The brown of the tea as I stir it and tell my mother, 'I want to go to Mecca'. The sincerity in my aunt's face when she says, 'he has called you, to save you. He loves you'.

Scene upon scene as her wet cheek pressed against mine. Our tears met for the first time ever. Becoming one.

The vulnerability in my mother's back as she stands in her ihram at the Turkish hotel. The strange faces on Ibrahim al-khalil road. The white marble floor of the Al-Haram mosque. The sound of nothing but 'oh Allah here I am' as I gaze at the Kaba for the first time. The knock in my knees when I fall to the ground, pleading for my life. The sight of my broken mother and father sobbing uncontrollably. The taste of the Zamzam water as it trickles down my burning throat. The crazy woman as she runs to the Kaba with her baby on her back. The KFC burger in the poor woman's hand. The moment I sit in front of the Kaba and feel like I am superwoman; untouchable. Cave Hira. The gutter on my left as I pray Jummah on the street.

She kissed me on my forehead. The snaps flickered erratically.

The night-walk towards Mina. The wet and humiliating feeling as I fall outside the toilets. The fuzziness in my stomach when Zia tells me of the great love story of Prophet Mohammad and Khadija. Ecstasy in the secluded area of Mina. The glaring sun descending in Arafat. The millions of pilgrims stretched across the plains of Arafat as they weep in terror. The pink palms of my trembling hands as I beg Allah to forgive me. My fear of the Day of Judgment and the sudden lack of care for my sorrows of the past. The beautiful sound of the beautiful man as he sings the Azaan. The roar of the pilgrims as they head to stone the pillars. The grey, defeated eyes of the fallen man as pilgrims trample on him. The pain from the heavy foot on my fingers as my death flashes before me besides the first pillar. The sight of my bloody feet as I whisper to myself, 'I don't want to die'. My long, obsessed fingers as they stretch to touch the Kaba in Mecca. The final grey stone rattling off the final pillar. The arms of my mother and father as they hug me and say, 'we are born again.'

A surge of emotion rose from my feet and straight through my eyes. They seeped with tears.

Reborn. Clichéd as it sounds, that is how I felt at that moment.

I sunk into the belief that this spiritual experience had cleansed me of all the impurities inside me. The dirt of depression, consuming hatred, red anger and endless sorrow were at that moment expelled from within me. Amongst those pilgrims, I did not care about the betrayal and heartbreak from Zameer. I did not care about the disappointment my work had given me. I did not feel hurt by Allah. The pains and memories of the past that were held inside me for so long, I could finally release. The gate of the prison had been prised open and the darkness of misery was set free into the black hole of the universe. None of it mattered anymore because there was so much more meaning to this life of mine.

But it was not only that.

In the eyes of God, the God that I found love for again, I was sin-free. Prophet Mohammad had said it. He had said that if a person performs Hajj his sins are removed and he is like a newborn baby. The miseries created by my sins had been incinerated in Allah's workhouse. My soul, my once black soul, has been washed and rewashed until it was whiter than snow, and in came Allah's glorious light.

I laughed.

I laughed a laugh that I never thought I would laugh again.

It was simply joy. A rare, liberating, moment of happiness.

I had something new.

This was my second chance of life and I vowed that I would live it differently this time. I was not quite sure how yet, but I made the promise to myself.

21

BEAUTY AND PEACE. TWO words that did justice to Medina.

We had said our farewell to Mecca a day after Hajj and had sat on a coach for sixteen tedious hours to Medina.

'Medina is a city of great significance to Muslims'. Layth had explained. *'It's brandished 'the city of Prophet Mohammad' and the 'second holiest city in the world'. It was Medina that Prophet Mohammad had fled to when he was driven out of Mecca during his prophethood by his enemies. It's here where he lived for years and where he attracted a few of the first of his followers'.*

On the first of the seven days we were to spend here, I awoke to the harmonic voice of an Imam making the dawn call to prayer.

'It's coming from the Masjid al Nabawi.' My mother shot up from her bed.

'Huh?'

'The mosque of the Prophet! The heart of Medina. It's built on his home and it's where his grave lies. Let's go. Let's go. Let's go see it!' You would think she was a six-year old about to go to Disneyland.

My parents and I stepped out of our extravagant hotel. All the hotels were lavish in this city according to my father. Marble walls, buffed floors, golden chandeliers, were the bare minimum.

Outside, I immediately noticed the quiet, odd softness of the air. The constant rumble I had heard in Mecca was absent here. Hushed. Calm. I was sure if I listened carefully I would be able to hear the sizzle of the bright sun on my skin.

We did not know the way to the mosque so we followed a small group of people who were all heading in one direction with prayer mats tucked under their arms.

Squinting, I saw that there was a lot more space in this city. Enough space to run around in a small circle without bumping into a weird stranger. With its high rise buildings and well-constructed roads the city was a long way from what it was like fourteen hundred years ago. Some parts of the earth were still sandy and bumpy, other parts were paved with white stone slabs. The long, yellow road that we walked down was lined with small one-man portable stalls. Souvenirs, fruits, Arabian robes, headscarves, sold again and again. The mix of modernity and old age culture gave the city a remarkable presence.

Another minute we walked before turning a corner and coming face to face with the mosque.

'Wow. It's exquisite.' My first utterance.

The mosque resembled an ethereal palace. A lavish two-storey white marbled building. So vast that it stretched out wider than my eyes could see. It had several sections and wings to it. On top of the building, in set corners, towered ten tall and slim minarets made of the same pure white marble. The tip of one minaret was green, setting out its importance above the others. Several white domes crept over the tops of the mosque and one larger green dome sat in the middle.

We crossed a black gate which stretched protectively around the entire mosque. Even the gate was exquisitely patterned, tips dipped in gold. The immense marbled courtyard, the size of several football pitches, gleamed like a newly set ice rink. The courtyard was lined with hundreds of twenty-foot-tall stone and marble lanterns, lest any part of this beauty be hidden in the dark. The outer walls of the mosque consisted of dozens of archways comprising of huge, meticulously designed and patterned golden doors that openly led into the mosque. Thousands of people walked across the courtyard like tiny robed ants. The mosque was a mirror of preened symmetry. Remarkably, considering its size, it was a delicate and detailed work of art.

'Apparently it's increased a hundred times in size since the time that it was built by the Prophet and now can accommodate half a million people,' informed my father. 'Fourteen hundred years ago it was only a square enclosure of thirty metres squared and was built with palm trunks and mud walls.'

'Wow! The transformation is phenomenal.'

A Saudi soldier hastily approached us. 'Ladies yalla,' pointing to the left. A segregation of the sexes, unlike in the Al-Haram mosque in Mecca.

We stepped onto the courtyard, shoes in our hands. Immediately an aura of peace seeped into my being. With unlimited leisure, my mother and I strode across our half of the courtyard. I outstretched my arms and raised my face to the sun, feeling the tranquillity of Jack and Rose as they sailed the calm sea on the Titanic. I turned three hundred and sixty degrees and let the glow of the burning star warm my body and soak in the serene ambience. There was no hustle and bustle here. No shoving. No pushing. No clatter, no noise. No sense of urgency. No impatience. The contrast between the atmosphere at the Al Nabawi mosque in Medina and the Al-Haram mosque in Mecca was striking. I wondered which I preferred. *Excitement or serenity?*

Taking a closer look at the visitors, it was apparent that the poor pilgrims I had seen in Mecca could not make it here. Visiting Medina was just an addition to our trip. It was highly recommended but not necessary. A luxury for the wealthier pilgrims. Knowing this, a soft stroke of guilt brushed over me momentarily.

Some women had found their comfort on the gleaming courtyard of the mosque. Others were heading indoors, away from the sweltering sun. We strode to the nearest entrance and were met by two large, veiled women. One of the women signalled for me to hand my backpack to her. Startled, confused and mildly protesting, I handed it over. She vigorously rummaged through it with her black gloves and then handed it back to me.

'They check for cameras and phones,' my mother said. 'They don't allow anyone to take pictures as it's seen as disrespectful.'

Stepping inside, was like stepping inside a grand royal palace. The marbled floor shimmered in chosen areas whilst others were protected by a thick, lustrous, red carpet. Hundreds of white marbled pillars, tops laced and patterned lavishly in real gold, rose before us. Huge marbled arches separated the pillars with a graceful elegance. Delicate chandeliers filtered from the high ceilings indulging my face and the faces of others with a golden light. Golden book shelves with green and gold copies of the Quran lined the walls. Hundreds of small people sat on the floor, heightening the enormity of the mosque's magnificence.

My mother and I quietly sunk into the soft red carpet and, whilst marvelling at its beauty, we did the seemingly best of all actions. We remembered Allah.

***

'Do you want to see Prophet Mohammad's grave?' Daania joined us at the mosque on the second day.

'What, we can actually see it?' I asked her. Baffled that the grave of this man, who was regarded so highly, was open to the public.

'Yeah, it's underneath that great, big, green dome you see outside, on top of the mosque. Come.'

Intrigued, my mother and I followed her. She led us to an area slightly further into the mosque and joined a small group of people sat on the floor. A woman, covered in black, wearing a white badge around her neck stood over them.

'She's taking them to see the grave. There are certain times that we can go to see it.' Daania whispered. Her brown eyes wide and bright with excitement. 'There's a small space around the Prophet's grave which is said to be the most virtuous piece of land on earth because it's a piece of *heaven*.'

I shot her a disbelieving look. *Heaven on earth? Yeah, whatever.*

'They say if you offer two nafils on that piece of land then it is as though you're offering them in heaven!' I noticed the faint glistening moustache on Daania's upper lip.

'Ok, hold up, hold up. A piece of heaven??! Scepticism marked all over my face. *Surely I would have heard about this.*

'Yes.' Confident, with a smug look on her face.

'A piece of heaven mum?' South Asian women as old as Daania were well known for their old wives tales. I was reluctant to use her as a reliable source of information.

'Yes, it's very true,' my mother nodding affirmatively. 'Prophet Mohammad said *'there is a garden from the gardens of Paradise between my house and my pulpit'*. And that area is around his grave.' My mother had a slight moustache too.

'Oh my God... A piece of heaven! What does it look like??' I was immediately itching to see it.

'You will see...' Daania replied coyly, turning one eye away from me.

'Heaven on earth? Is it covered with flowers that we've never seen before? Or is it laced with diamonds and jewels?? Or is it just a smoky bit of air?? And how come I've never heard of this before?? How big is this space?' I persisted with Daania. Never a patient person, being teased only turned me into a pest.

Before she could answer my questions – not that she had any intention of doing so – we were ushered by the white-badged woman. The fiftyish women shot up and eagerly tiptoed after her in the silence. We walked a few steps and she signalled for us to sit down again. Twenty or so minutes later she moved us a few paces down the mosque before we obediently sat down again. A couple of hours were spent like this. We sat up and sat down several times, each time being moved deeper into the far end of the mosque.

The white-badged, long nosed woman did not say a word in all this. In fact no one said a word but only flicked their prayer beads in deep concentration. Baffled. Like bubbling water in a saucepan, my anticipation to get to the Prophet's grave and stand on the piece of heaven heightened with each delayed minute. I wanted to see this great man's grave. I wanted to see this piece of heaven.

'Yala.' The woman in charge whispered for us to rise and follow her again. She was now joined by three other white-badged women. We scurried after them in silence for a few minutes until we saw a large, meshed gate ahead of us.

A few feet wide, the inside of the mesh was obscured by a green cloth. Above the cage, a large wall that was engraved with golden Arabic scripture. Large, exquisitely decorated pillars stood on the sides of this mesh. The green dome, which I had seen outside the mosque, blanketed the area like an umbrella whilst little perched birds peered through the gaps. A couple of hundred women bustled around this place whilst others prostrated or raised their hands in prayer.

'That's it. He lies behind the meshing,' said Daania, her voice full of awe.

'Wow! Erm... but can't we actually see the grave??'

'No, no one can.'

'Oh...,' disappointed. Imagining a gravestone, soil, flowers. Not a meshed gate.

The hushed frenzy taking place right besides the meshing caught my attention. Women shoved and pushed each other to get to the edge of the obscure gate. Through the many feet and legs I spotted a green carpeted area that they were trying to clamber on to.

'That's the piece of heaven!' Daania gushed.

'What?' looking at her as though she had lost her mind.

'Yala! Yala!' The badged women urged us to quickly move on and out.

'Quick! Try and get onto the green bit and offer two nafil!' Daania pushed my mother and I into a wedge of women.

My bubbling excitement had burnt the saucepan dry. Gravely

disappointed at being faced with a green carpet in place of heaven and a meshed gate in place of Prophet Mohammad's grave, I still made my way forwards. *I've waited three hours, playing the sit-up-sit-down game for this, so I'd better make the most of it.*

The carpet heaven was lined with women. Being quite slim, I managed to squeeze into a corner on the edge of the green. 'Oh Allah's Prophet, may the peace, mercy, and blessings of Allah be upon you.' I whispered. I looked down at the carpet that was probably bought at £21 per sqm. *Maybe the Prophet had meant what he said in a symbolic manner? Or perhaps it's a disguised heaven so not to dazzle us humans?*

Either way, I took my chances. I prostrated in the direction of the Kaba with my forehead on the heavenly green carpet and closed my eyes. I submerged myself in the moment and imagined actually being in paradise. A sweet marshmallow smell wafted from underneath the gate and I smiled a silly smile. 'Allah, give me heaven for real!'

***

It was a privilege to be in the city of Medina, so close to Prophet Mohammad's body. This was the greatest man to have ever walked on earth according to Muslims and I got to stand so near him. Realising over the last few days how remarkable this man was, the honour was earnestly felt.

I had never met him, just like the other Muslims here, yet I found that I loved him. I reminded myself that I loved him because he wept day and night for me, begging Allah to save me and the rest of his people. I loved him because he might be the person who will save me from hell on the Day of Judgment, if he has not already with his prayers and his message. I loved him despite having never met him, because he had loved me despite having never met me. This man might turn out to be my blessed saviour one day.

Strange as it may seem, his love, his presence, was sincerely felt in this city by me. Said to be a man that radiated tremendous peace and love, I felt that peace and love here. In the mosque, where I spent most of my time, the serenity that transmitted through the marbled floor was invisible to the eye and unexplainable to the mind.

The people in the mosque walked and sat so graciously. They were gracious just like I had heard he was. Even the cleaners were polite and cheerful. Just like I had heard he was. People ran to the sweepers with riyals in their hands begging them to take their money as charity. They were charitable just like I had heard he was. Some came to the mosque having travelled ten or twenty miles per day, by foot, just to be here and pray their five prayers. They were patient and dedicated just like I had heard he was. And when I visited the modern shopping centre and cultured markets, the owners and traders were overly courteous. Just like I had heard he was. The book shops were always full of people buying books on Islam. They sought knowledge just like he did. And in the shopping areas, when the call to prayer was made, the whole city came to a standstill whilst the devotees paid their minimal dues to God. They were devoted to God just like he was. Their lives revolved around Allah. Just like his did.

He may have died, but everywhere and in everything, his legacy, peace, love, still remained here in Medina. In fact, it seemingly did more than just remain. It travelled the globe for fourteen hundred years and touched billions of people.

***

'Wow.'

On my last day as I sat in the courtyard on my prayer mat in the afternoon, 'wow' was my single word for those few hours. With my pearl prayer beads in hand, I did nothing but bask in the immense beauty and peace around me. That beauty, that peace, seeped through my ears, my eyes and stirred my heart like a soft feather in a gentle breeze.

In silence, I listened to the soothing beautiful voice that resonated through the city from the minarets of the mosque when the Imam made his sweet call for the afternoon prayers. In silence, I closed my eyes and let the voice flow through my ears, ooze like honey into my soul. His voice, like many of the Imams' voices here, was soft, melodious, sensational. His every tuneful word gently rustled my heart and blew into it a warm emotion.

In silence, I stared at the wonders around me. *These beauties surround me every day and I've always been blind to them.* Life was always hectic at home. Errands to run, work to do, people to see, sleep to catch up on. Engrossed in the rat race I never took time to stop and stare at the marvels of life around me. I had denied my eyes and ears to such simple, free pleasures for years.

The sky, how vast and mysterious it is... The birds, how they spread their wings and soar over the land so enviably... The sun, how it gives warmth and light to the whole world ... produces day and night... How it glitters on the polished marble of this mosque... This pregnant woman, how from a tiny, tiny, tiny sperm and egg, a foetus began to form arms, legs, eyes and a brain inside her belly... And after nine months will become a human being... A human being...! How ants even conceive... Do they feel...? These children who sit and play in the mosque... how they laugh at the silliest of things... Do ants laugh? This crying woman, how her tears are formed just from her invisible thoughts... How did Allah do all this...? And me... look at these hands I raise as an expression of submission... And look how I talk to God as if he is my new best friend...

William Henry Davies was right. He was right all along when he wrote his famous poem and my all-time favourite; 'Leisure'.

> *'What is this life if, full of care,*
> *We have no time to stand and stare.*
>
> *No time to stand beneath the boughs*
> *And stare as long as sheep or cows.*
>
> *No time to see, when woods we pass,*
> *Where squirrels hide their nuts in grass.*
>
> *No time to see, in broad daylight,*
> *Streams full of stars, like skies at night.*
>
> *No time to turn at Beauty's glance,*
> *And watch her feet, how they can dance.*
>
> *No time to wait till her mouth can*
> *Enrich that smile her eyes began.*
>
> *A poor life this is if, full of care,*
> *We have no time to stand and stare.'*

I had had no time to stand and stare.
But now I watched.
In awe I watched the clear, blue sky leisurely reform its colour;

it's blue deepening to an orange, red and then purple. I watched the transforming sun move and descend behind the minarets and domes of the Medinian mosque. I watched this magnificent palace spark its thousands of lanterns, one by one, and dazzle the whole city. I watched packs of birds fly across the land to take rest for another night. I watched as the moon crept out behind the dark blue sky and graced the world with its elegance. I watched as the stars unveiled their glitter and counted each wish we made. I watched people, these thousands of fascinating servants of Allah, rise at the precise moment of dusk in complete submission to their creator. In wonder, I watched every detail of this beautiful scene slowly unfold before my very eyes.

It was a poor life I had lived indeed, when, full of care, I had taken no time to stand and stare.

22

A RARE SMILE EMERGED on my face. A smile that spoke a thousand words, in a thousand languages.

Staring out of the window of the plane home, this time I was not searching for that glimmer of light. The glow of the sun graced every surface of the plane. Darkness and clouds had taken a bow. The world I flew over did not scare me anymore. With the weapon, with the shield of my prayer, I was ready.

I reclined under the warmth of the sun and played back the moment in Mecca when I had bidden farewell to the Kaba. And made my final wish.

***

In the starry night, I strode towards the celestial palace, the Al-Haram mosque. Its peaceful aura and luminosity drew me towards it with an effortless charm.   A cool breeze kissed my cheeks as I savoured this serene and dream-like moment for the final time. The grandeur, the shimmer, the radiance, the purity, the unexplainable ambience of tranquillity of this palace could not have belonged on the cold and hard grounds of earth.

'It sits as though its rightful place is only in heaven,' whispering to my parents. 'Amazing... how it still takes my breath away...'

The scene of my entrance played out like a slow motion movie. I was an Arabian Queen walking into her palace towards her jewel. With my bare right foot, I lightly stepped onto the glistening marble courtyard. The coolness rushed up my body sending bitter-sweet shivers through my veins. Instinctively I pushed my shoulders back. Lifted my head up.

Through the regal archways, I walked along the shimmering, marbled, ivory path created by the imperial white pillars. Thousands of glints, sparkles, beaming off the chandeliers and glossy walls lit my eyes. Amidst the grandiose, I was tiny. Yet I was a queen. A queen walking to the most precious jewel she will ever see.

I hold my breath. My heart pauses. Body tense. As I wait in anticipation for the first glimpse of this ruby.

There it was – a hint of black, shimmering, silk cloth. The swarming people, the lavish interior, become a blur.

Hypnotised, my glazed eyes transfixed on the mesmerising Kaba. My desire to see more, insatiable. Pushing me to pace further. But not faster. The golden Arabic scripture, scrolled over the black jewelled cube, coyly uncovered itself. As I walked through the final archway and entered the centre courtyard I knew nothing would break me away from its magnetic pull.

I gasped for breath as its complete beauty enthralled me. The large black cube shrouded in the finest black, silk cloth, laced with exquisite golden Arabic scripture, stood regally. The stars, the moon, reserved their radiance for only this. Thousands of people, thousands of unseen angels circulated it in its honour. Its sacredness, its exquisiteness surrounded my body like a flash of electricity. Its beauty penetrated my soul and stirred it to a soft rising elation.

A feeling of invincibility rushed through my veins once more. The past became a memory. The future was no longer a worry. And the present; that surely was a gift.

My eyes still glazed, I exhaled 'subhanallah,' raised my palms and let two tears fall.

In that long moment, I put the pieces together. The pieces of my journey.

It was in desperation that I travelled those three thousand miles to make a wish. A lost woman. My heart bled in my chest. Dreams lay in pieces. And my hope in God was no more. But they all said it was a *'life changing journey'*. They said it was the *'land of wishes'*. A final, drastic attempt to save myself. I packed my bags. Leaving with the words of my aunt ringing in my ears; *'he has called you, to save you. He loves you'*.

I travelled.

I travelled to the Kaba; the monument that the Muslim world revolves around, where billions over the years had come to make a wish. I stood at the place where the world began, where the first man had walked, where God's ray of blessings were said to shine. I raised my hands like a beggar. A desperate beggar. Bowed my head in the humility of my ihram. Dropped to my knees, just like the most beloved man of Allah had done. And I wept. I wept like I had never wept before. And I said to him 'oh Allah, here I am...' Unbeknown to me, it was then that he had begun to save me. To save me from the miseries I had come from. And when I made my first wish for eternal happiness, it was then that a dead hope stirred in my heart.

When I turned and saw my mother, my father and thousands of other men and women from all over the world weeping uncontrollably; it was then that I saw that I was surrounded and always had been surrounded, by people who were suffering just like me. They too had wishes. They too had broken dreams. When I looked down at my simple robe, the same robe that millions had been wearing, I realised that my life on this earth was insignificant. My problems, my worries, my miseries were trivial. Today's worries would be tomorrow's memories. And in a hundred years I would be forgotten. Life is short. In came perspective and humility.

As Daania and my mother stood with me in the queue outside KFC, I realised that Allah did not betray me. He loved me. All the misery that I had been inflicted with, the pain, the hot tears, was as a result of two things; a test or a punishment. I saw that Allah had given me depression in my career, heartbreak through Zameer to either test my faith in him or punish me for my wrongs. He had tested his most beloved human, Prophet Mohammad, with severer torture. But he loved him. So surely he loved me too? As my creator, I realised that it was his right to test and punish. But he did it so I would learn. So I would become stronger in my faith. Become a better person. He did it because he loved me.

It was in the same queue that the errors of my ways had become as stark as a burning match in the dark. I had failed his test by rejecting him. Reacted to his punishment by delving deeper into a life of sin. It had explained why the dark pit that I had first become trapped in only ever got darker as months went by.

When time stood still that night besides the Kaba, my father made me see that the hurt that I had suffered over the last year should be the least of my worries. With more sinning I had more pain to face – another fifty or so years of my life, the moment of death, possibly thousands of years in my grave, fifty thousand years of the single Day of Judgment and zillions of years in hell. Actually, an eternity. And each agony would be increased a hundred-fold. My past year of hell was nothing in comparison to what more may come. He made me see that.

On the day of Arafat, the terror of the Day of Judgment and Hell was so immense that I made not a single prayer for the end of my existing miseries. In that moment I did not care for them at all. Zameer, my job – they were nothing. With the chaos of the Day of Judgment before my very eyes, I begged Allah to simply forgive me for my bad deeds over the past years of my life and not send me to hell.

It had made a mark.

It had become the most moving, most memorable moment of my life.

During the time of stoning I had watched the sad eyes of a dying man as he dropped in front of me. I, myself, came so close to death. In that moment I realised that death was as close to me as my feet. When my tiny heart stops beating, be it today or tomorrow, that would be the end of me. The pains of my life would become meaningless as I come face to face with new kinds of torment. I saw that death was no respite and I was hell scared of it. I was not ready to die.

But it was on the final day, when I laughed like a pure baby, that I was enveloped by a new, powerful hope. I saw that Allah did indeed love me. He had indeed started his plans to save me. He had not specifically saved me from the heartbreak of Zameer or the disappointment of my life as a lawyer, but he changed my manner of thinking.

He showed me how short this life is.

He made me fear the unthinkable misery of hell and made me yearn an eternity in heaven. He made me want to be a good person. And he had given me a second chance to do that. He allowed me to rewind my life and start again as though it had never happened. With a 'thank you Allah', I promised to live life the right way.

On that final day, I looked at the Kaba, and I realised that to live the right way would be to simply fight against bad and stand by good. To keep off the path that leads to hell, walk on the path that leads to heaven.

Heaven. All I wanted was heaven.

I unfolded the scrap piece of paper in my hand that I had written a poem on the night before. I read it out to Allah, and on this night, it became my most meaningful prayer.

'O Allah... love me! so

Never a lonely tear falls in vain
Sleep meets my aching pain
Deaf the haunting cries of rain

O Allah... love me! so

Burned is that accursed's demise
Let him hate for I am deep in despise
Die before I, I am so sick of his lies

O Allah...love me! so

All you are to me, I bid the rest goodbye
Your name I breathe with every sigh
Your passion floods this desire in I

O Allah... love me! so

Death does not creep in dreaded dismay
Fear? Your compassion will not betray
Make the call, take me, take me away

O Allah... love me! so

Dreams are not just 'I dream'
Honeys of heaven, a euphoric extreme
Ribbons of happiness, alas untie the seam

O Allah... love me! so

I am loved, enough if only by you
Free I am, it is you I pursue
Now hear me O Allah... for I love you!'

Calmly, I folded the paper and turned away from the magical
jewel.

I walked a few paces outwards. But a niggling feeling made me
turn back once more.

I gazed at the spellbinding golden black.

In that entranced moment a wild desire cascaded into my heart.

A wild ambition.

A wild dream.

My final wish.

'Oh Allah... love me as one of your dearest. Make me... make me one of the *best* of mankind.'

With that, I turned around and walked away.

23

OVER A YEAR HAS passed.

On a cold, northern beach of England, I sit and watch the ferocious waves crash under the grey, stormy sky. With my pen and fluttering writing pad in hand, I inhale the frosty air, gaze out far and across the horizon, and ask myself the unavoidable question.

Am I happy?

No.

What is happy? I pull out my iPhone and Google the term 'happy'. Wikipedia tells me that *'to be happy is to be pleased, delighted or glad about something'*. Am I pleased, delighted or glad about life?

No.

I am not happy.

How can I be happy when I am still a player in the rat race?

Every morning I pry my tired eyes open and think, *'another day, another dime to be made'*, and, having not slept enough, I drag myself out of bed with a look of death. How can I be happy when, even though I have left the law firm I used to work for and set up my own business, there is still the realisation that so much of my day and life is wasted on meaningless work? Work. Simply to pay the bills and put food on the table. Working, not to live, but to merely exist.

How can I be happy when Satan has risen from the dead?

'You look exactly the same!' Sarah said to me a few weeks after I returned. Yes, I do look exactly the same. Sat on the wet beach, I am in my blue skinny jeans and purple Firetrap top. My face is blushed with make-up as my loose wanton hair blows across it in the wind. As much as I had felt humble and liberated in my modest white Islamic robe and headscarf in Saudi, the incessant lure of Top Shop, Selfridges has been irresistible. And so has the temptation of parties and concerts. I cannot help but enjoy the strumming of One

Republic's guitar. The fingers on Alicia Keys' piano. I thought I had killed Satan the day I threw my final stone on the third pillar. But no one told me he had more lives than a cat. How can I be happy when my will is too weak to break free from the chains of my perilous desires and fight the wretched leech?

How can I be happy when that man on the white horse that I dream of day and night has still not arrived?

'How you doin?' Yes, men still waltzed into my life promising the jewels of love, just like Zameer had. Guys who only chase legs for temporary pleasures, until they get bored. Or men who lack ambition, intelligence or even a simple sense of humour. How can I be happy when I only ever seem to meet philanderers or disappointments but no one that has the charm to say 'take my hand'?

How can I be happy when the world I live in is in such a mess?

The poor scramble for a cup of clean water whilst the rich hoard their wealth buying themselves crystal encrusted helicopters, without a thought of sharing. Innocent people are still dying in the needless wars of today. Each second there is a child, a woman in the world that is crying in pain. Pain that is unjust. How can I be happy when there is this hatred, anger, jealousy, greed, evil, oppression in the world that I am a part of?

How can I be happy when I am dying?

Yes, I am dying.

Every day I take a step closer to death. With my 'anti-ageing cream for young women', I stare in the mirror each morning grieving over my failing skin. Wrinkles are forming around my eyes. My youth and beauty is diminishing before me and there is nothing I can do to stop it. How can I be happy knowing that death is as close to me as my feet? Another day, another fifty years, what does it matter? It will come to me. Even the powers of every person, every machine on this planet put together would not be able to prevent my death. How can I be happy knowing that all those I love will eventually leave me? Like Nafeesa did. Or I will leave them. How can I be happy when any good that I might have in this life will, one day, inevitably end?

How can I be happy when a whole new terror might await me after death?

The fear of my soul being ripped out of me when I die, the crushing of my body in my grave, the mayhem of the Day of Judgment, the incessant torture of an eternal hell – it is still as immense as the day it was in Arafat. These thoughts, at times, are unbearable. How can I be happy when I know what may lie ahead yet I still do not seem to have the ability to stick to the rules for another few years to save myself from an infinity in hell? How can I be happy when I am in constant fear? Fear, that should I die tomorrow an irreversible torture may begin.

No, I am not happy.

Deep inside I am not happy. And I know I never will be.

My life, and this world, is full of imperfections. Sadness. Improvising from a famous saying, even if you put the moon in my right hand and the sun in my left, happiness will never rest in my heart. Because the fear of death will always follow it.

But that is not to say that I am miserable.

I still laugh when I watch The Simpsons on TV. Still make fun of my friends, the good ones, when they attempt to dance. Have bursts of giggles when my young cousins run around the park chasing butterflies. Watch the latest movies at the Odeon cinema. Eat from the best of restaurants with a non-alcoholic cocktail by my side. I smile a lot more now too – Zia had said it is a good deed. And knowing that life is short, life is very short, I do not take events that occur in life too seriously anymore.

But, most of all, I am hopeful.

Channel 4 aired a series of documentaries on the Hajj and dubbed it as *'The Greatest Trip on Earth'*. That it was for me. And as many had claimed it to be, 'life changing' it was indeed for me. Hajj gave this despairing woman, who thought she would never see light again, hope.

The words of Zia are embedded in my memory. *'Fear his wrath but hold onto the rope of Allah's mercy with hope'.*

Hope is my oxygen.

Hope, that if I bear the imperfections of life, worship Allah and try to give Satan a kicking now and then, he will put heaven in the palms of my hands. Heaven, where I believe is the only place pure and endless happiness can exist.

I do not live anymore to pursue the happiness of my next fifty years. I do not dream of becoming a hot shot lawyer, finding fame, becoming a billionaire. I have a career yes, but it is no longer what my hopes of happiness revolve around. I still want a life partner but my hopes of happiness do not revolve around that anymore either. My hopes of happiness do not rely on any worldly matters.

Holding onto the rope of Allah's mercy, my hopes of happiness revolve around him. The one who promises not to disappoint me should I play my cards right. As corny as it sounds, he is now the core of my life.

Allah. My creator. My sustainer. My destroyer.

With this new meaning to life, I chase a new dream. I desire his love and I desire his heaven. In fact, I desire the *best* of his love and the *best* of his heaven.

So I hog the bathrooms to wash myself, now offering all five obligatory prayers. Believing that the sole purpose of my existence is to worship Allah, the least I can do is take a few minutes out of the daily rat race, the meaningless chases, to pay my dues to him. Even if it means going out a little later than usual, skipping a lunch meeting, missing a TV programme or forsaking sleep in the morning. If those people in Mecca and Medina can kick paying customers out of their shops and let the burgers in their food huts burn in order to worship Allah, then so can I. They are my inspiration. If I can offer my prayer in the stifling heat almost on top of a horrid gutter without feeling humiliated, then I can offer my prayers anywhere on the streets of Britain without embarrassment. I am an inspiration to myself.

And when I step onto my prayer mat, I escape the swirls of life and submerge myself into my bubble, where there is just me and my Lord. I prostrate in the direction of the Kaba, and imagine that I am there again. I am invincible again.

My mother and I now hang out like best friends. She is the person who is valued the most by me. A right she has acquired through her love and through the laws of Islam. We go shopping together, I take her to restaurants and, with heaven being said to be at the feet of mothers, I even massage her feet. The sight of her cowering body and teary face when we stood outside the Kaba for the first time will not leave me. I try to keep her happy.

My father, holding the key to the doors of heaven, has also become blessed with my pleasantness. I make him a cup of tea now and then.

And my brothers? Well, I blessed them with the knowledge that it is their duty as Muslim men to look after me. So I send them off to the shops to buy me treats whilst shouting out *'I am a diamond!'*

Taming my ego and refraining from thinking that I am better than others or someone is not good enough for me has not been easy. A person with an ounce of pride will not enter heaven apparently. Recalling the moment in Muzdalifah when, prince or pauper, we were all brought down to the same level and exposed as nothing but servants of Allah, I force humility upon myself. I tell myself that I am nothing special over someone who is less intelligent, less pretty, less wealthy, less interesting. It gives me a satisfying pleasure though, when I realise that I am better than Queen Elizabeth and Beyoncé if the gold of my good deeds is weightier in the eyes of Allah.

Single and flirty I may be, already once burnt, I do my best to stay away from illicit romances. I now believe that only in the safe haven of marriage will my body and my heart be free to love. I have faith and patience in the promise Allah makes in the Quran; *'Good men are for good women, and good women are for good men'*. It is a promise that I am holding onto. The love story of Prophet Mohammad and Khadija has inspired me. Left me with longing. I am waiting for Allah to write my great love story. My man on the white horse will come with God's will. I am sure of it.

Life without love has an emptiness to it. Loneliness creeps up at these vulnerable times. I try to chase away the feelings, remembering the time when I had once said to Allah, *'I do not care for the love of others. I only want your love'*. Life without love does have an emptiness to it. But life without God has a deeper emptiness to it.

He is with me. He has given me all I have. He loves me more than anyone could ever love me, seventy times more than my mother apparently. Surely that should be enough for me?

Speaking of men. *'Zameer. Who's Zameer?'* is my response whenever my friends mention him. He is now nothing but a distant memory. Once a bitter woman consumed with hatred, I do not hate him anymore. Allah is said to hate the person who hates, so I have rid of those ill feelings. In fact, I have done more than that. I have shocked myself and I have forgiven him. Despite the hurt he had caused me I have forgiven him because if Allah had forgiven all my sins when I completed Hajj, then surely I can only repay him by forgiving those who had wronged me? Prophet Mohammad loved and prayed for his enemies and so… well, that is pushing it a little far. There is no way I am going to do that.

Two and a half per cent of my savings I gave to charity in Ramadan last year. That was the obligatory for every Muslim. But I do more and make a steady donation every month to Islamic relief, Oxfam, Unicef, NSPCC and other worthy causes. At the surprise of others, I have also pledged to give half of my company's profits to charity. Whether half of my profits turn out to be ten pounds or a million pounds I do not know. But I hope I can make some sort of difference. Seeing the poor and crippled in Mecca, the lady at the foot of KFC, the man on the grounds of Mina, I knew that I did not deserve good things any more than they did. I am just one of the undeserving lucky ones. I want to share that undeserving luck. What is an extra pair of shoes to me when I can feed a family in Ethiopia for a month? What is a new car to me when I can build a few houses for the homeless in Somalia?

The grim honesty the media reveals of those suffering from famine, floods, earthquakes, bombings, murders, rape, still saddens me. But now, when there is nothing in my power that I can do, I pray. I send them a selfless prayer and take comfort in the fact that one day justice will be done. One day these weeping people will laugh like kings and queens. One day their oppressive torturers will scream in burning pits.

A fiery woman I am. Always a fiery woman. To control my temper is virtually impossible at times. Doing some reading of my own since my Hajj trip, I have come to know that anger is actually a grave sin. Fearing the anger of Allah, I stick pins in cushions instead of getting angry when my friends lie to me, fight with me or when someone eats that chocolate fudge cake I had hidden in the corner of the fridge for days. Ok, in all honesty, sometimes I will pinch the greedy liars until I hear their screams...

'The pens have been lifted and the ink has dried, know that what hit you could not have missed you and what missed you could not have hit you'. Prophet Mohammad's words speak to me when certain events bring me down. My new MINI Cooper was damaged in a car accident. I failed to win an important contract for my business. I try my best to be patient and not waste my time grieving. God has willed for whatever to happen to happen and the forces of a million people would not be able to come in the way.

What is meant to be will be.

As a woman I PMS pretty badly and that is when I am most prone to feelings of depression. Bills, broken nails, the future of my business, the death of my pet canary, old memories – I can become depressed about anything and everything. I even worry about the extinction of polar bears when I am PMSing. Whatever it may be that brings a tear to my eye, the dawning words of my mother on Ibrahim al-khalil road embrace me again. *'It is a test or a punishment'.* Nodding my head, I accept these tests, these punishments. I stay steadfast and faithful to Allah. Besides, what is the point of feeling depressed over such matters or worrying about the future when, glancing at my toes, I could drop dead tomorrow?

Ingratitude is still my greatest flaw. I never seem to have enough clothes, shoes, money, food, health, gadgets. The old wise man I met in Mecca, Mr Raul; I still remember him. The eyes of the poor man in Mina; I still remember them. As Mr Raul had taught me, I imagine my reaction if I baked a cake for my mother out of love and she threw it back in my face screaming 'it's horrible!' I imagine Allah's reaction when out of love he has given me all that I have and sees that I still complain. I do not want him to be displeased. I do not want him to turn me into the pleading poor man. Given that, I would like to now say a quick 'thank you Allah, for everything'.

The desire to do what everyone else seems to be doing – wearing that outrageously short, little, black dress, having a tattoo, dancing the night away in Ibiza, drinking tequilas – gnaws at me all the time. Life is not fair. I cannot do what I want but must follow the rules of Islam. Life is not fair.

But then, who said life is fair? Prophet Mohammad openly admitted that this life is a paradise for non-believers who can liberate all their desires and a prison for the believers who must restrain their desires. I tell myself; what is another zero to fifty years of a life of loose imprisonment when it would mean avoidance of an endless imprisonment in hell and freedom of desires in heaven, for an eternity? The historic characters of Islam had sacrificed their children and lives for Allah, so surely I could sacrifice a few nights out? Besides, I had cried too many tears of fear and forgiveness and made too many promises in Arafat to let it go to waste. And I had had too many near-death experiences when stoning Satan to let that scumbag win over me and make a fool out of me again.

Life is not fair but life is too short to waste on things that I will most certainly regret. People now say to me, '*you only live once, let your hair down!*' I reply, '*I only live once, to get it right! When I drop it'll be too late to go back*'.

Life is short.

Above everything, I do the best of all deeds effortlessly. I do not walk around with pearl prayer beads in my hand like I did in Mecca. But when I am driving to work, waiting in a queue at the supermarket or best of all, when I am sat on this beach now taking time to appreciate the beauty around me, I whisper good words about Allah. I tell him he is the greatest and that all praise and glory is for him.

He will love me for that.

My greatest power has become prayer. It has become my weapon, my shield. Whatever I want, I ask Allah for it and only him. Asking him has become a form of power as well as a form of worship. Through my sufferings and my journey of Hajj I realised the powerlessness of man and woman and how everything comes from God. I have wishes, desires, that no human can seem to fulfil. When I had raised my hands before the Kaba I was convinced that Allah was going to accept my prayers. I was convinced that he would have accepted a wish to walk on water or fly in the sky had I asked. 'He can do anything surely', I tell myself. 'He created the world did he not?' Today, when I cup my palms before me and make a wish, I convince myself again that with the power of prayer I can change my destiny and anything is possible.

Absolutely anything.

And when Allah seemingly does not accept my wishes, like when I asked him to take me travelling around the world but he did not, I do my utmost best not to despair in his ability to accept my prayers. My friend, Sully, said to me recently, *'Allah always accepts the prayers of a believer. He does it in three ways; either by granting the wish in the form requested or by instead removing a difficulty that was about to face him, such as an illness or loss, or by reserving the grant of the wish in heaven'.* Even Prophet Mohammad, as Allah's most beloved, once cried out when being tortured *'when will come the help of Allah?'* Even he sometimes did not get what he wanted straight away. Every wish of mine may not be granted how I want it to be granted. I accept that and accept the tests that such denial brings, but I maintain my faith in Allah and continue to ask him.

And when all else fails, I whisper to myself, 'I will have it in heaven'. It makes me feel better.

Life is quite simple really.

Life is short.

Life is simple.

Allah created me to just love. To love him and to love others. And there are thousands and thousands and thousands of ways to show that love. So as the days tick along I give myself meaning and a sort of contentment in my short life by doing just that.

I will love him, and I will love you for the sake of him.

But all along I am chasing his love.

All along I am chasing his heaven.

And until I get there, I will keep telling myself to dream the wildest dream, and stand behind it the wildest belief. One day, one day, it will happen.

***

A dreamer; day and night, I dream the same dream.

One night, when Allah wills, the sound of thunder will stir me from my sleep. I will gaze up at the deep, mysterious sky but the stars will say not a word. Lightening will strike and blind me for a brief moment of confusion. I will open my eyes again and there he will be. The man on the white horse. Tall, steely and perfectly carved.

The epitome of man.

He will hold out his hand and smile the most charming smile. 'Our time has come...,' he will whisper, 'take my hand.' Mesmerised, I will reach out my delicate fingers and lightly touch his.

The stars will twinkle, the moon will witness and love will cast its magical spell. He will clasp my hand with his perfect strength, gaze into me with his deep, soulful eyes and raise me up to his horse. He will look back once and say 'my diamond... let's go.'

Through the rising dawn I will travel the world with him. I will adopt children in Mexico to save them from the rats on the streets. I will give cures to the weak in Africa, suffering from AIDS, malaria. I will build huts for the homeless grieving from the floods in Pakistan. I will bake warm bread for the famine-struck in Ethiopia. I will pull away young innocent children from the mines in Palestine. I will throw into space the guns and swords of the murderers in the Middle-East.

I will make the world smile.

I will become great.

One of the best of mankind.

Once my work is done, I will sleep like a queen for years or for centuries, until Allah opens his shimmering doors of heaven. The incandescent white light will instantly indulge me and raise me up into the cool, soft air of Paradise. The sweetest scent will seep into my nose and send shivers of pleasure into my soul. A hum of euphoria and ecstasy will envelop me, making the promise to stay for eternity.

As light as light, I will first glide towards them and throw myself into their embrace. My mother, my father, my sister, my man and all those that I had loved and lost on planet Earth. In the reflection of their glistening eyes I will see the most beautiful being ever. Beauty that would surely blind a man of today. I will click my fingers and soft white wings will sprout from my sides. I will then do what I have always wanted to do.

I will fly.

I will soar into the white skies of heaven and roam the luscious gardens of paradise at the speed of light. I will catch a shooting star with my exquisite hands and kiss the moons with my gracious lips. Like a breath, I will land on my magnificent palace, encrusted with dazzling diamonds and glittering jewels. I will swim under the waterfalls of honey and in the seas of melted chocolate surrounding my abode. Angels will wait on me bringing me the most delectable of foods, the most pleasurable of wines never known to man. I will pose on my throne and beckon the beautiful singing man to caress my ears with his euphonic harmony once more.

Then, the most spellbinding and awaited moment will emerge. The moment when I finally meet the One that I had devoted my life on earth to. When I lay my eyes on him, I will whisper, 'O Allah, an infinity of words could not describe what I see.'

And forever I will be... happy?

No...

'Happy' is a word of planet Earth.

The word that I wish to write, it does not yet exist.

It will come to me in heaven.

I will tell you then...

ACKNOWLEDGEMENTS

It goes without saying that this book could never have been written without the will of Allah. So I would firstly like to thank you, Allah, for giving me the means to experience this beautiful journey and to share my story. I could not have done it without you.

Many people have helped me turn my story into this written form.

I thank you my family for your support and encouragement throughout these years. There have been many ups and downs, but you remained loyal and faithful like the truest of kin.

Faizel Vohra, you are one of the most selfless friends I have. Thank you for all your input, your editorial skills and your encouraging words. Tony Seddon, thank you for your editorial input. Rob Conroy, I truly appreciate you giving your time to me. Thank you to Lukman Umarji, Suleman Chotia and Safwan Adam, and your respective friends.

The input from the members of the First Writers group has been invaluable in the writing of this book. Alan Whelan, John Boydell, Ed Christiano, Marilyn Chapman and Diane Wilkinson, when you read this I am sure you will realise how indebted I am to you. Thank you for your time and your critique.

There are many others who have graced my life during the key moments of writing this book. You know who you are and I hope my gratitude reaches you.

And finally, thank you mum. The powers of my being could never express how blessed I feel to have had you in my life during this time. I will thank you for the rest of my life, and more. This was for you.

A NOTE ON THE AUTHOR

Safiya Hussain was born and currently lives in Lancashire, England. She is now an award winning entrepreneur and runs her own business.

You can join Safiya on Twitter @SafiyaHussain

www.NewAgePublishers.co.uk

www.ThreeThousandMilesforaWish.co.uk

Lightning Source UK Ltd.
Milton Keynes UK
UKOW050407160812

197624UK00001B/2/P